The European Union and National Defence Policy

Have pressures from the integration of Europe resulted in a shift in national defence policies? Have developments in integration affected the way in which policy is made at the national level? Is national defence policy inclining increasingly towards co-operative action?

Focusing on the role that European integration has played in shaping the defence policies of various European countries, this book fills a surprising gap in existing studies. The editors have brought together an impressive array of contributors, who consider the pressures on state policy emanating from the process of integration. The book is divided into three distinct parts: the first outlines the tortuous history of attempts to link defence with European integration and highlights some recent initiatives. The second part includes studies of the four larger member states – France, Germany, Italy and the United Kingdom, as well as a chapter on The Netherlands – providing an insight into the different national factors that condition the impact of EU action. The final part considers the key questions of nuclear weapons and arms procurement policies.

The national defence policies of European states are currently undergoing a period of radical transformation. This, the second book in *The State and the European Union* series, sheds light on an increasingly important and topical aspect of contemporary European security and will be essential reading for those studying European Politics, Public Policy and International Relations.

Jolyon Howorth is Professor of French Civilization and Jean Monnet Professor of European Political Union at the University of Bath. **Anand Menon** is Lecturer in the Politics of European Integration at the Oxford University Centre for European Politics, Economics and Society and Professeur Invité at the Institut Supérieur des Affaires de Défense, Université de Paris II.

The State and the European Union series
Edited by Anand Menon, *Oxford University, Centre for European Politics, Economics and Society*, Hussein Kassim, *Birkbeck College, London* and David Hine, *Christ Church, Oxford*

This new series presents books based on an ESRC-funded interdisciplinary seminar series on the theme of state autonomy in the European Union. The series considers the impact of the EU's institutions, policy processes and laws on the policies of member states. The series will consider issues related to the nature of policy formation in order to assess the impact of the EU on the member states in this sphere. The primary focus is on France, Germany, Italy and the United Kingdom.

The European Union and National Industrial Policy
Edited by Hussein Kassim and Anand Menon

The European Union and National Defence Policy
Edited by Jolyon Howorth and Anand Menon

The European Union and National Macroeconomic Policy
Edited by Anand Menon and James Forder

Beyond the Market
The European Union and National Social, Environmental and Consumer Protection Policy
Edited by Hussein Kassim, Anand Menon and David Hine

The European Union and National Defence Policy

Edited by Jolyon Howorth and
Anand Menon

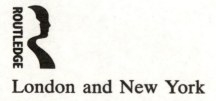

London and New York

First published 1997
by Routledge
11 New Fetter Lane, London EC4P 4EE

Simultaneously published in the USA and Canada
by Routledge
29 West 35th Street, New York, NY 10001

Typeset in Times by Intype London Ltd
Printed and bound in Great Britain by
Mackays of Chatham PLC, Chatham, Kent

British Library Cataloguing in Publication Data
A catalogue record for this book is available from the British Library

Library of Congress Cataloguing in Publication Data
A catalogue record for this book has been requested

ISBN 0–415–16484–2 (hbk)
ISBN 0–415–16485–0 (pbk)

Contents

Illustrations

Figures

Tables

Contributors

Filippo Andreatta is a post-doctoral research fellow at the Faculty of Political Science, University of Bologna.

Johannes Bohnen is a doctoral candidate at Oxford University.

David Chuter is a Research Associate at the Centre for Defence Studies, King's College, London.

Stuart Croft is Professor of International Relations at the University of Birmingham.

Lawrence Freedman is Professor of War Studies at King's College, London.

Christopher Hill is Montague Burton Professor of International Relations and Political Science at the London School of Economics.

Jolyon Howorth is Professor of French Civilization and Jean Monnet Professor of European Political Union at the University of Bath.

Anand Menon is Lecturer in the Politics of European Integration at the University of Oxford Centre for European Politics, Economics and Society and Professeur Invité at the Institut Supérieur des Affaires de Défense, Université de Paris II.

Alfred van Staden is Director of the Netherlands Institute of International Relations, 'Clingendael' (The Hague) and Professor of International Relations at the University of Leiden.

Trevor Taylor is Professor and Head of the Department of Defence Analysis and Security Management at the Royal Military College of Science, Cranfield University, Shrivenham, UK.

Preface

This volume is based on a series of research seminars, funded by the Economic Social Research Council, on 'State Autonomy in the European Community', held in Oxford in the academic year 1993–1994. The seminars examined the impact of European Community action on the content of national policy and on the relationships between actors at the national level, with the aim of assessing the implications of EC policy for the member states and the extent to which their autonomy has been affected. The seminars, which were interdisciplinary, addressed developments in the following areas: industrial, financial and service sectors; social policy; environmental protection and consumer policy; macroeconomic policy; and defence policy. The impact of EU membership on national administrative systems was also the subject of a seminar.

Neither the research seminar series nor this book would have been possible without the support of ESRC Award No. A 451 264 400 248.

Acknowledgements

We would like to acknowledge the efforts of David Hine and William Wallace, who made this project possible, and to express our thanks to two of the series editors, Hussein Kassim and David Hine, for their support, help and encouragement throughout the preparation of this volume. We are grateful to the principal and fellows of St Edmund Hall and to the staff at the Social Studies Faculty Centre of Oxford University who co-staged in April 1994 the seminar on which this volume is based. Finally, we should like to thank all the participants at the seminar for making it a stimulating and successful event. Our greatest debt is to the contributors to this volume for their patience in coping with the two editors, whose inadequacies were compensated for by the administrative skills of Jill O'Brien and Jane Wyatt.

Introduction

Anand Menon[1]

This is the second volume of a series which examines the impact of the European Union on its member states. It shares with the others in the series the aim of evaluating the ways, if any, in which the process of European integration has impacted on both the substance of national policy and the way in which that policy is made. The volume on industrial policy (Kassim and Menon 1996) pointed out how little work has been done on the subject of the effects of integration on the state. This is, if anything, all the more true of defence. The vast majority of studies carried out on the relationship between defence and integration concentrate solely on the moves made towards the creation of a European defence identity, ignoring the question of whether achievements to date have exercised an impact on the national level.

None the less, the EU's impact on the nation state is an important element of integration. Andrew Moravcsik has recognised as much, classifying 'substantive domestic policy adjustment' as one of the crucial elements of the integration process, in that 'policy co-ordination is most significant where it imposes greatest adjustment on domestic policy' (Moravcsik 1994: 479). Indeed, much of the contemporary debate on defence within the context of the ongoing Intergovernmental Conference (IGC) on institutional reform has hinged on whether the West European nation states could ever agree to alienate decision-making power and hence the ability to reshape national defence policy in a collective supranational body.

DEFENCE, INTEGRATION AND THE STATE

There are two aspects to the issue of the impact of European integration on the member states. First, how has the substance of policy at the national level been affected by European-level institutions and policies? Have pressures resulting from the progress of integration resulted in a shift in national defence policies? Second, have developments in integration affected the way in which policy is made at the national level? Is there any evidence, for instance, of national military elites picking up 'habits of co-operation' which in turn have the effect of inclining national policy increasingly towards co-operative action?

A conceptual tool we have found useful in attempting to ascertain the degree of impact of integration on the member states has been that of autonomy. By this we do not in any sense seek to imply absolute national defence self-sufficiency. Indeed, a convincing case can be made for the assertion that the notion of an autonomous national defence policy is something of an illusion. The coming of the nuclear missile revolutionised warfare and impinged severely on state autonomy. Certainly, the concept of nuclear deterrence may have proved successful in preventing the use of these weapons, and hence protecting national territory. Yet, as deterrence is all about bargaining with a potential adversary concerning the possibility of nuclear use, national defence is no longer something that can be assured by the state acting in isolation. Thus, as the development of gunpowder undermined the defensibility of the mediaeval fortress, long-range weapons of mass destruction have undermined the 'hard shell' of the contemporary state (Herz 1957).[2] According to some, we have witnessed 'the final demise of the impermeable territorial state and its boundaries ... in the military sphere' (Kahler 1987: 290). This was perhaps all the more true of a western Europe confronted with a huge military threat from the East and reliant on American protection.

In this volume, we employ the notion of autonomy, as developed in Eric Nordlinger's seminal work on the subject (Nordlinger 1981). According to this view, the state 'is autonomous to the extent that it translates its preferences into authoritative actions' (Nordlinger 1981: 19). One problem inherent in Nordlinger's analysis of autonomy is that it focuses solely on societal constraints on the state, thus ignoring those pressures which may emanate from outside the state's own boundaries. This is unsatisfactory for all policy areas, but especially for one which deals primarily with the outside world. Broadening the notion of autonomy to encompass both domestic and external forces provides us with a useful tool to determine which constraints affect the ability of a state effectively to formulate and implement a defence policy of its own choosing.

Another area in which it is useful to refine Nordlinger's original analysis concerns the state itself, whose preferences, in his formulation, are taken as in some sense 'given'. Clearly this is problematic. The existence or absence of consensus over preferences amongst those various individuals who together form the state is an important determinant of the ability of the state to translate these choices into policy. Internal divisions may well mean public authorities are unable to pursue a coherent strategy, so rendering the state somewhat disadvantaged in squabbles with societal actors over policy outputs and reducing its ability to translate its own preferences into authoritative actions. The chapters that follow, therefore, do examine, where necessary, the complexity of state preference formation, with a view to ascertaining whether the very workings of the state machinery itself have evolved, perhaps as a result of exogenous pressures.

The concept of autonomy serves our purposes in several respects. First, it allows us to differentiate between desired and imposed policy change at the national level. Policy adaptation can occur for any number of reasons, not least because it corresponds to a shift in policy preferences. The concept of autonomy also allows us to differentiate between policy change resulting from integration which accords with state preferences and change which does not. In the former case, Europe does not entail a reduction in state autonomy, whereas in the latter it clearly does. To give a practical example, the decision by the European Commission to block the proposed merger between de Havilland and ATR represented a constraint on the autonomy of the French state to carry out its preferred industrial policy. On the other hand, whilst the deregulation of British industry which occurred in the 1980s was completely consistent with the deregulatory thrust of EC industrial policy at the time, it also corresponded to the preferences of the Thatcher government. National policy outcomes tallied with the requirements of European-level policy and the British state did not, in this instance, find its autonomy circumscribed.

Moreover, the use of autonomy helps us to avoid the problems that arise when, as is often the case, the notion of sovereignty is used as the basis of assessments of the impact of European integration on the member states. Using autonomy allows us to concentrate on *de facto* state capacities rather than on *de jure* legal authority. In other words, we can concentrate on whether governments have the power to adopt certain policies or achieve certain objectives, rather than whether they have the legal right to do so. Whilst in no way undermining sovereignty, integration may impact on autonomy by, for instance, increasing the ability of states to turn preferences into policy through acting as part of a collective.

A final necessary clarification concerns the nature of defence policy itself. In talking about defence policy, we are, in reality, referring to several interrelated yet often distinct strands of policy. First, a distinction must be made, as with all policy sectors, between rhetoric and actual policy. It is important to distinguish between the rhetoric used by national officials, which may appear to have taken on a more 'European' hue, and practical policy choices which are made and implemented. Thus, when the French Prime Minister asserts that 'all aspects of defence are concerned, in one way or another, with the European dimension: the organisation of our forces, our intelligence and logistical capabilities, our industries, our equipment policy' (Juppé 1995), one would need to examine the reality closely before taking this at face value.

Second, actual as opposed to declaratory policy can itself be subdivided. At one extreme, war fighting is clearly a central aspect of defence policy. Beyond this, however, are several increasingly 'routine' aspects of this sector, ranging from nuclear to conventional strategy, to the organisation and deployment of military forces, to procurement policy. Clearly, different strands of policy are vulnerable in different ways to different pressures. Some aspects of defence policy, such as procurement, involve the direct participation of societal actors (for instance private companies) in the policy process (through activities such as lobbying for contracts); the constraints on state autonomy in this context will be very different from those manifest in areas such as nuclear strategy where the state is virtually the sole actor. Similarly, whilst the absence of an EU-level military policy limits the impact of integration on, say, military strategy, procurement policy may well be affected by developments in civilian sectors such as industrial policy.

Having examined the nature of state autonomy as it pertains to defence, we now consider how that autonomy can be circumscribed.

CONSTRAINTS ON THE AUTONOMY OF THE STATE

The focus of this volume is on the role European integration has played in shaping national defence policies. The contributors, therefore, were asked to concentrate on the pressures on state policy emanating from the process of European integration. Defence, however, as Jolyon Howorth illustrates in his chapter, has not developed the complex and powerful institutional framework at the European level that characterises many other policy areas. Therefore the scope for formal institutional impact on national policy is limited. In contrast to other policy sectors where the supranational institutions and EU law exercise a very real impact on the national level, as far as defence is concerned the progress of integration is registered as much in terms of rhetoric and bold intentions as through practical institutional (let alone legal) developments. A more amorphous issue is the role played by the ambitions and intentions of some to move further towards integration in shaping national defence policy. It may well be, for instance, that policy makers will assume future moves towards defence integration from ambitious declarations such as those contained within the Maastricht Treaty. This will lead them to 'factor in' the European dimension even where practical steps have not yet been taken. Hence, the current attempts being made by President Chirac to restructure the French arms industry are partly predicated on the expectation that national firms will soon have to compete in a European arms market.

The authors in this volume have also tried to consider the relative importance of pressures emanating from the European level compared to the other forces which act on the autonomy of the state. As suggested in the discussion of the concept of autonomy, two additional categories of constraint on the autonomy of the state can be identified: first, those imposed by the workings of the external environment; and second, those emanating from within the borders of the nation state.[3]

International pressures can take many forms, ranging from the influence of the structure of the international system (bipolarity) on state action, to the shifting technologies and capital and corporate mobility associated with globalisation. A further issue, given the centrality of NATO to discussions of national security, is the role of international organisations other than the EU and of extra-European states. Such external factors do not necessarily affect all states equally. Domestically, a whole panoply of forces acts on the state, ranging from the influence of powerful arms companies to that exerted by peace movements and trades unions.

Of the three sets of pressures on policy discussed here – domestic, international and European – it is the second that has been the focus (at least implicitly) of most attention in the literature on defence policy. Students of defence matters have traditionally tended to look at national defence policy as a response, or series of responses, to shifting international conditions, though many studies tend to make this assumption implicitly rather than explicitly. Indeed, game theory, based on the notion of unitary states interacting in an environment they dominate, has 'been elevated to the exclusive status as the paradigm of security studies' (Cederman 1996: 2). Similarly, theorists of international politics have tended to point to questions of security as best exemplifying the systemic constraints on state action.

That this has been the case is perhaps unsurprising given the over-whelming constraint on national defence policy that was the Cold War. As one observer has put it:

> no European country *can* have an independent defence policy if the potential adversary is the Soviet Union; for fighting the Argentines in the South Atlantic, perhaps, or the Libyans in Chad, but not for keeping out the Russians. The independence of any European country is contingent on the independence of its neighbours. Therefore the starting point for any European defence policy is the concept of alliance. Not just a purely declaratory alliance either; nor an alliance whose practical arrangements are maintained *sub rosa* by the military while denied by the political elite; nor an alliance where total loyalty is somehow combinable with total independence of national decision-making; nor, because of the speed with which danger could erupt, can it be an improvisatory alliance. A real alliance means integration in advance.
>
> (Davidson 1988: 151)

Such an alliance, moreover, had to include the only Western power capable of deterring Soviet aggression – the United States. However, since 1989 this has all changed. As the burden of the Cold War has been lifted, so Europeans have come increasingly to talk in terms of equipping Europe with a defence capability of its own. The profound changes that occurred after 1989 affected not only international pressures on European states. Within these states, these changes may also have eased some of the constraints on groups seeking to influence policy outcomes by removing the all-encompassing threat facing Western Europe and hence placing defence issues back within the framework of legitimate political debate and dispute. The particular interest of this study at this time is that it enables us to examine the changing nature of the constraints facing the state while these are in mutation.

As far as the EU itself is concerned, we did not, in undertaking this volume, expect to discover that it played as central a role in shaping national defence policies as it does in some other policy areas. In itself, this does not negate the validity or value of the study, in that defence provides a useful contrast to the other sectors investigated in the series and will improve our understanding of integration through a consideration of the differential impact it exerts across policy sectors. Moreover, given the prominence accorded to questions of defence in debates over integration in recent years, it would be fair to expect to find at least some evidence of European influence over national policy. In this respect, we can usefully distinguish between the different kinds of impact that could be looked for.

First, the relationship between integration and the state can have various implications for the autonomy of the latter. In some cases, state autonomy is clearly reduced by integration as national decision-making competence is watered down or supplemented by European institutions. At other times, however, EU action may actually enhance state autonomy (for a strong statement of this, see Moravcsik 1994). The gains of collective action may outweigh an individual state's loss of decision-making autonomy as the collective manages to achieve goals no longer feasible for a single state. This would be the case if it were found that the EU allowed members the financial and technological means – clearly unavailable to each of them individually – to protect themselves against missile attacks.

This hypothetical example also serves to illustrate that the EU may exercise an impact through its interactions with other pressures coming to bear on the state. In this case, the effects of advancements in weapons technology which render states vulnerable to attack are mitigated through collective European-level action. The same may be true of domestic pressures. In some cases, the Union may serve as a justification, or alibi, for policy initiatives; in others as a scapegoat to be blamed for unpleasant policies which displease powerful domestic lobbies. François Mitterrand, for instance, made a virtue out of necessity by explaining his 1983 U-turn on macroeconomic policy in terms of a renewed desire to strengthen and enhance European integration.

The EU's impact on national defence policy will not always be direct. While in many cases one would expect developments in defence co-operation at the European level to feed back into national policies, this is not always the case. European initiatives in other spheres could also have an impact on defence policy: we could expect, for instance, that the convergence criteria for economic and monetary union, by necessitating greater fiscal parsimony, may well have played a part in shaping national defence budgets. Moreover, the effects of European-level activity may not be felt, in the first instance, at the level of the state itself. Action taken at the European level may alter the behaviour of private actors, which in turn influences state behaviour. The creation of a European Armaments Agency, and increasingly urgent talk of the need to remove barriers between heavily insulated national armaments markets, could spark a round of mergers between defence-related firms, in much the same way that the Single European Market scheme provoked a flurry of intra-European mergers and takeovers in late 1988 by holding out the prospect of a larger market.

Finally, it is important, in our quest for traces of European influence on national policy, not to make the mistake of attributing any signs of an increased pro-European enthusiasm on the part of member states to this influence. Indications that national officials are starting to favour further moves towards bestowing a defence role on the EU may well not be explicable in terms of the impact of Europe itself. Often, international pressures (doubts about the continued American commitment to Europe, the prevalence of regional conflicts in a post-Cold War international system and so on) or domestic factors (shrinking budgets), may lead governments to adopt this attitude. European outcomes are not necessarily the result of European pressures.

THE STRUCTURE OF THE BOOK

The first chapter provides an empirical background to the subject. Howorth, in chapter one, outlines the tortuous history of attempts to link defence with European integration and highlights recent initiatives whose effects on the national level the later chapters investigate.

A number of country studies follow. They provide a comparative national perspective on the question of EU impact. Four chapters are devoted to the larger member states – France, Germany, Italy and the United Kingdom. Howorth, Bohnen, Hill and Andreatta, and Chuter respectively point to the very different factors that have shaped and continue to shape defence policies in these countries. They show how different histories and geographies have led to very different outlooks on, and responses to, European defence integration. David Chuter's insightful cultural deconstruction of the British defence establishment's almost visceral anti-European instincts points to one factor which may help to explain why, whatever the pressures and whatever their prominence, state preferences may be slow to change. Alfred van Staden then examines the pressures on Dutch defence policy, giving an idea of what the question of defence autonomy means for a small state without real power potential in this field. The survey of countries is not exhaustive, and an obvious lacuna is the absence of any chapter dealing with a neutral state. The countries chosen, however, provide enough contrast to allow a judgement on whether and, if yes, which national factors condition the impact of EU action.

The volume then looks at two key issues in the contemporary debate over defence, integration and the nation state. It underlines the point that defence is a sector of tremendous diversity in which the pressures acting on one segment of policy may differ radically from those on others. The question of nuclear weapons, investigated by Croft, is a crucial one. This is so not only because of their perceived connections to autonomy in both Britain and France, but also because of repeated recent claims, emanating in particular from Paris, regarding the need for a European deterrent in order to have a European defence. Croft examines the debates in Britain and France and analyses the often contradictory pressures at work on the nuclear stances of these two states. Taylor considers the pressures on national procurement policies, often considered the 'soft' end of defence policy. His analysis serves not only to illustrate the various constraints that hinder as well as promote more europeanisation of national policy, but also makes clear the links between defence and the economic questions touched on by other books in the series.

National defence policies in Western Europe are undergoing a period of radical transformation. Even now, some seven years after the end of the Cold War, it is clear that statesmen have, in many if not most cases, failed to come to grips with the full implications of that momentous watershed in international affairs. Whilst clearly not presenting an exhaustive study of defence policy in Western Europe, this volume will cast light on an increasingly important and topical aspect of contemporary European security: the role of the European Union in influencing the shifts in national policy currently underway.

NOTES

1 The author would like to acknowledge the support provided by ESRC Research Grant R000221254 which has enabled him to carry out research on the pressures affecting national defence policy.

2 It is the combination of weapons of mass destruction along with the means of their delivery which has successfully undermined the notion of national defence. The one without the other simply would not have the same effect: the initial stages of the development of the *force de frappe* saw a French nuclear force that depended for its delivery on *Mirage* attack bombers whose range implied the necessity to refuel over Warsaw Pact territory. Clearly, the possibility of a successful mission against Russian soil was therefore limited.

3 This is not to claim that it is possible to distinguish clearly between these, as they often overlap or can be mutually reinforcing. For example, technological developments, which can be viewed as a systemic phenomenon affecting all

states, by increasing the technological complexity of warfare, can strengthen the position of specialist groups at home, so making it harder for political leaders adequately to understand, and hence refute, their claims and demands.

REFERENCES

Cederman, Lars-Erik (1996) 'From Primordialism to Constructivism: The Quest for Flexible Models of Ethnic Conflict', paper prepared for delivery at the meeting of the American Political Science Association, San Francisco, 29 August–September 1996.

Davidson, Ian (1988) 'A new step in Franco–British co-operation', in Boyer, Y., Lellouche, P. and Roper, J. (eds) *Franco-British Defence Co-operation: A New Entente Cordiale?*, London: Routledge.

Herz, J. (1957) 'The rise and demise of the territorial state', *World Politics*, 9, 473–93.

Juppé, A. (1995) 'Declaration of general policy by the Prime Minister, Alain Juppé, Paris, National Assembly, 23 May 1995', text supplied by the French Embassy in London.

Kahler, M. (1987) 'The survival of the state in European international relations' in Maier, C. *Changing Boundaries of the Political: Essays on the evolving balance between the state and society, public and private in Europe*, Cambridge: Cambridge University Press.

Kassim, H. and Menon, A. (1996) 'Introduction', in Kassim, H. and Menon A. (eds) *The European Union and National Industrial Policy*, London: Routledge.

Moravcsik, Andrew (1994) *Why the European Community Strengthens the State: Domestic politics and international co-operation*, Harvard University Centre for European Studies Working paper series, no. 52.

—— (1993) 'Preferences and Power in the European Community: a liberal inter-governmentalist approach', *Journal of Common Market Studies* 31:4, 473–523.

Nordlinger, E. (1981) *On the Autonomy of the Democratic State*, Cambridge, MA: Harvard University Press.

1 National defence and European security integration

An illusion inside a chimera?

Jolyon Howorth

The history of European integration since 1945 is indissociable from the history of attempts to create a relatively autonomous European security and defence identity (ESDI). This assertion requires four important clarificatory comments. First, the notion of 'European integration' embraces all bilateral and multilateral activities between and among the states of (for the moment mainly Western) Europe. It is much more than the history of the EEC/EC/EU; but it is much less than the advent of something many British commentators call 'federalism'. Second, ESDI is 'indissociable' from that history in that the desire to secure the peace internally as well as externally was the primary motivation for European integration in the first place, and also in the sense that most of the landmarks of the integration process have been accompanied by a security dimension. Third, the ESDI concept itself requires several comments. Pressure for its gestation has come overwhelmingly from France. The delightfully equivocal notion of 'identity' is a semantic attempt not to tread on any institutional toes. ESDI is an assertion by the European states of the desirability and legitimacy of their quest for more concerted influence over issues affecting European security.[1] This was perhaps most concisely stated in article 4 of the October 1987 'Platform on European Security Interests' agreed by the WEU members at The Hague.[2]

However, and this is the fourth clarificatory point, the assertion of that concerted influence has always been qualified by the parallel contention that Europe's security can ultimately be guaranteed only through the Atlantic Alliance. Hence the use, in my opening sentence, of the notion of 'relative autonomy'. Implicit in it is the proposition that ESDI should provide Europe with a security capacity which would place it in a state of relative political and military non-dependence on Washington – without the relationship degenerating into one marked by disagreement or conflict. This has always been implicit rather than explicit in the formulation of the ESDI concept, as typified by the 1987 Hague Platform:

It is our conviction that a more united Europe will make a stronger contribution to the Alliance, to the benefit of Western security as a whole. This will enhance the European role in the Alliance and ensure the basis for a balanced partnership across the Atlantic. We are resolved to strengthen the European pillar of the Alliance.

(WEU 1987: 41)

In theory, this objective was endorsed by NATO in the 1991 'New Strategic Concept':

The development of a European security identity and defence role, reflected in the strengthening of the European pillar within the Alliance, will not only serve the interests of the European states but also reinforce the integrity and effectiveness of the Alliance as a whole

(Ganz and Roper 1993: 205–17)

Yet the problem of 'autonomy' has constantly bedevilled the entire debate on ESDI. Against those (mainly in Europe) who argue that a more powerful Europe would make for a stronger Alliance, are those (mainly in America) who insist that any increase in European autonomy constitutes an inevitable weakening of the Alliance. The Bush administration in particular suspected that the pressure for relative autonomy concealed a desire to break free of the Atlantic Alliance (Kelleher 1995: 188). Hence Bush's famous admonition at the Rome NATO summit in 1991: 'If your ultimate aim is to provide for your own defence, the time to tell us is today!' That comment sits uncomfortably with the text of the New Strategic Concept. ESDI, if it has any meaning at all, implies some measure of autonomy. Nobody has yet shown how autonomy is compatible with integration.

Moreover, as the Reflection Group framing the 1996 agenda for the Inter-Governmental Conference (IGC) discovered, the forging of a viable ESDI is a fine balancing act involving a variety of international players most of whom have different agendas.[3] To date ESDI has remained something of a chimera, even though, as this volume demonstrates, strategic discussion in Europe over the past ten years has been largely informed by attempts to bring it into being.

Since 1949, there has been no such thing as 'national defence' in Europe. The technology of weapons systems, the internationalisation of security institutions, NATO's integrated command structure, growing interdependence at every level, and the ever broadening definition of security – all these have consigned to the history books earlier approaches to the 'military' 'defence' of the 'nation'. Only at the most abstract level did the theology of nuclear deterrence allow certain European states (France and Britain) the luxury of claiming that their own national security was safe in sovereign hands. What this would have meant in practice must remain conjecture. But there are experts aplenty – former apostles of NATO doctrine such as Henry Kissinger, McGeorge Bundy and Robert McNamara among them – who have argued that nuclear weapons 'serve no military purpose whatsoever' (McNamara 1983: 79). François Mitterrand was once pressed by Mrs Thatcher about his willingness to 'go nuclear' if Soviet troops ever overran NATO's front-line defences and bore down on Bonn. He sought refuge from the dilemma in the not entirely casuistic argument that the implications of such a scenario would be that both NATO and deterrence had failed and that, therefore, he (France) would be obliged to reassess the situation (Mitterrand 1988: 60). The point here is that, despite assertions of 'national independence' in the nuclear field, the advent of nuclear weapons effectively created a single strategic and security space in Europe, the breach of any part of which would affect the security of the whole. In that sense also the concept of national defence has long been at best a misnomer, at worst a logical contradiction. On the surface, a volume such as this one, which aims to scrutinise the impact of European security integration (a chimera) on national defence policy (an illusion), ought to be a very short one.

The illusion of national defence and the chimera of European security integration are both largely explained by the existence and reality of NATO. To date, both national and continental dimensions of security have been utterly subsumed within the Atlantic Alliance. The fact that, for most of the post-war period, most of the European nations have felt more comfortable than uncomfortable with that arrangement does not conceal the reality that the arrangement itself has been considered unsatisfactory by several states at different times and for different reasons. The principal grievance has been a sense of power imbalance within the Alliance and the suggested remedy has usually involved some scheme or other for producing greater equilibrium between the two sides of the Atlantic (Smith 1984; Treverton 1985; de Porte 1986; Alford and Hunt 1988). Hence, the pressure towards ESDI.

From the outset, the French were the prime movers. As early as 1934, Charles De Gaulle, in his *Vers l'Armée de Métier*, had argued for an integrated European security structure. After the War, the creation of some sort of West European security and political union became a constant feature of Gaullist pronouncements (Bozo 1996; Howorth 1996). The Treaty of Washington in 1949, together with the onset of the Korean War a year later, both implying German rearmament, galvanised European thinking on how best to establish the correct balance between Germany and Europe, and between Europe and the USA. The result was the Pleven Plan for the European Defence Community (EDC). This French plan gave rise to a French counter-proposal. For De Gaulle, as for Jean Monnet (the author of the Pleven Plan), Europe could not be Europe without its own army. Yet, during the passionate debates of 1950–4, the dichotomy was not between 'European' defence (Monnet/ EDC) and 'national' defence (De Gaulle) but between two contradictory perceptions of how effectively 'European' the different models would be.

Both projects sought to create the greatest possible measure of European military integration.[4] Both had enormous weaknesses, which their respective critics did not fail to highlight. For Monnet, De Gaulle's vision of an integrated European army retaining a multiplicity of national commands was either a cover for an attempt at French hegemony or a recipe for disaster. For De Gaulle, Monnet's *apatride* troops, marching to the orders of Brussels-based supranational technocrats, was a recipe both for military disaster and for permanent American hegemony. Both critiques were well-founded. Neither scheme had much future, their detailed operational requirements were wanting in all sorts of ways. In the end, what Europe got was the modified Treaty of Brussels and *de facto* NATO hegemony.

Once installed as President, De Gaulle immediately relaunched various initiatives aimed at restoring the balance in European–American relations and at laying down the groundwork for greater European co-operation. In particular, the Fouchet Plan (1960–2) and the Franco–German Treaty (1963) both aimed in rather different ways at the fundamental objective of forging a more unified European defence entity. Both failed primarily because they left unresolved the question of future relations between such an entity and the USA (Soutou 1992; Maillard 1995: Ch. 7; Bozo 1996). The issue was raised again under the Pompidou presidency as part of a general thrust towards European political union. Pompidou and Edward Heath had, from the outset, engaged in top secret negotiations about defence (including nuclear) co-operation, the details of which were only revealed in 1994 (Roussel 1994: 652–9). One of their prime motivations was concern about American economic pressures on Europe as the old Bretton Woods order collapsed. It was ironic, therefore, that in his April 1973 address launching the 'Year of Europe', Kissinger should specifically stress the need for 'linkage' between American security protection for Europe and European acquiescence in (or even concessions towards) American economic leadership. French Foreign Minister Michel Jobert's plans to relaunch the Western European Union as a counterweight to Washington within the Atlantic Alliance once again came to nought because the more Atlanticist European partners, although nervous about American intentions, were even more nervous about the shorter-term implications of ESDI (Cogan 1994: Ch. 7).

By the end of the 1970s, after a decade of European political co-operation (Nuttall 1992), four years of European frustration with the vacillations of the Carter administration, coupled with apprehension in the face of growing Soviet assertiveness around the globe (culminating in the December 1979 invasion of Afghanistan), prompted renewed interest in ESDI.

In many ways it was the Europeans who took the lead in generating the strategic debates of the early 1980s. Helmut Schmidt's 1977 speech to the International Institute for Strategic Studies on the need for intermediate nuclear force (INF) disarmament in Europe was followed by Giscard d'Estaing's hosting of the four power summit in Guadeloupe in January 1979. The latter prepared the ground for NATO's December 1979 decision to deploy INF weapons in Europe which in turn triggered the 'Euromissiles crisis'. As Reagan replaced Carter and the two superpowers confronted each other over missile deployment or disarmament in Europe, and as European governments directed their fire against their domestic peace movements, however, the prospects for a new initiative on ESDI faded momentarily. They resurfaced with a vengeance in 1983 and 1984 as several historical factors coalesced. After deployment of the Euromissiles in 1983, European governments were able to take their minds off their domestic peace movements. They were, however, immediately confronted by a new problem. The Strategic Defence Initiative (SDI) appeared to undermine the American nuclear guarantee to Europe through the deployment of space-based anti-missile defence systems which would protect American soil while leaving Western Europe exposed. Moreover, the unilateral manner in which President Reagan had announced this initiative underscored once again the extent of European dependency. The Western European Union was relaunched (WEU 1987; Gamble 1989; Dean 1994: Ch. 11).

The most significant question immediately raised by the revival of WEU was its relationship with NATO and with Washington. Reagan continued to shock the Europeans with his unilateral initiatives – notably through his meeting at Reykjavik in November 1986 with Mikhail Gorbachev. That meeting came close to undermining the entire strategic basis of Atlantic security, with Reagan being prevented from agreeing to Gorbachev's proposal for total nuclear disarmament only by a rearguard action on the part of his advisers (IISS 1986–7: 56–65). Yet the Europeans still shrank from accepting a French proposal to draft a full-blooded 'European security charter'. Instead, they confined their objective to strengthening the European pillar within NATO. Militarily, however, apart from one or two largely symbolic developments such as the Franco–German brigade and the joint minesweeping force in the Gulf, it meant little more than a statement of intent: 'to develop a more cohesive European defence identity which will translate more effectively into practice the obligations of solidarity to which we are committed' (WEU 1987: 37). The Cold War was not yet over and opportunities for joint military action other than in peripheral theatres such as the Gulf were still extremely rare. Politically, the quest for ESDI reflected a threefold ambition on the part of most WEU countries: to reinforce the integration process recently accelerated by the Single European Act; to offer a European voice in matters connected with arms control and disarmament; and to offer a European view on relations with the Soviet Union via the Conference on Security and Co-operation in Europe (CSCE). These ambitions not only responded to endogenous European strivings for greater integration. They also reflected the growing sense of concern in Europe that, from an exogenous perspective, the harmony of West–West relations could no longer simply be taken for granted; nor could responsibility for relations between Europe and other areas of the world – including Russia – be forever delegated to Washington.

These developments accelerated rapidly after November 1989 with the fall of the Berlin Wall. For a brief moment, France, once again taking the lead in pushing for ESDI, appeared to be challenging US leadership in the European security area. However, Franco–American clashes over the reform of NATO (Grant 1996), dramatic though they appeared at the time, amounted in the first instance to a conflict over the relative priority to be accorded to the political and to the military. The French view was that clear political objectives should be set before discussing military restructuring. The American view appeared to reverse those priorities. Throughout 1990 and the early part of 1991, one might have been forgiven for thinking that Paris saw WEU as a potential alternative to NATO rather than as a complement (Delors 1991). But several developments forced a radical rethink on that score and gave rise to the process which is the subject of this volume's enquiry.

First, the 1991 Gulf War forced Europe in general, and France and Germany in particular (albeit in very different ways), to face up to their own inadequacies on the security front (Howorth 1994; Yost 1993; Kaiser and Becher 1993). The lesson learnt here was that the Europeans were nowhere near ready to ensure their own security, but it was essential for them to begin to get their act together. The second development was the qualitative leap forward taken by the European nations at Maastricht. This contained contradictory implications in security terms. On the one hand, the Maastricht Treaty overtly asserted the need for a European common foreign and security policy (CFSP). On the other hand, the rigorous convergence criteria agreed on for the planned move towards economic and monetary union (EMU) in effect meant that European governments were going to have to cut back significantly on government spending. The third development was the emergence of strong political pressure in all countries for a post-Cold War 'peace dividend'. This, combined with the need to reduce state deficits, made it very difficult for European governments to contemplate financing the pursuit of auton- omous security. The fourth, and in many ways the most significant development, was the experience of former Yugoslavia. Not only did the Europeans realise again that in diplomatic and military terms they were still pygmies; they also interpreted US reluctance to become involved in Bosnia as a sign of resurgent isolationism. The result was a move towards energetic reassertion of the indivisibility of security on both sides of the Atlantic. One final major development was the arrival in the White House of a new president who did not share the hegemonic assumptions of previous American administrations. Bill Clinton seemed happy to allow the Europeans to develop ESDI – on condition that it complemented rather than contradicted NATO. That, as we have seen, had always been the greatest challenge to the framers of ESDI. But the fact that Washington now appeared to endorse the legitimacy of the attempt constituted a major breakthrough. Since 1994, all NATO, WEU and European partners have actively been seeking the magic formula which would allow the flowering of ESDI in a way which would enhance rather than weaken the Atlantic Alliance. This volume analyses key aspects of that process.

Prior to the late 1980s, the impact on national defence policies of European (as opposed to NATO) considerations was minimal. It was limited mainly to a number of joint military procurement projects whose rationale was usually (and overtly) maintaining a foothold in the upper reaches of high-technology industrial development and avoiding sub-contractor status *vis-à-vis* the USA (Creasey and May 1988; Hébert 1991: Ch. 9; Sharp and Shearman 1987). It is true that, throughout the 1980s, Franco–German defence 'co-operation' had acquired a high profile, the two countries having decided, for their own and often quite different reasons, to intensify their security dialogue (Friend 1991; McCarthy 1993). However, developments in this area were more symbolic than real. Even the creation of the *Force d'Action Rapide* in 1983 (a significant political gesture from Paris to Bonn) was stronger on symbolism than substance (David 1984). Moreover, on several really substantial issues (the role and purpose of French 'prestrategic' nuclear weapons; the joint production of a new fighter aircraft and a new battle-tank) 'nationalist' positions prevailed over any hypothetical European ones. In Britain, the 1980s saw a series of major arguments within the defence establishment between the rival advocates of the Atlantic and European options. In every significant case, the European option lost out.

It is therefore all the more remarkable that, within five years of the fall of the Berlin Wall, most of the main European security actors have begun to devote the highest priority to the European perspective in defence policy and planning. In Germany we have witnessed not only a modification of the constitution in response to European demands, but also a cultural sea-change marked by the emergence of a new concept – *Europafähigkeit* (Europe-compatibility) – as the central strand in German defence thinking. In Holland, which traditionally eschewed WEU and Europeanisation as little more than a French agenda for self-aggrandisement, the post-1989 period (particularly since 1994) has been marked by accelerated Europeanisation in procurement, deployment and doctrine. In Italy also, where previously a NATO culture reigned supreme, there has been a growing Europeanisation of security discourse. In France, the radical defence reforms announced in February 1996 were, as presaged in the *Livre Blanc* of 1994, predicated quite explicitly on the imperatives of Europeanisation. This is also true in the previously sacrosanct realm of nuclear policy, where the concept of *dissuasion concertée* (concerted deterrence) has become the quasi-official rationale for a continuing nuclear effort.

Forging a common European nuclear capability and policy will be no easy task, but the prospect is now considerably more real than it was only five years ago. The Europeans may not quite be faced with the stark choice posed by the French *Livre Blanc*: 'With nuclear weapons, European defence autonomy is a possibility; without them, it is out of the question' (*Livre Blanc* 1994: 98). But nuclear weapons are clearly on the European agenda where only a few years ago such a proposition would have seemed impossible. In particular, the need for a joint European approach to non-proliferation and test ban negotiations has brought the issue to the fore. The obstacles to a common approach are legion. But the issue itself is unlikely to go away. The main area in which rapid developments have recently begun to take place, however, is in procurement. The restructuring and rationalisation of the European defence industry is an objective to which all governments pay notional allegiance. Even the British government seems finally to have decided that participation in the European Armaments Agency is not only unavoidable but actually desirable.

Which brings us to the UK: as so often, it is the exception which proves the rule. The British defence establishment's almost visceral anti-European instincts point out the serious limitations on meaningful European security integration, at least in the short term. Britain arguably possesses – still – the best trained and most efficient fighting forces in Europe. Without their contribution, any ESDI would be incomplete. Britain's position within the spectrum of options being discussed at the IGC remains resolutely 'anti-European' in the sense that the London government alone objects to *any* proposals which might lead to the merger of WEU and the EU. And yet, even the British government accepts the need for ever greater co-operation and concertation on security matters between the members of WEU (*Partnership of Nations* 1996: 20).

Much may now hinge on the practical military consequences of the largely political agreements reached at the Berlin meeting of NATO foreign ministers in June 1996. The key to the future is the notion of Combined Joint Task Forces (CJTFs), first mooted at the breakthrough meeting of the North Atlantic Council (NAC), in Brussels in January 1994. What was formally agreed in Berlin was that, henceforth, the WEU countries will be able, on their own, to deploy NATO resources to conduct military operations with which the USA does not wish to be involved. There are two conditions and a number of qualifications to this arrangement. The conditions are that the proposed WEU operation must receive the prior political approval of the NAC and that NATO should, throughout the course of the operation, maintain a watching brief over its development. The qualifications concern the type of NATO hardware which will be available to the Europeans: anti-aircraft systems, some elements of command, control, communications and intelligence, and AWACS. It is unclear whether more sensitive hardware, long-range transport aircraft and satellite intelligence will automatically be available. There will no doubt be much hard bargaining over the coming months and years. As always, the sticking point is the stage at which autonomy is deemed not to strengthen but to weaken the alliance. The increasing europeanisation in national defence policies is primarily geared to developing the capacity to act quickly and effectively to contain and resolve any Balkan conflicts. Only in the long term can Europe guarantee the security and stability of its hinterland. For the present, however, WEU countries appear to have both the political desire and the diplomatic green light to try to develop such a military capacity. Some will continue to treat such a prospect with scepticism. Many laughed politely when, in 1949, the German constitution proclaimed national unity as its first goal. As in that case, the long term may be the only framework for judgement.

In the longer term, four readily identifiable factors will help inform the outcome. First, the success of the current IGC is critical. If the Europeans cannot even agree among themselves on the institutional framework within which to set their intended CFSP, there is little chance of ESDI becoming a reality. Latest indications are that a reasonable level of consensus is emerging within the IGC around certain key issues: strengthening policy planning staffs; the appointment of a senior person with responsibility for CFSP; more flexible application of unanimity rule in decision-making in order to avoid stalemates; financing of joint actions from the EU budget; the inclusion in the Maastricht Treaty of 'Petersberg tasks' (covering intervention in crisis areas for humanitarian and peace-keeping purposes); the development of links between the EU and WEU with a view to future integration of the latter into the former. If agreement can be reached on the means of implementing those decisions, then the prospects of endogenous progress towards ESDI are reasonable.

Second, the decision of the Clinton administration, in August 1996, to punish European firms maintaining links with countries such as Libya and Iran re-emphasised the volatile nature of the shared values underpinning the Atlantic community. The possibilities for US–European tensions are legion: the growing importance of domestic priorities; negotiations within the World Trade Organisation; relations with Russia, China and the Middle East; competition in high-technology, particularly defence-related, industries; and even on cultural issues (Gordon 1996). In the working out of these difficulties, two potentially contradictory pressures are leading to the same strategic conclusion. US reluctance to remain involved, on the ground, in messy European peace-keeping operations, coupled with a sense of the need, nevertheless, to assert the steadfastness of Atlantic values suggest that a compromise involving serious rebalancing of the Alliance would be in the interests of both sides. From the European angle, this paradox is reflected in the growing awareness of the need to keep the Americans involved in securing European security but to do more of their work for them.

Third, what of Russia? NATO expansion to the East, as ardently desired and promoted in Prague, Budapest and Warsaw as it is abhorred and resisted in Moscow, is set fair to be a major strategic question for the early part of the next century. How will the Europeans, particularly the Germans with their new-found diplomatic clout and their growing military muscle, respond to the challenge of co-managing with Washington a development which is clearly interpreted in very different ways on the two sides of the Atlantic. Would the emergence of an ESDI be regarded in Moscow as more reassuring or more threatening than a robust implementation of Partnership for Peace?

Finally, the Europeans face numerous challenges arising from militant Islam. The arc of instability which runs from the Bosphorus to the Red Sea and back to the Atlantic presents innumerable challenges for the embryonic ESDI. The possibility of a major upheaval almost anywhere along that crescent at any moment in the foreseeable future will immediately bring into play the need for both policy co-ordination and, conceivably, military co-operation.

As the chapters in this volume show, Europe is gradually becoming aware of itself as an international actor. The end of the Cold War and the replacement of a single, apocalyptic, yet somewhat abstract threat with a series of less momentous crises around the periphery have forced the United States and the EU to rethink the basic structures of their alliance. To become aware of oneself as an actor is one thing. To play the part – particularly in a world made infinitely complex by multiple patterns of interdependence – is quite another.

NOTES

1 The acronym ESDI acquired general currency only in the post-1989 period and it could be considered anachronistic to use it to refer to the earlier period. But, as shorthand for the many attempts to bring about greater European defence co-operation or integration, it is both neat and not inappropriate.
2 'We remain determined to pursue European integration, including security and defence and make a more effective contribution to the common defence of the West. To this end, we shall:

  • ensure that our determination to defend any member country at its borders is made clearly manifest by means of appropriate arrangements;
  • improve our consultations and extend our co-ordination in defence and security matters and examine all practical steps to this end;
  • make the best possible use of the existing institutional mechanisms to involve the Defence Ministers and their representatives in the work of WEU;
  • see to it that the level of each country's contribution to the common defence adequately reflects its capabilities;

- aim at a more effective use of existing resources, inter alia by expanding bilateral and regional military co-operation, pursue our efforts to maintain in Europe a technologically advanced industrial base and intensify armaments co-operation;
- concert our policies on crises outside Europe insofar as they may affect our security interests.'

(WEU 1987: 43)

3 The single conundrum of relations between EU and WEU occupies the vast majority of the Reflection Group's report on security issues and has generated numerous bulky official documents. The options are as polarised as their promotion by different protagonists is vigorous. Both the Reflection Group and the WEU Council canvass three basic options. The first, promoted increasingly vigorously by the UK, pleads for the status quo: the maintenance of an autonomous WEU, along with the promotion of practical arrangements for ever closer co-operation between that body and the EU at every institutional level. The second, promoted by a majority of countries, including France, Germany, Belgium and Spain (plus the Commission and the European Parliament) proposes a phased merger between EU and WEU and the transfer to the former of all the functions currently carried out by the latter. The only nuance of difference between countries promoting this option concerns timing. The third option varies from text to text. The Reflection Group structures it as a division within WEU between 'Petersberg tasks' (covering intervention in crisis areas for humanitarian and peacekeeping purposes) and 'Article 5 tasks' (involving the security of Europe as a whole and requiring the engagement of American forces). The latter would remain the remit of an autonomous WEU, while the former would revert to EU jurisdiction, either through politically or legally binding directives, or through transfer to the EU of part of WEU's functions. The WEU Council thought any third alternative would offer three avenues for the transmission of EU decisions to WEU for implementation: stronger Council 'guidelines'; EU 'instructions'; 'legally binding link'. Whatever the relative merits of these various alternatives to the two starker choices of autonomy or merger, it is clear that their *raison d'être* is twofold: a) to facilitate a process eventually leading to merger; b) to allow greater flexibility for neutrals to participate in peacekeeping and other security operations.

4 De Gaulle has wrongly been accused of opposition to the principle of an integrated European defence. In fact, he wanted a much more far-reaching structure than that proposed under the guise of the EDC. For a start, he insisted that a European army must include Britain – as well as all the other nations excluded from the EDC (De Gaulle 1990: Vol. 2, 566). Secondly, he wanted a very high degree of integration:

> from the perspective of European defence, it is of the highest practical necessity that the countries involved should adopt the same strategic plans and should place in common all those resources which can be merged without depriving the various armies of their body and their soul: infrastructure – that is to say airports, ports and communications systems; the structure of combat units; weapons systems; the productions of certain materials; command structures; joint general staffs, etc., every means of co-operation which would allow for the ideal association of nations in a confederation of states.

(De Gaulle 1990: Vol. 2, 590)

REFERENCES

Alford, J. and Hunt, K. (eds) (1988) *Europe in the Western Alliance. Towards a European Defence Entity*, London: Macmillan.

Bozo, F. (1996) *Deux Stratégies pour l'Europe: De Gaulle, les Etats-Unis et l'Alliance Atlantique*, Paris: Plon.

Cogan, C. G. (1994) *Oldest Allies, Guarded Friends. The United States and France since 1940*, Westport: Praeger.

Creasey, P. and May, S. (eds) (1988) *The European Armaments Market and Procurement Cooperation*, London: Macmillan.

David, D. (1984) *La Force d'Action Rapide en Europe: Le Dire des Armes*, Paris: FEDN.

Dean, J. (1994) *Ending Europe's Wars: the continuing search for peace and security*, New York: 20th Century Fund.

De Gaulle, C. (1990) *Discours et Messages*, Paris: Plon.

Delors, J. (1991) 'European integration and security', *Survival*, March/April.

De Porte, A. (1986) *Europe between the superpowers: the enduring balance*, New Haven, CT: Yale University Press, 2nd ed.

Friend, J. W. (1991) *The Linchpin: French–German Relations, 1950–1990*, New York: Praeger.

Gamble, I. (1989) 'Prospects for West European security co-operation', *Adelphi Paper* No. 244.

Ganz, N. and Roper, J. (eds) (1993) *Towards a new partnership: US–European Relations in the post-Cold War era*, Paris: WEU.

Gordon, P. H. (1996) 'Recasting the Atlantic Alliance', *Survival*, 38/1, Spring.

Grant, R. P. (1996) 'France's new relationship with NATO', *Survival*, 38/1, Spring.

Hébert, J-P. (1991) *Stratégie Française et Industrie d'Armement*, Paris: FEDN.

Howorth, J. (1994) 'French policy in the conflict', in Danchev, A. and Keohane, D. (eds) *International Perspectives on the Gulf Conflict*, London: Macmillan.

—— (1996) 'France and European security 1944–1994: re-reading the Gaullist "consensus"', in Chafer, A. and Jenkins, B. (eds) *France from the Cold War to the New World Order*, London: Macmillan.

IISS (1986–7) *Strategic Survey 1986–1987*, London: IISS.

Kaiser, K. and Becher, K. (1993) 'Germany and the Iraq conflict' in Gnesotto, N. and Roper, J. *Western Europe and the Gulf*, Paris: WEU.

Kelleher, C. (1995) *The Future of European Security: an interim assessment*, Washington, DC: Brookings.

Livre Blanc sur la Défense (1994) Paris: 10/18.

Maillard, P. (1995) *De Gaulle et l'Europe*, Paris: Tallandier.

McCarthy, P. (ed.) (1993) *France and Germany 1983–1993: The Struggle to Cooperate*, London: Macmillan.

McNamara, R. (1983) 'The Military Role of Nuclear Weapons: perceptions and misperceptions', *Foreign Affairs*, 62/1.

Mitterrand, F. (1988) Speech in *Propos sur la Défense* No. 5, Septembre–Octobre.

Nuttall, S. (1992) *European Political Cooperation*, Oxford: Clarendon.

A Partnership of Nations (1996) London: HMSO (Cm 3181).

Roussel, E. (1994) *Georges Pompidou 1911–1974*, Paris: Lattes.

Sharp, M. and Shearman, C. (1987) *European Technological Collaboration*, London: Routledge.

Smith, M. (1984) *Western Europe and the United States. The Uncertain Alliance*, London: Allen & Unwin.

Soutou, G-H. (1992) 'Le Général de Gaulle et le plan Fouchet' in [ICDG ed.], *De Gaulle en son Siècle, Vol. 5. L'Europe*, Paris: Plon.

Treverton, G. F. (1985) *Making the Alliance Work. The United States and Western Europe*, London: Macmillan.

WEU (1987) *The Reactivation of WEU: Statements and Communiqués 1984 to 1987*, Paris: WEU.

Yost, D. (1993) 'France and the Gulf War of 1990–1991: political–military lessons learnt', *Journal of Strategic Studies*, 16/3.

2 France

Jolyon Howorth

There are several major difficulties in deconstructing the relationship between French and European security policy. The first, and most obvious, is that 'European policy', in so far as it exists, has tended to be primarily French in conception and impulsion (see Chapter 1, p. 12). This is as true of security policy as of any other field of policy and it has been the case virtually since 1944 (Howorth 1996a). However, and this is the second difficulty, pressure from Paris in favour of the creation of some sort of European Defence and Security Identity (EDSI), sustained and imperative though it has tended to be, has not always been complemented by any actual Europeanisation of French defence policy and planning. There is a related problem, to which I shall return, of defining what might be meant by the 'Europeanisation' of a nation such as France's 'national' defence policy. A third problem is the discrepancy between discourse and reality. An uninformed observer called upon to read the major documents, texts and speeches emanating over the last few years from the command centres of French defence planning – whether the seat of the presidency at the Elysée Palace, the office of the Prime Minister at the Hôtel Matignon or the ministry of defence on the rue Saint Dominique – might be forgiven for believing that French and European defence policy were nearly identical.[1] France tends to treat defence and security policy as if she were acting for the whole of Europe. Paris has a long tradition of calling the shots on the continent and a combination of French resource inputs, military and industrial capacity and grandiose security ambitions puts France in a class of its own. But therein lies another problem. Despite the rhetoric, France's defence thinking on certain key issues (nuclear policy, alliance policy, resourcing, industrial policy and conscription) has often been visibly out of step with the majority of its European partners. Paradoxically, this appeared at first to change quite rapidly in 1995 with the advent of the neo-Gaullist President Jacques Chirac. His defence reforms of February 1996, which amount, as we shall see, to a veritable revolution, are explicitly and repeatedly justified and presented as a response to the urgent need for 'Europeanisation'.

This brings us back to the meaning of such a concept. Claims of

'Europeanisation' need to be closely scrutinised. In the area of defence and security, there are no European institutions with sufficient political or military autonomy to influence directly a centuries-old national policy-making process such as that of France. Gaullism, as the epitome of national preoccupations, has often been presented in caricature. But De Gaulle did demonstrate that, with sufficient political will, a state can chart an independent path. In France, the 'impact' of Europe seems to register in two main ways. First, there is a sense of correlation between historical developments across the continent and developments at home. This has been particularly strong since the 1980s. Second, relations between France and other individual countries draw her into a network of interdependent relations with other states. These processes make the conceptualisation of security policy outside a wider European context impossible. In that sense, the very process of European integration exercises an influence over policy makers. Faced with this reality, a state such as France can seek to pursue one of two approaches: either to play the new international game of co-operation according to realist rules and seek to maximise national advantage along zero-sum lines; or to accept that what is taking place is a form of genuine integration which involves, as François Léotard put it, an attempt to bring about a 'mutualisation' of power where every national actor gains. France has probably moved, in recent decades, from something close to the first approach to something close to the second.

THE 1980S AND THE EMERGENCE OF 'EUROPEANISATION'

The crisis over Intermediate Nuclear Forces (INF) in the early 1980s was instrumental in resuscitating a 'European defence entity' which had been moribund, along with the Western European Union (WEU), since the 1950s. The differences of opinion between Europe and Washington over key aspects of foreign policy, and particularly over policy towards to the Soviet bloc, persuaded most European leaders that the time had come to think afresh about the long-delayed European pillar of the Atlantic Alliance. Although President Mitterrand had stood resolutely shoulder to shoulder with Washington over the 'Euromissile' crisis, France initiated a revival of the WEU through a series of important meetings leading to the 'Platform on European Security Interests' signed at The Hague in October 1987 (WEU 1988). This revival was probably best typified by Franco–German defence co-operation, discussions about which intensified throughout the 1980s, notably through the establishment of a Franco–German Defence Commission (1982) and then Council (1988) as well as through the launch of the Franco–German brigade in 1989 (Friend 1991; McCarthy 1993; Howorth 1992). It was at French insistence, with German backing, that a clause was inserted into the Maastricht Treaty (Title V, Article J.4) establishing a common foreign and security policy (CFSP) to deal with 'all questions related to the security of the Union, including the eventual framing of a common defence policy which might in time lead to a common defence.' The WEU was designated 'an integral part of the development of the Union' and requested 'to elaborate and implement decisions and actions of the Union which have defence implications'. There is a large element of symbiosis between French and European defence planning. This symbiosis developed strongly throughout the 1980s under the twin impulses of a resurgent Europe and an American leadership believed to be switching its strategic priorities away from Europe to the Pacific rim.

The 'endogenous impetus towards Europeanisation' should not, however, be exaggerated. Prior to the fall of the Berlin Wall, the emphasis was on streamlining the European pillar of NATO, rather than on producing an independent West European defence or security policy. The 1987 WEU 'Platform' drawn up at The Hague was a clear attempt to maintain the fundamentals of a NATO-based security system, while reasserting the rights and responsibilities of the European nations under the modified Brussels Treaty. Close coupling with the United States remained at the heart of the doctrine – which was predicated upon the persistence of a massive and identifiable threat from the East. This effectively ruled out any attempt to rethink the bases of European security. Moreover, French defence policy itself, although deeply committed at the level of discourse to the forging of a new European order, remained relatively unaffected – in terms of planning and procurement – by that objective. The 1987–91 *loi de programmation militaire* (LPM), brought in under Prime Minister Jacques Chirac, had involved massive expenditure on prestige 'national' programmes. These included a new generation of nuclear submarines, a nuclear-powered aircraft carrier, the new Leclerc battle tank, and the astronomically expensive 'red-white-and-blue' fighter plane, *Rafale* (Howorth 1990: 126–7; Gordon 1993: 158–60). France's ambition, at that stage, seemed much closer to maximisation of national advantage than to anything more genuinely integrationist.

It was the collapse of the USSR, Warsaw Pact and the entire Cold War system which provided an exogenous, and qualitatively new, impetus towards Europeanisation. The French took an early lead in arguing, from within and without NATO, that the Alliance should undergo a fundamental review, beginning with a political analysis of the new world situation and leading to a shift in strategic approach and military planning. At a meeting with George Bush at Key Largo, Florida, on 19 April 1990, François Mitterrand proposed the convening, towards the end of that year, of a NATO summit intended to initiate a grand strategic review based on a new political analysis of the world. It was not coincidental that, on the same day, the French President and Chancellor Helmut Kohl formulated their joint proposals on European monetary union and European political union, including the suggestion that Europe should 'define and implement a common foreign and security policy' (Kohl and

Mitterrand 1990: 76). France understandably felt that the tide of history was turning in her favour.

In the immediate aftermath of the fall of the Berlin Wall, Washington and Paris both argued in favour of strategic review, but in very different ways. In the confusion of these years, there were many crossed wires, a considerable degree of mutual misunderstanding and an excessive polarisation of positions (Andréani 1995: 892). The French were thought to be pressing for a radical restructuring of NATO, based on a reduced political role for the Alliance and concomitant military adjustments, the emergence of an increasingly autonomous European security entity and a significantly increased role for the Conference on Security and Co-operation in Europe (CSCE), complemented by Mitterrand's brainchild, the European Confederation.[2] In other words, the French were thought to be trying to challenge NATO's predominance in European security (Cogan 1994: 177–95; Gordon 1993: 165–78; Grant 1966: 59). Washington's position, on the other hand, implied continued American political hegemony over a gradually extended Alliance, accompanied by rapid military changes within NATO intended to reassure Moscow and to cater for intervention in out-of-area operations. Analysts had a field day commenting on this very public Franco–American shadow-boxing, but to date there has been no comprehensive scholarly analysis of what was in large part a chapter of misunderstandings.[3] In the event, history conspired to reduce the 'French agenda' (whatever it actually was) to a sideshow. The collapse of the Soviet centre put paid to any French hopes of projecting CSCE to centre stage. The Gulf War removed any doubt as to which country in the world could aspire to the status of a military superpower. And the Yugoslav debacle called into question the European Union's capacity to conduct a unified – let alone an autonomous – regional security policy. As long as George Bush remained in the White House, Atlantic relations followed a pattern of 'business as usual'.

The advent of a new United States President of a new generation, in the person of Bill Clinton, produced a new situation. The NATO summit in January 1994 provided a breakthrough in trans-Atlantic relations in that, for the first time, it encouraged the emergence of the European security entity called for in the Maastricht Treaty and even welcomed the notion of a common European defence policy.[4] For the Europeans, and particularly for the French, there now seemed to be everything to play for, particularly in the context of the 1996 Intergovernmental Conference (IGC). Within months of the 1994 NATO summit, the French government published a major defence review in the shape of a *livre blanc* (the first since 1972) and this was rapidly followed up by a new military programme law (LPM) covering the period 1995–2000. After the election to the presidency of Jacques Chirac in 1995, a further, and radically different, LPM covering the years 1997–2002 was put before Parliament in May

1996. The cardinal feature of all three documents is, at least on the surface, Europeanisation.

In his Preface to the 1994 *livre blanc*, Prime Minister Edouard Balladur noted that, 'with the coming into effect of the Treaty on European Union, our defence policy must in fact contribute to the gradual construction of a common European defence' (*Livre Blanc* 1994: 6). A French contribution to the construction of a common European defence is not exactly the same thing as the 'Europeanisation' of French national defence planning. But, in his own preface to the *livre blanc*, the UDF Defence Minister François Léotard, a fervent advocate of European integration, went further. France's aim, he insisted, was to create a European defence

> not by playing off one State against another, but by bringing about, for the first time in the tormented history of this old continent, a *mutualisation of power* (*mutualisation de la puissance*) in the service of the defence of Europe and of a common security for the States engaged in its construction. This ambition lies at the heart of the new *livre blanc*.
>
> (*Livre Blanc* 1994: 10)

What exactly is meant by 'mutualisation of power'? We do not know, since Léotard lost his job with the advent of Chirac and soon emerged as a critic of the 1996 LPM which he considered insufficiently European. He also opposed the abolition of conscription suggested in the LPM. However, lack of European dimension was hardly a feature of President Chirac's speech to the *Institut des Hautes Etudes de Défense Nationale* (IHEDN) on 8 June 1996. He stressed that the 1996 LPM

> is framed by a great European ambition. This European dimension affects, first and foremost, our conventional forces [but it is] equally present in our nuclear deterrence [and] in the restructuring of our armaments industry. . . . Finally, the same European ambition underpins France's initiatives in favour of the construction of a new continental security architecture
>
> (Chirac 1996)

There is little doubt about the underlying message. France wishes Europe to adopt what Paris conceives as a European security policy. Is it possible to disentangle the rhetoric and the reality, the national and the European dimensions? Moreover, is there continuity between the European vision of the cohabitationist Mitterrand/Balladur administration and that of the Chirac/Juppé tandem?

French defence structures, concepts and policy have changed, particularly in the mid-1990s, as a result of this European agenda. For a nation which, ever since the 1960s, has prided itself on what was presented (rightly or wrongly) as a growing political consensus on the Gaullist precepts of national independence and non-integration into multilateral defence structures, the implications of the new approach appear on the surface to be far-reaching. They affect the perception of 'security', nuclear doctrine, overall strategic doctrine, institutional adjustments, procurement policy, intelligence and 'prevention' and the defence industry.

THE 'EUROPEANISATION' OF FRENCH DEFENCE POLICY

The new definition of 'security'

Underlying the new European discourse is a conceptual shift from 'defence policy' *per se*, with its overwhelmingly military emphasis, to a broader understanding of security which embraces economic and indus-trial policy as well as diplomatic, cultural, educational and other dimensions. The principal sources of tension in the post-Cold War world are now seen in France as stemming from disequilibria between the rich areas of the world and the poor. Interdependence is perceived not simply as a feature of the economic and industrial systems of the advanced market economies, but also as a desirable foundation for regional and international stability. Whereas previously, both prior to the nuclear age and throughout the Cold War, it was simple to define and plan for the protection of 'vital national interests', in the post-Cold War world such threats and risks as do exist are thought to stem above all from indirect causes such as economic chaos, social and demographic instability and their attendant political upheavals. Moreover, France believes these risks are shared, primarily by her EU partners: 'It cannot be ruled out that, as the interests of the European nations converge, France's conception of her vital interests will eventually coincide with that of her neighbours' (*Livre Blanc* 1994: 49). Europeanisation, for Jacques Chirac, involves 'drawing all the consequences of a community of destiny, of a growing interpenetration (*imbrication*) of our vital interests' (Chirac 1996: 12). But the new feature of this approach to security is that these mutual interests are also shared by the EU with the regions on its periphery, such as Central and Eastern Europe and the Mediterranean seaboard.

> It is in our interest to engage [with the Mediterranean countries] in economic, political and cultural relations which will help them to [. . .] reduce political tensions and the reasons behind emigration. In this case, a good co-operation policy is our best guarantee of security.
>
> (Lamassoure 1995: 4)

It was France which took the lead in proposing this broad definition of security as the basis for the new 'Mediterranean Pact' which emerged from the Barcelona Conference in November 1995 (Barbé 1996; Howorth 1996b). Where defence was more or less infinitely divisible, security is thought to be essentially indivisible. As the 1997–2002 LPM put it: 'Pro-gress in the construction of Europe has reinforced the political, economic and social links between the states involved to such a point that their security interests are difficult to distinguish' (*Projet de Loi* 1996: 4/55). How does this approach affect military planning and procurement?

Nuclear doctrine

Stuart Croft (pp. 141ff) examines the general problems involved in moving towards a European nuclear policy. For France, with its traditional insistence on independence and autonomy, that problem is even more difficult than for the UK. Analysis of the 'nuclear debate' in France reveals the limitations of doctrinal evolution in this sphere (Tertrais 1994; Garcin 1995; *Relations internationales et stratégiques* 1996/1; *Trimestre du Monde* 1996/1). The 1994 *Livre Blanc* states boldly that

> the issue of a European nuclear doctrine is destined to become one of the major questions in the construction of a common European defence. . . . Indeed, with nuclear weapons, Europe's defence autonomy is possible. Without them, it is out of the question.
>
> (*Livre Blanc* 1994: 98)

Such a doctrine is linked in the French mind to European integration and to the development of a European identity. It is generally considered to be at best a medium to long-term prospect.

Since 1989, however, there has also been another development in French thinking about nuclear strategy. It has taken place without any reference to France's European partners. It concerns the adaptation of nuclear doctrine and systems to meet the hypothetical threat posed by various forms of unspecified (but presumably Third World) state terrorism. Various specialists have recently advocated reversal of France's traditional approach which insisted that nuclear weapons were not for actual use but were designed to allow a 'weak' state to deter a 'strong' one (*la dissuasion du faible au fort*). The new thinking has reversed this dictum by conceptualising nuclear weapons as a deterrent for use by the strong (France) against the weak (perhaps Iraq or Libya). The ultimate threat would be of precision nuclear attacks on the infrastructure of any hostile state attempting to hold France (or perhaps the West) to ransom (*la dissuasion du fort au faible*) (Yost 1995; Howorth 1995). David Yost has offered the useful distinction in this context between those in France who are in favour of a 'more operational' approach to nuclear issues and those who stick to a 'less operational' approach. This shift in nuclear thinking represents a fundamental break with traditional Gaullist precepts, and runs counter to thinking among the majority of France's European partners. In 1993–4 Defence Minister Léotard, Prime Minister Balladur and President Mitterrand combined their efforts to reassert nuclear orthodoxy by blowing the whistle on the 'more operational' lobby.

But apostles of restraint, such as Pascal Boniface who situated the debate in an overtly European context, were rare. Boniface argued:

> there is a fundamental contradiction between the prospect of the Europeanisation of French nuclear forces and the risk of shifting towards a nuclear policy which would no longer be purely deterrent. Our European partners will not follow us in the direction of nuclear use concepts which we have ourselves always rejected in the past.
>
> (Boniface 1993)

The likelihood of France's officially shifting towards this 'more operational' doctrine seemed momentarily to have increased during the commotion caused by President Chirac's resumption of nuclear testing in 1995, especially since many of his closest advisers were associated with that doctrine. On 10 September 1995, however, Chirac categorically denied that France would ever move towards such a doctrine and appeared to have definitively re-established the orthodoxy of deterrence in French discourse (Boniface 1995 and 1996).

None the less, French nuclear doctrine is being modified under the impetus of the European debate in a number of other directions. The most intriguing development is the notion of *dissuasion par constat*. This is usually translated (erroneously in the view of its authors) as 'existential deterrence' (Le Borgne 1987; Fricaud-Chagnaud 1986). It offers an approach which might find a receptive ear not only among the non-nuclear members of the EU but also in Britain. It assumes growing interdependence at every level between the nuclear and non-nuclear states of the Union and, consequently, asserts the logical impossibility of identifying any 'vital national interests' of a given state (including France). It presupposes both the continued existence of nuclear weapons (and nuclear weapon states) in the European theatre, but also the existence of serious conventional forces acting as a guarantee against surprise attack or nuclear blackmail. The notion is developed at some length in Fricaud-Chagnaud's recent book on French defence policy, whose provocative title – *Mourir pour le Roi de Prusse*? – symbolically posits the starkness of the security dilemma now facing France (Fricaud-Chagnaud 1994). The approach is said to avoid the pitfalls of most others, such as 'extended deterrence', 'concerted deterrence' or 'shared deterrence'. It is, however, these other concepts, particularly concerted deterrence, which are most in evidence in the various fora where these matters are discussed (Zadra 1992; Bozo 1992; *Relations internationales et stratégiques* 1992).

Since 1995, the semi-official formula chosen by the French government has been concerted deterrence (*dissuasion concertée*). Its curtain-raiser was a speech by Alain Juppé, then Foreign Minister, in January 1995 (Juppé 1995a), and it acquired semi-official status in the summer as the government strove valiantly to justify the resumption of nuclear testing by arguing that the tests were in the interests of Europe as a whole

(Juppé 1995b). The irony is that it has been, once again, the neo-Gaullist Chirac who appears to have broken with a precept of classical Gaullism. Most attempts to theorise the new concept have stressed three points. The first is that Europe cannot simply ignore the nuclear reality. Ergo, 'Europe' must – and will eventually decide to – remain a nuclear entity. Second, the political problems involved in persuading the EU fifteen of the legitimacy, credibility and 'legibility' of nuclear deterrence are enormous, particularly following the tests. No direct attempt at persuasion should therefore be made and France should seek alternative avenues through which to raise the nuclear discussion. Third, the most propitious avenue may be the imminent discussion among Europeans on non-proliferation and a total test ban (*Politique Etrangère* 1995/3). It is therefore via this 'back-door' that France should draw her EU partners into discussion on a concerted European nuclear doctrine (Bozo 1996; Fricaud-Chagnaud 1996; Boniface 1996).

For the moment, there is only one EU partner keen to talk. The Franco–British Joint Commission on Nuclear Policy and Doctrine was formally established as a permanent group in July 1993 after the London summit between François Mitterrand and John Major. The Commission, composed of about five officials from each side, representing the two Defence and Foreign Ministries, meets about three times a year, although the supporting group, responsible for drafting position papers, meets more regularly. Discussions have focused on two types of issues. First, there has been detailed mutual exploration of each side's nuclear doctrine. Discussions have centred on actual nuclear policies rather than on shifts which may or may not occur. This has given rise to the (apparently surprising) mutual recognition that, despite mutual irritation during the Cold War period, the nuclear doctrines of the two countries are similar and largely compatible. Second, discussion has taken place about topical issues of nuclear relevance such as the Non-Proliferation Treaty, arms control and shifts in the nuclear doctrines of other states. Research and development and procurement issues have been excluded from the agenda. The work of the Commission is, of course, classified but well-placed sources suggest that, in discussions about the conditions under which 'European deterrence' might acquire some political and operational meaning, there has been agreement that a coincidence in the 'vital interests' of EU countries concerned would be an indispensable preliminary. There has apparently been no formal discussion of specific hypothetical scenarios (such as an 'Islamic threat'), but it is difficult to imagine that such issues will remain out of order. Moreover, the Commission's work has proved relevant to discussions within NATO's Defence Group on Proliferation dealing with the role of deterrence against proliferators. Above all, the Commission developed excellent internal working relationships in which both sides soon discovered that reaching serious agreement on nuclear doctrine ought not to prove particularly problematic.[5] On 30 October 1995, John Major and Jacques Chirac declared the commonality of their two countries' vital interests (*Financial Times* 31 October 1995) and in May 1996 this was implicitly extended to Germany as well (Boyon 1996: 60).

What 'Europeanisation' might mean to France's traditional insistence on the national dimension of the nuclear deterrent is not yet clear. All prominent French officials regularly insist that France is willing (and presumably able) to put her nuclear forces at the service of Europe. The debate on this issue, precisely because it is (for France) the most difficult and the most sensitive, has only just begun. But the fact that it has begun is indicative of the distance already covered from what is commonly understood as 'Gaullism'. As Frédéric Bozo has concluded. 'For France, in deterrence as in everything else, Europe must therefore be considered above all as the means of proceeding to an indispensable redefinition of her power status' (Bozo 1996: 100). The logical corollary to this is a veritable revolution in overall strategic doctrine.

Strategic doctrine

Prior to 1994, the relationship between France's nuclear and her conventional weapons was constructed around two strategic precepts. First, the doctrine of deterrence, born of superpower confrontation and the nuclear stalemate, insisted on the notion of 'no-war' (non-guerre) or 'refusal of battle' (refus de la bataille). For the French, the function of nuclear weapons was to prevent wars, not to fight them (as was at least theoretically envisaged under NATO's doctrine of flexible response). The corollary of that first strategic precept was the second: that conventional forces also were intended to prevent wars rather than to fight them, more specifically to prevent the resort to nuclear weapons. Thus, French strategic doctrine aimed first and foremost at the *sanctuarisation of national territory*. This relationship between the uses of nuclear and conventional forces has, since 1994, changed radically. The *Livre Blanc* made this explicit. The chapter on defence strategy argues that since nuclear weapons are henceforth likely to play a significantly less central role in strategic planning, whereas conventional weapons are likely to be very much more in evidence (and also in use), the relationship between the two is explicitly 'inverted' (p. 94). Indeed, the *Livre Blanc* even goes so far as to hint that, whereas previously, conventional weapons were regarded as tactical support systems for the strategic nuclear deterrent (neither of which was intended for use), today it is conventional weapons which are regarded as strategic:

> One might even say that, in these scenarios, the nuclear deterrent will guarantee that the conventional forces are not short-circuited: the role which the latter played in the Cold War is now played by nuclear

forces; thus there is no rupture in strategic doctrine, but an evolution in the respective roles of nuclear and conventional means as a function of different scenarios.

(p. 95)

However, as we have already noted, the debate on the potential *military use* of nuclear weapons (possibly in support of conventional weapons) is not only embryonic and extremely problematic, but was actually foreclosed by Chirac himself in September 1995.

It is therefore interesting to observe that these thoughts on the inversion of the strategic relationship between nuclear and conventional weapons, while constituting a large section of the 1994 *Livre Blanc*, have shifted in the documents accompanying the 1996 reforms. While they remain implicit in those texts insofar as the nuclear deterrent clearly plays a far less important role in future strategic planning than does the reconfiguration of conventional forces, the only explicit reference to the relationship between nuclear and conventional forces in the 1996 LPM keeps all options open: 'The respective weight and articulation of the four principal operational functions – deterrence, prevention, projection, protection – will vary according to the situation. It would be dangerous to freeze them into a single configuration and into one inflexible strategic model' (*Projet de Loi* 1996: 6/55). The explanation for this change appears to be that the intellectually satisfying exercise of strategic inversion conducted for the *Livre Blanc* was soon perceived to have negative consequences for the development of an integrated European strategy: France's partners are less keen to embrace a constraining strategic relationship with the French nuclear panoply than are the thinkers in the rue Saint Dominique. Hence the total flexibility in the new LPM. We shall encounter a similar shift between 1994 and 1996 when we examine the structures of the French armed forces. But the main conclusion to be drawn from this, once again, is that European considerations are driving the debate. Before examining the procurement and restructuring implications of the new strategic approach, it is necessary to examine the institutional framework within which it will be set.

The institutional framework

The strategic and doctrinal changes we have just analysed have been accompanied by a radical restructuring of the institutional framework. This has involved two main aspects. The most important has been the decision to abolish conscription and to opt for a fully professional army. This has involved abandonment of the radical restructuring of the armed forces which was planned for but never implemented under Balladur/ Léotard. I shall return to this aspect shortly. The second major aspect has been the influence of developments within the EU/WEU/NATO nexus. This has been studied in some detail elsewhere (Grant 1993 and 1996) and it is not my purpose to revisit those details. However, it is important to understand the European dimension of the new institutional thinking. I stressed earlier that the apparent quarrel between France and the United States over the degree of autonomy which any European defence identity might enjoy was a form of shadow-boxing. Even at the height of the 'misunderstandings' in 1991–2, there was never any serious prospect of NATO and WEU/ESDI going in separate directions (Bozo 1995a: 867). The formula 'separable but not separate' used at the January 1994 NATO summit to characterise the CJTF arrangements cut through a great deal of potential confusion. Jacques Chirac commented in 1993 that 'the necessary rebalancing of relations within the Atlantic Alliance, relying on existing European institutions such as the WEU, can only take place from the inside, not against the United States, but in agreement with it' (Grant 1996: 63). It was a lucid statement of the reality. Laurence Martin and John Roper, in an important study, have similarly argued that

> in the most important case – NATO – progress towards common European policies offers the best way of offering the United States an acceptable framework within which to remain committed to European security and the stability of Europe's wider neighbourhood without remaining unacceptably entangled in the lesser vicissitudes of European politics.
>
> (Martin and Roper 1995: 5)

There can be no doubt that France's gradual reintegration into NATO in 1995 and 1996 is a response to several factors, each of which is informed by a European perspective. The first is a recognition that, in the new post-Cold War world of multiple risks and theatres of military intervention, France can do little on her own: 'The analysis of the risks and threats of the future shows that we must be capable ... of projecting ourselves jointly with our European and Allied partners towards distant and varied theatres, both within and outside Europe' (*Projet de Loi* 1996: 7). Further,

> the international dimension is inescapable not only because, politically, the framework for any engagement can only be multinational, but also because the overall deployment of the necessary means, particularly airborne, is now beyond the scope of any single country.
>
> (Boyon 1996: 19)

The lessons of Bosnia have been digested.

In particular, France believes that there are likely to be future circumstances where the Europeans might wish to intervene militarily in an operation with which the United States does not wish to be militarily involved. The elaboration of CJTF is predicated on the European objective of creating, in peace-time, a permanent and visible WEU-centred structure within NATO with its own command structure, general staff and support facilities. As the French Foreign Minister, Hervé De Charette, stressed in his speech to the key NATO ministerial conference in Berlin in June 1996:

> [These developments] are not just a French initiative. They make no sense unless they reflect the aspirations of all the European countries. I am delighted that this is now clearly the case. The degree of European solidarity which was manifest throughout our meetings, allowed us to conduct an exemplary discussion with our American friends.
>
> (De Charette 1996a: 35)

The exceptionally positive interpretation which was placed on the outcome of the Berlin meeting by the French government may yet prove to be somewhat hyperbolic. A great deal remains to be decided at the technical, institutional and political levels. But what France does appear to have achieved is a general recognition, in NATO and WEU, that the distinction between 'Article V tasks' and 'Petersberg tasks' is a valid one,[6] that it demands an institutional division of labour and that the most appropriate way of proceeding is via CJTFs. This is even more significant in European terms in that, as the French minister pointed out in his press conference after the Berlin meeting, the Petersberg tasks 'are of real importance because in practice they are the ones which, in future, have every chance of being carried out' (De Charette 1996b: 37).

As France accelerated her reintegration into the 'new NATO', some interpreted this development as a gradual abandonment of her forty-year struggle to create an EDSI in favour of playing a greater world role via the Atlantic Alliance. This was categorically denied by those negotiating, within NATO, the French 're-entry'.[7] For the French government, the renovation of NATO and the consecration of WEU are two sides of the same coin. 'On the one hand, we wish to give WEU full operational credibility, which it has hitherto lacked, by allowing it recourse to Alliance resources. On the other hand, we want this more credible WEU to fulfil its role as the armed force of the European Union' (De Charette 1996c: 19). This is the other institutional thrust to the Europeanisation of French security policy. Throughout the second half of 1995 and the early part of 1996, France's proposals for institutional reform within the context of the IGC were limited to unspecific suggestions. These included that there be an increase in qualified majority voting on condition that there be a re-weighting of votes in the Council; that the Treaty produced by the IGC include a political solidarity clause in the defence field (which would short-circuit the problem of the neutrals); that any agreement cater for the possibility of various 'ad-hoc coalitions' and other bi- or multi-lateral arrangements; and that efforts be made to merge WEU with the EU. After the NATO Berlin meeting in June 1996, French diplomatic initiatives became more proactive. Partly in collaboration with Germany, France took the lead in pressing for: the inclusion of Petersberg tasks in the remit of the Maastricht Treaty; the inclusion in the Treaty of a security-solidarity clause; the reinforcement of the role and competence of the Council of Ministers in all defence matters; the empowerment of the Council to define the aims and objectives of the European Union in the defence and security field; the reinforcement of WEU's operational powers; and the eventual merger of WEU and the EU (De Charette 1996c). How is this French approach reflected in the restructuring of its internal forces?

Internally, the armed forces have been regrouped in new inter-service command structures to allow for an integrated approach to the combat missions of the post-Cold War world. The main feature has been the breakdown of former rigid divisions between the services, which are now organised in broad inter-service commands: Intelligence, Command and Communication, and Force Projection. This shift has been paralleled in budgetary terms. The defence budget is being broken down into inter-service 'modules'. Even the centuries-old separate 'écoles de guerre' have been merged into a *Collège Interarmées de Défense* (*Armées d'Aujour-d'hui* February 1993). The three services each have a specific role to play in several or all of the four main functions of the professional armed forces: deterrence, prevention, projection, protection. The army, for instance, henceforth comprises four 'Forces': an armoured force, a mechanised force, an armoured rapid intervention force and an infantry assault force.[8] All of these will gradually be optimally configured for intervention, primarily in Europe. In addition, France is in the process of establishing, with Italy, Spain and Portugal, various integrated force structures (air, land and sea – EUROFOR and EUROMARFOR) leading to a Mediterranean Rapid Reaction Force. Moreover, in October 1995, John Major and Jacques Chirac inaugurated the Franco–British Euro Air Group based at High Wycombe to co-ordinate international and European missions of various sorts. The first commander is a French general. France has thus situated herself at the heart of a European network of integrated military units involving the main countries of the EU. For a country which once held to the rejection of integrated command structures as a point of principle, this is a considerable shift.

However, the restructuring envisaged under the 1995–2000 LPM and that introduced only eighteen months later as LPM 1997–2002 are significantly different. This is so notwithstanding claims of seamless continuity written into the texts of the latter document.[9] Much of the difference follows from professionalisation and budget cuts, which are not concerns of this chapter. But from the perspective of Europeanisation, it is interesting to note that whereas, in the previous plan, there were three overall commands for the entire armed forces – Europe, overseas and special operations – these specifications have now disappeared. Likewise, the army was previously structured around three corps of which one was the Eurocorps. All specific reference to the Eurocorps in the 1996 LPM has disappeared. How can one explain this anomaly – particularly in a document which robustly claims to be inspired by the need to Europeanise? The Germans, in particular, were very concerned about the disbandment of the 1st armoured division which constituted the main French contribution to Eurocorps. They were equally concerned about the excessive attention (as they saw it) paid in LPM 1996 to force projection. Some interpreted this as expressing a French predilection for 'colonial' operations, mainly in Africa and the Middle East. As the German Defence Minister quipped: 'the Eurocorps is not the Afrikakorps'. French officials went out of their way to reassure their German counterparts that the Eurocorps remained one of their top priorities, and the difference was temporarily reconciled for the Franco–German summit in Dijon in June 1996 at which it was announced that the two countries were formulating a 'common security and defence concept' which would remove any remaining distance between the military plans and objectives of their respective armed forces. This 'common concept' was to be announced at the end of 1996. The root explanation for the Chirac reforms is, however, probably relatively simple. They were in large part a response to budgetary pressures which increased as a result of the economic convergence criteria for monetary union.

Although the broad outlines of a new professional army had been (more or less) thought through, the detailed implications had not. It is almost certainly the case that Paris was still not sure in mid-1996 precisely what contribution it could best make to Eurocorps. The French parliamentary report on LPM 1996 implies that any one of the new army's four 'Forces' could be assigned to Eurocorps (Boyon 1996: 35). The indications are that the main structural features of the French 'Army of 2015' are maximum flexibility for collaboration with allies wherever the need is felt. How does this ambition translate into procurement?

Europeanisation and procurement

The Chirac reforms of 1996 had a considerable impact on procurement. The aim to reduce defence spending by FFr100bn has affected 'Europeanisation' in contradictory ways. The proportion of the defence budget allocated to nuclear forces, which had risen to more than 30 per cent in the mid-1980s and dropped back to 24 per cent by 1990, fell precipitately to 10 per cent in 1996.[10] Since 1990, most of the 'national' nuclear programmes planned in the 1980s have been cut, postponed or drastically reduced. The Chirac reforms accelerated this process by scrapping the surface-to-surface missiles on the *Plateau d'Albion*, scrapping the short-range *Hades*, closing down the nuclear test sites in Polynesia and closing the fissile materials plants at Marcoule and Pierrelatte. As we have seen, this reduced nuclear programme is now explicitly presented as a contribution to the security of Europe.

The remainder of the budget can usefully be broken down in two ways: either between the three armed services (plus the *gendarmerie*); or between the three main operational functions: prevention, projection, protection. Perhaps the best way of gauging the impact of 'Europeanisation' is by assessing the evolution of priorities in the major procurement programmes. For the army, the *Leclerc* heavy battle tank programme has been drastically scaled down from an initial target in 1987 of 1,400 units to 650 in 1995 and then to 400 in 1996. In fact, only 307 will be produced during the 1997–2002 planning period. Despite concern from Germany that, yet again, France is proving less than committed to holding her share of the front-line in any major tank battle in Europe, this massive reduction in the *Leclerc* programme seems broadly in line with European strategic planning assumptions, which are not predicated on the imminence of a mass tank battle. By comparison, the light armoured vehicle programme (*VBM* and *VBCI*) is being maintained at the 1987 target of 600. This system has proved its effectiveness both in Kurdistan and in former Yugoslavia and an entire family of slightly different models is now under construction in co-operation with both Germany and the UK (Boyon 1996: 101). The picture is less clear where helicopters are concerned. In response to the disappearance of the tank threat from the Warsaw Pact, France inverted her priorities in favour of the 'support and protection' *HAP* (anti-helicopter) version (as opposed to the anti-tank *HAC* version) of the Franco–German *Tigre*. Research and development funds for these two programmes are set at FFr5bn over the planning period. However, the numbers actually ordered have shrivelled to virtual insignificance (only 25 *HAP*s are budgeted for before 2002 and no *HAC*s). It is a similar story for the *NH-90* transport helicopter, again a Franco–German product. Although FFr2.6bn has been allocated for research and development, none will be ordered until after 2003. This has infuriated the Germans, who see French cuts as adversely affecting their own procurement plans.[11] Clearly, the constraints of economic and monetary union are coming into conflict with the imperatives of CFSP. The stated objective for the 'Army of 2015' is to be able to project into a more or less distant combat zone either 50,000 professional soldiers in a single theatre or 35,000 in a major theatre with another 15,000 destined for a secondary theatre. The explicit assumption behind these projections is that French troops will be fighting in conjunction with other national contingents under either a UN, a WEU or a NATO mandate (*Projet de Loi* 1996: 4/ 55–5/55). In the 1994 *Livre Blanc* six scenarios for intervention are sketched out. They are: a regional conflict not threatening France's vital interests (Europe, Mediterranean, Middle East); a regional conflict which could threaten France's vital interests (Europe, Mediterranean, Middle East); a threat to the territorial integrity of France's overseas possessions;

implementation of bilateral defence agreements (mainly in Africa); oper-
ations in favour of peacekeeping and international law (again, mainly
Europe, Middle East and Africa, but also possibly the Far East and even
Latin America); and the re-emergence of a major threat to Western
Europe. Apart from the third and fourth, all cite Europe as their main
theatre of concern (*Livre Blanc* 1994: 109–18).

Turning to the air force, there is a major problem. It is called *Rafale*.
In the most exhaustive report so far on this system (Darrason 1996: 18),
the global cost has been estimated at FFr193.4bn. With a target of 320
planes (including 86 of the naval version), crude arithmetic costs the
plane at over FFr600m per unit. This can be set against the annual budget
for the entire Air Force of FFr37bn. The lessons of this episode for 'state
autonomy' are, to say the least, instructive! The reasons *Rafale* was chosen
in preference to the five-nation European Fighter Aircraft were overwhelmingly to do with a perceived desire to protect national interests.[12]
Since that decision was taken in August 1986, the French state has learnt
the hard – budgetary – way that such an ambition is probably unrealisable
in today's world.[13] The 1996 LPM confirms the target of a first consign-
ment of 12 naval *Rafales* for 2002, with a further 15 envisaged (plus an
initial 33 of the air version) for 2005. There are many in the higher
reaches of the defence establishment in France – including, apparently,
the Chief of Air Staff, General Rannou (*Valeurs Actuelles* 25–31 May
1996; *Le Monde* 26–27 May 1996) – who believe that the Air Force
version of *Rafale* will be abandoned and only the naval version ever be
deployed (Interviews, Paris, June–July 1996). *Rafale* is certainly the last
major 'red, white and blue' weapons system likely to be developed in
France. The 1994 *Livre Blanc* states bluntly that 'no major future conventional armaments programme seems able to escape the logic of
[European] co-operation' (*Livre Blanc* 1994: 192).

The *Rafale* saga also had indirect consequences for the overall credibility of France's desire to play a leading part in the creation of a viable
European armed force. It led, for budgetary reasons, to the temporary
abandonment of French involvement in the European transport aircraft
which the French recognise is indispensable if Europe is to approach
'autonomy' in logistics. However, agreement was reached at the Franco–
German summit in June 1996 to finance the transport plane from private
sources and build it as a European venture linked to the Airbus company
(*Le Monde* 7 June 1996).

The Navy should see the launch of the new generation nuclear-powered
aircraft carrier *Charles de Gaulle* (scheduled for July 1999), but until the
Rafale comes on stream in 2002 the carrier will be without air protection.
No decision has been taken to order a second vessel, despite the unanimous opinion of naval strategists that a credible fleet air system requires
a minimum of two carriers. A Franco–German carrier has been mooted
(Sautter 1996). Moreover, the new generation of *Horizon* class anti-

aircraft frigates is being produced in co-operation with the UK and Italy with a scheduled delivery date of 2005. The aspiration is to contribute to the creation of a unified European navy with power projection capabilities across the globe (Buissière 1995).

The 1996 LPM does confirm deployment of a wide range of new, sophisticated weapons systems and many of them have been devised, reconfigured or prioritised to meet the requirements of the new crisis-driven combat missions of the post-Cold War era (Lanxade 1994). It may be an exaggeration to suggest that moves towards European integration in defence are the principal driving force behind these new deployments. Yet, the French shift towards emphasis on conventional weapons for power projection constitutes a radical departure in defence policy from the heyday of 'Gaullism'. Clearly, at doctrinal, programmatic and operational levels, this shift represents a *de facto* convergence between French defence planning and that of WEU and NATO. Convergence (rather than integration) is the essential feature. However, if the current rate of convergence continues, there will come a time when it is difficult to distinguish between the main features of the defence policies of the countries involved.

The role of prevention

One of the most significant features of recent French procurement plans is the emphasis on intelligence-gathering capabilities and command and control systems. The most painful lesson learnt in Paris from the Gulf War was the fact that, as the then Defence Minister, Pierre Joxe, put it, without American satellites the French armies in the Gulf were effectively 'blind' (Yost 1993; Howorth 1994). Accordingly, since 1991, France has placed the utmost priority on the acquisition by Europe of a relatively autonomous space-based intelligence and command capability. In the 1996 LPM, 'prevention' is elevated to the status of one of the four operational functions of French defence planning (along with deterrence, projection and protection). There is no doubt that France's new strategic approach, involving the acceptance of multiple combat missions in a European context, has been a major impetus behind her plans for a European space capacity. The French space budget rose tenfold between 1987 and 1995, to more than FFr5bn. Between 1994 and 1995, the space budget rose by 23.4 per cent.[14] Despite programme setbacks (ambitious plans for a European space shuttle – *Hermes* – were drastically scaled down in 1992), a major breakthrough came in December 1995 when the Germans finally agreed to participate financially in the French-driven European space programme. This allowed Chirac to make savings on the space budget in the 1996 LPM, but the programme remains extremely ambitious. The *Helios 1a* military observation satellite, which will give Europe (limited) autonomous intelligence data, was launched in July 1995. The WEU satellite monitoring centre at Torrejon in Spain was inaugurated in April 1993. French plans for the Horus radar observation satellite have now been Europeanised with Germany as the major partner. A variety of other space-based projects are on the drawing board. German partici- pation, however tentative, was always seen as a precondition for wider European involvement, and the signs are that the latter will now follow. Indeed, the new generation of other intelligence-related systems (such as the replacement for the *Syracuse* telecommunications system) is set to become a Franco–Anglo–German programme (Paecht 1996: 107). France seems to have taken the lead on a European military-space programme and eventually, through sheer force of example, to have dragged her partners along with her. The 1996 LPM states explicitly that the space programme cannot exist other than as a European co-operative venture (Boyon 1996: 70). WEU is keen to acquire its own extensive space facilities, but remains dependent on the Franco–German lead (WEU 1996a and 1996b).

The defence industry and europeanisation

It is in the field of the armaments industry that the discourse on the European imperative becomes universal. Without exception, the recent major texts on weapons procurement for the twenty-first century stress not only the desirability but the inevitability of European co-operation.[15] In a major speech on procurement policy in September 1994, the then Defence Minister François Léotard outlined a three-point plan:

First, to consolidate our national industry by giving it the necessary means to forge European alliances . . .; Next, to conduct these Euro- pean-wide industrial alliances in the tightest possible synergy with the co-operation programmes. Finally, to agree on a division of labour among the European states for non-strategic programmes.

(Léotard 1994: 64)

Despite these assertions, France still produces 75 per cent of her weapons systems within the confines of the Hexagon (Conze 1995: 10); and the economic, social and political problems involved in industrial restructuring and conversion are considerable. Yet the brutal industrial restructuring ordered by President Chirac in February 1996 was as industrially neces- sary as it was politically controversial. France's major competitors, particularly the US, the UK and Germany, had all recently completed major industrial restructuring exercises, creating, in effect, a small number of 'lean, fit' national giants. The 1994 merger between Martin-Marietta and Lockheed, for example, created a company bigger than the entire French aeronautics industry with a turnover equivalent to one-third of the entire European aeronautics industry. France alone continued to protect and tolerate inefficient and loss-making nationalised defence companies dependent on national orders. Yet, if Europe as a whole was to avoid mere sub-contractor status in relation to the US, then transeuropean restructuring, mergers and takeovers were necessary. In an effort to give France some chance of dominating the two main sectors in which she still operated competitively – electronics and avionics – Chirac made two decisions. He ordered the rapid merger of the profit-making Dassault and the loss-making Aérospatiale in order to produce one industrial giant around which – hopefully – other European partners (MBB, BAe etc) might be forced to gravitate. And he ordered the privatisation of Thomson CSF, gambling on provoking a series of mergers among French companies in the sector prior to the constitution of a (French-led) European group capable of competing with US defence manufacturers.

These initiatives provoked two types of reaction. The Germans at first responded negatively to the defence review. For on the one hand, the review slashed procurement budgets on which Germany's own defence and industrial programmes were partly dependent, while, on the other hand, it asked France's main partners to delay further European defence restructuring until France had got her own house in order. Chirac's measures provided an ironic start to the life of the long-delayed Franco–German Armaments Agency. It required the personal intervention of President Chirac and Chancellor Kohl, and an unplanned extension of the regular Franco–German summit in June 1996, before agreement could be reached simply to hold further discussions in late 1996 on the future division of tasks in the European defence industry. These meetings heard a constant refrain that the stakes for the whole of Europe were simply too high for the political will of the leaders not to prevail.

This insistence was not missed by the British, who had hitherto been reticent about joining the Armaments Agency. In March 1996, even the staunchly anti-European Defence Secretary, Michael Portillo, had been won over to the view that the prospects were highly attractive. Britain duly joined the Agency and co-operated with the French and Germans in the production of a European armoured personnel carrier. In May 1996, as a prelude to the privatisation of Thomson-CSF, British Aerospace and Matra merged their missile production in a £1bn deal. This led, in July, to the British government's abandoning its traditional preference for American partners: it announced it would participate in the three-nation programme to produce a European cruise missile. Although agreement on rationalisation of the European armaments industry remained distant, the French decisions in February 1996 seemed to produce a European dynamic with precisely the desired effect (Gray 1996).

France will no doubt fight to gain as big a share of the European armaments pie as she can. So far, the content has revolved around advanced systems for Europe's putative army and air force. The future of the naval shipyards will prove to be the next major test. France might claim a competitive edge in submarines, aircraft carriers and advanced frigates. As for other areas, the future looks bleak. She will not win every skirmish in the campaign to create a European defence industry. Her long-protected and heavily state-centred procurement procedures will have to undergo painful adjustment. But France under Chirac accepts the need to go through a restructuring of its defence industries. The European project ultimately depends on it.

CONCLUSION

France is intensely committed to the creation of an integrated European defence structure and to a common foreign and security policy. Throughout the period of the Cold War, and particularly from the 1960s onwards, while never losing sight of the objective of a European security entity, France nevertheless pursued policies which stressed autonomy and national decision-making processes. This began to change in the 1980s, but since 1989 there has been rapid and significant movement. Conceptually, 'defence' is being replaced by 'security' as the guarantor of stability – and security is interpreted as a collective endeavour and collective goal. Doctrinally, where both nuclear and conventional weapons are concerned, there have been important shifts in the direction of convergence, sharing and even integration between France and some of her European partners. In terms of force missions and military involvement, the previous record of immobilism has been replaced by an almost frenetic activism. And virtually none of this activism is unilateral. France is the largest single contributor to UN missions throughout the world. In terms of weapons development and procurement, there is a seemingly irresistible move towards European co-operation. In terms of medium to long-term aims, the vision of an increasingly autonomous European defence entity tied in to intricate new security treaties with both the US and Russia is becoming the object of a new consensus. France may not yet have abandoned her national defence structures and programmes. But the evolution of defence thinking at every level is increasingly conditioned by the supposition that, sooner or later (and preferably sooner), France's entire approach to questions of defence and security will be properly integrated with that of her European neighbours. To that extent, French defence policy has already been profoundly and irrevocably affected by the debate about something called Europe.

NOTES

1 'Our defence policy . . . and this is our conscious choice, must be situated in the perspective of a European defence, without which we would be faced with nothing but a constant exhaustion of our resources, our willpower and our capacities,' the Defence Minister, François Léotard, said when presenting the

1995 defence budget to parliament in November 1994, *Propos sur la Défense*, November 1994, p. 6. Similarly, the 1997–2002 *Loi de Programmation militaire*, presented to parliament on 13 May 1996, is 'totally framed within a European perspective'. French defence policy, the document continues, 'lies at the heart of a network of solidarities and interests which are increasingly turning Western Europe into a common strategic space'. Assemblée Nationale, *Projet de Loi relatif à la programmation militaire pour les années 1997–2002*. No. 2766, 6–7.

2 Mitterrand's proposal of 1 January 1990 was for all the countries of continental Europe to form a vast 'Confederation' through which to engage in every form of exchange. Attempts to launch the Confederation, at a special conference in Prague in June 1991, failed owing to resistance from the Central and Eastern European countries, who saw it as a kind of antechamber effectively excluding them from the EU; they were also perturbed by the exclusion of the USA.

3 There is an urgent need for a scholarly re-evaluation of the discussions between the major allies (particularly France and the USA) in the period November 1989 to December 1992. While there was clearly a mutual jostling for position in the emerging 'new world order', it is an exaggeration to suggest that France assumed (still less hoped) either that NATO would disintegrate or that the projected EDSI would be independent of, or separate from, the Atlantic Alliance.

4 Declaration of the Heads of State and Government participating in the meeting of the North Atlantic Council held at NATO HQ, Brussels, 10–11 January 1994, reproduced in *Survival*, Spring 1994, pp. 162–7. See in particular articles 3, 4, 5. In reality, this was not that different from what had been written into Article 3 of the London Declaration on a Transformed North Atlantic Alliance on 6 July 1990: 'The move within the European Community towards political union, including the development of a European identity in the domain of security, will also contribute to Atlantic solidarity and to the establishment of a just and lasting order of peace throughout the whole of Europe.' Text reproduced in *Survival*, September/October 1990, 469.

5 I am grateful to several officials from the Ministry of Defence for their willingness to discuss these issues with me.

6 Art V tasks are those which would involve the security of Europe as a whole and would require the engagement of American armed forces. 'Petersberg' tasks are those defined at a WEU meeting outside Berlin in June 1992 and cover intervention in crisis areas for humanitarian and peacekeeping purposes.

7 Author's interview with the Head of the French mission to NATO's Military Committee, General Jean-Paul Pellisson, Brussels, 22 January 1996.

8 Under the previous – Léotard – LPM of 1995–2000, the Army was structured around *three* rather different *Corps*: the *Corps blindé mécanisé*, based in Lille; the Force d'Action Rapide; and the *Eurocorps*.

9 Both the *Loi de programmation militaire* itself and the parliamentary report which helped it through the National Assembly repeatedly stress that the new law is the logical continuation of the prescriptions in the 1994 *Livre Blanc* and in the 1995–2000 LPM (*Projet de Loi* 1996: 7; Boyon 1996: 15).

10 The picture is clearer if we look at actual expenditure.

Year	Overall Budget FFr millions	Nuclear forces FFr millions
1987	169, 200	36, 050
1991	194, 548	42, 952
1992	195, 268	40, 446
1993	197, 916	26, 906

1994	193, 828	23, 164
1995	194, 262	22, 387
1996	185, 800	18, 900

It is difficult to compare percentages with precision. The French defence budget has always been broken down into many different components but, to make matters worse, with the restructuring of the forces in 1993 along modular rather than service lines, the figures changed quite dramatically from 1994 onwards. Each year in February, the SIRPA publishes a compendium, *La Défense en Chiffres*. In 1992, the percentage allocated to nuclear forces, which had been dropping by about 1 per cent per year for several years, was recorded as 21 per cent. In 1993, it was recorded under the new scheme as 14 per cent and in 1995 as 11 per cent. However, in some versions, a figure for 1993 of 21 per cent is cited, but this is 21 per cent *of equipment allocations* (Titre V) rather than 21 per cent of the entire budget.

11 In the National Assembly report on the LPM, the *HAC* target was quoted as 100 (down from 140 in 1987) and the *HAP* target at 115 (up from 75 in 1987) (Boyon 1996). However, the Senate report on the LPM estimated these targets respectively at 50 and 75 (Villepin 1996). See, on this, *Le Monde*, 17 June 1996.

12 A former engineer with the Royal Aircraft Establishment at Farnborough, David Oldfield, is currently producing a definitive study of the *Rafale* story as a Ph.D. dissertation at Bath University.

13 The costs of sophisticated weapons programmes, particularly in terms of research and development, are rising exponentially. The Chief executive of Martin-Marietta, Norman Augustine, calculated that, by the year 2043, on current trends the US Defence Department would only be able to afford one single combat aircraft – to be used four days a week by the Air Force and three days a week by the Navy. This 'Augustine's Law' – is outlined in Jean-Paul Hébert, *Stratégie française et industrie d'armement*, Paris, FEDN, 1991, p. 113.

14 See *Armées d'Aujourd'hui*, No.197, February 1995, special issue on the defence Budget, p. 53. On French space policy in general, see Hugh Dauncey, 'The Making of French Space Policy, 1979–1992', Ph.D. dissertation, University of Bath, 1994. For the official French view, see *Avis présenté au nom de la Commission de la Défense Nationale et des Forces Armées sur le projet de loi des finances pour 1994*, Assemblée Nationale, Tome V. Défense: Espace et Communications, No.583, 7 October 1993.

15 'For industry, the creation of a European defence is an imperative and an opportunity' – *Livre Blanc*, p. 192; 'there is not a single [defence] industrial sector which, in future, should not ally with other Europeans' – François Léotard, speech to Centre des Hautes Etudes de l'Armement (CHEAr), 14 September 1994, in *Propos sur la Défense*, No.45, September 1994, p. 45; 'a reinforcement of international co-operation is indispensable because ... France alone will not be able in future to sustain the complete range of technological and military materials' – Edouard Balladur, speech to IHEDN, 8 September 1994, in Ibid., p. 42; 'It is obvious that given the necessary industrial scale in the field of weapons and given convergence in economic interests, European co-operation is the natural framework in which the nations of the Union should equip their armies' – Henri Martre, former head of DGA, 'L'Industrie française d'armement dans la tourmente', *Défense Nationale*, March 1995, p. 18; 'European construction is an indispensable element in taking up the challenge of cost reduction and in avoiding structural disarma-

ment' – Henri Conze, current head of DGA, in *Armées d'Aujourd'hui*, No.196, January 1995, p. 12.

REFERENCES

Andréani, J. (1995) 'Les Relations franco-américaines' in *Politique Etrangère*, 1995/4: 891–902.

Barbé, E. (1996) 'The Barcelona Conference: launching pad of a process', *Mediterranean Politics* 2.

Boniface, P. (1993) 'Dénucléarisation rampante ou retour à la suffisance nucléaire?', in Pascallon, P. (ed)., *Quelle Défense pour la France?*, Paris: Dunod.

—— (1995) 'Essais et doctrine nucléaires', *Relations internationales et stratégiques* 20 (hiver).

—— (1996) 'La dissuasion européenne: enjeux et perspectives', *Relations internationales et stratégiques* 21 (printemps).

Boyon, J. (1996) *Rapport fait au nom de la commission de la défense nationale et des forces armées sur le projet de loi (No.2766) relatif à la programmation militaire pour les années 1997–2002*, Paris: Assemblée Nationale (No. 2827).

Bozo, F. (1992) 'Une doctrine nucléaire européenne: pour quoi faire et comment?', *Politique Etrangère* 2.

—— (1995a) 'La France et l'Alliance: les limites du rapprochement', *Politique Etrangère* 1.

—— (1996) 'Dissuasion concertée: le sens de la formule', *Relations internationales et stratégiques* 21, 93–100.

Buissière, R. (1995) 'L'Europe: puissance navale?', *Défense Nationale*, February: 99–110.

Chirac, J. (1996) 'Discours du Président de la République, M. Jacques Chirac, devant l'IHEDN', Paris, 8 juin 1996, reproduced in French Embassy, London, *France: Statements*, SFC/96/138; and in *Défense Nationale* Juillet–Août 1996.

Cogan (1994) *Oldest Allies: Guarded Friends: The United States and France since 1940*, Westport, CT: Praeger.

Conze, H. (1995) Interview in *Armées d'Aujourd'hui* 196, January.

Darrason, O. (1996) Assemblée Nationale *Rapport d'information sur le Rafale*, National Assembly 13 May.

Davidson, I. (1992) 'A Classic Striptease', *Financial Times*, 14 January.

De Charette, H. (1996a) French Embassy, London: *Statements* SFC/96/133 Berlin, 3 June.

—— (1996b) French Embassy, London: *Statements* SFC/96/134 Berlin, 4 June.

—— (1996c) French Embassy, London: *Statements*, SFC/96/140 Berlin, 10 June.

De la Gorce, P-M. (1993) 'Présentation', *Défense Nationale* (February 1993) devoted to 'Le Nucléaire Militaire'.

Fricaud-Chagnaud, C-G. (1986) 'L'Europe de la dissuasion et des solidarités actives', *Stratégique* 29.

—— (1994) *Mourir pour le roi de Prusse?*, Paris: Publisud.

—— (1996) 'Dissuasion concertée: vers un partenariat stratégique', *Relations internationales et stratégiques* 21, 88–92.

Friend, J.W. (1991) *The Linchpin: French-German Relations 1950–1990*, New York: Praeger.

Garcin T. (1996) 'La France et l'arme nucléaire après la gurre froide' *Le Trimestre du Monde*.

Gordon, P. (1993) *A certain Idea of France: French security policy and the Gaullist legacy*, Princeton, NJ: Princeton UP.

Grant, R. P. (1993) *The Changing Franco-American Security Relationship: new directions for NATO and European defense co-operation*, Arlington, Va: US CREST.

Grant, R. P. (1996) 'France's new relationship with NATO', *Survival* 38/1.

Gray, B. (1996) 'An elusive moving target', *Financial Times*, 14 May.

Howorth, J. (1990) 'France since the Berlin Wall: defence and diplomacy', *The World Today* 46/7.

—— (1992) 'France and the Defence of Europe: redefining continental security' in M. Maclean and J. Howorth (eds), *Europeans on Europe: transnational visions of a new continent*, London: Macmillan.

—— (1994) 'French Policy in the Conflict', in Alex Danchev and Dan Keohane (eds), *International Perspectives on the Gulf Conflict*, London: Macmillan.

—— (1995) ' "Hirochirac" and the French nuclear conundrum', *French Politics and Society* 3.

—— (1996a) 'France and European Security (1944–1994): rereading the Gaullist "consensus"', in T. Chafer and B. Jenkins (eds), *France: from the Cold War to New World Order*, London: Macmillan. (An earlier version of this essay appeared as 'France and the Quest for a West European Security Entity (1944–1994): fifty years, one agenda', in *Proceedings of the Western Society for French History*, Vol.21 (1994): 255–73.

—— (1996b) 'France and the Mediterranean in 1995: from tactical ambiguity to inchoate strategy', *Mediterranean Politics* 2.

Juppé, A. (1995a) 'Quelle horizon pour la politique étrangère de la France?', *Politique Etrangère*, Printemps, 247.

—— (1995b) article in *Figaro*, 26 August.

Kohl, H. and Mitterrand, F. (1990) Statement in *La Politique Etrangère de la France*, March–April.

Kolodziej, E. (1994) 'French Nuclear Policy: adapting the Gaullist legacy to the post-Cold War World', in Michael Mazzur and Alexander Lennon (eds), *Toward a Nuclear Peace: the Future of Nuclear Weapons*, Boston: St Martin's Press.

Lamassoure, A. (1995) speech to the colloquium of the *Centre d'Etudes et de Perspectives Stratégiques*, 11 April 1995, in the French Embassy, London *France: Statements*, 18 April.

Lanxade J. (1994) 'Rôle et emploi des armes de précision', *Défense Nationale*, November 27–32.

Le Borgne, C. (1987) *La Guerre est morte mais on ne le sait pas encore*, Paris: Grasset.

Léotard, F. (1994) *Propos sur la Défense*, No.45.

Livre Blanc sur la Défense 1994, Paris: 10/18.

Martin, L. and Roper, J., (eds) *Towards a Common Defence Policy*, WEU: Paris.

McCarthy, P. (ed) (1993) *France and Germany 1983–1993. The Struggle to Co-operate*, London: Macmillan.

Politique Etrangère (1995/3), Special issue on non-proliferation.

Projet de Loi (1996), Projet de loi (No.2766) relatif à la programmation militaire pour les années 1997–2002, Paris: Assemblée Nationale.

Relations internationales et stratégiques (1992) No.6, 'L'Avenir de la Dissuasion nucléaire'.

Relations Internationales et Stratégiques (1996/1) No.21, Special dossier on 'La France, la Dissuasion et l'Europe'.

Sautter, P. (1996) 'Construisons un porte-avions avec l'Allemagne', *Le Monde*, 7 June 1996, 14.

Schmidt, P. (1993) *The Special Franco–German Security Relationship in the 1990s*, Paris, WEU, Chaillot Paper No.8.

Tertrais, B. (1994) *L'Arme nucléaire après la guerre froide*, Paris: Economica.

Le Trimestre du Monde (1996/1) No.33, special dossier on 'La France et l'Arme nucléaire'.

Yost, D. (1993) 'France and the Gulf War of 1990–1991: Political–Military Lessons learnt' in *Journal of Strategic Studies*, Vol.16/3.

—— (1995) 'Nuclear Weapons Issues in France', in John C. Hopkins and Weixing Hu (eds), *Strategic Views from the Second Tier: the Nuclear Weapons Policies of France, Britain and China*, New Brunswick, NJ: Transaction Publishers. Yost's condensed version of that same study, 'Nuclear Debates in France', *Survival*, Vol.36/4, Winter 1994–5: 113–39.

—— (1996) 'France's Nuclear Dilemmas', *Foreign Affairs*, 75/1, January/February 1996, 108–18.

WEU (1988) *The Reactivation of WEU: Statements and Communiqués 1984–1987*, Paris: WEU.

—— (1996a) Assembly of WEU, *A European Intelligence Policy* Document 1517, 13 May 1996.

—— (1996b) Assembly of WEU, *WEU and Helios 2*, Document 1525, 14 May 1996.

Zadra, R. (1992) *European Integration and Nuclear Deterrence after the Cold War*, Paris: WEU (Chaillot Paper No.5).

3 Germany

Johannes Bohnen

INTRODUCTION

Germany has, in recent years, been one of the strongest proponents of strengthening the defence element of European integration. This chapter shows not only that this German commitment has increased since 1989, but also helps explain why this has been so. An examination of the various pressures that impinge on German security policy shows how security discussions and initiatives at the European level have impacted on German policy. In particular, and paradoxically, European pressures served to increase Germany's autonomy in the field of defence. They gave the government more room to manoeuvre and enhanced Germany's influence over its partners. While Europe has by no means been the most important constraint on state autonomy, it has, especially in recent years, increasingly impinged on domestic debate and so affected policy outcomes.

GERMANY AND EUROPEAN DEFENCE

Since the founding of the Federal Republic, Bonn has taken a positive view of the goal of including security and defence policy in the process of European unification (Stratmann 1992: 31). However, the evolution of German thinking on the proper relationship between defence and European integration was influenced by its desire to preserve the paramount role of the United States within NATO. German integration in both European and Atlantic structures involved both complementary and competitive elements. At times European and Atlantic designs conflicted with each other. Germany did not object to discussing questions of defence policy, for example, within the context of European political community. Given its dependence on the US and NATO, however, its main interest was to work towards a common foreign and security policy rather than any military co-operation within the European Community framework.

There are numerous examples of Germany being caught between Atlantic and European designs for European security. The European

Defence Community could have married the Atlantic and European elements of German security shortly after the War. But, after its accession to NATO, German interest in including defence in the process of European integration decreased significantly. German governments became increasingly concerned about the anti-American undertones of European defence initiatives. The years between 1958 and 1963, in particular, witnessed divergent approaches to the most appropriate structures for European defence co-operation. These stemmed largely from differing US and French designs and ambitions.

Following the failure of the second Fouchet Plan, de Gaulle turned to Germany to secure France's political leadership in Europe. The Élysée Treaty signed on 14 January 1963 laid down arrangements for Franco–German collaboration in many areas, including foreign and defence policy. As is well documented, however, the anti-American implications of the Gaullist approach troubled the German Bundestag. This led it to reaffirm Bonn's commitment to its transatlantic bonds via the inclusion of a strongly pro-NATO preamble to the Treaty text. This dampened de Gaulle's ardour considerably, prompting him to turn away from such schemes for European collaboration. Nevertheless, many German politicians felt a certain sympathy for Gaullist ideas. They appealed to Strauss as well as to Konrad Adenauer by holding out the prospect of greater emancipation from American leadership. However, at the end of the day, Bonn's freedom of action was constrained by its dependence on the US.

During the late 1970s and early 1980s, a combination of common European and distinct national motives brought closer West European security and defence co-operation back onto the agenda. The WEU's reactivation in 1984 was partly due to frictions in the transatlantic relationship intensified by US President Ronald Reagan's strong anti-communist rhetoric and the quarrels over the Strategic Defence Initiative (SDI), the US plan for a space-based anti-missile system. Partly, too, it came about because France realised that Germany's struggle over the deployment of intermediate nuclear forces (INF) made French participation in a common European response necessary. Paris feared that German public opinion, influenced by the peace movement, would drift towards pacifism and neutralism. The domestic security consensus which had existed in Germany during the 1970s was slowly eroding. The Social Democratic Party (SPD) was increasingly at odds with the US and NATO, which were felt to have embittered the political climate between East and West. Thus, one motivation for WEU revitalisation was the desire to 'tie Germany in'.

Germany's support for WEU reactivation also increased in this period, particularly after the 'Genscher–Colombo' plan to further develop EPC had failed in 1981. Genscher aimed to secure the fruits of *Ostpolitik* and the goal of unification under the cover of a European policy of détente. The initiative failed, however, and, whilst Germany was never happy with

the solution of strengthening WEU as an independent defence organisation outside the EPC framework, the Germans did try to use it as a
means to bring the French closer to NATO without putting Atlantic
commitments in danger. In fact, the basic pattern of German defence
policy from 1966 onwards has turned on how best to achieve a balance
between the US (and Britain) and France – or between the 'NATO
option' and the 'Euro option'.

In October 1991, almost two years after the Berlin Wall came down,
France and Germany launched an initiative in which their stated aim was
to include defence in the process of European integration through the
eventual merger of the WEU with the EU and the creation of the so-
called Eurocorps (Europe Documents 1991). France, for the first time,
agreed to the concept of military integration. The initiative, which took
Germany's American and British partners largely by surprise, indicated
a German policy more assertive than in the days of the Cold War. Bonn
was now confident that the old German desire to include security in the
process of European integration could be realised and that a distinct
military component could be established in the long run.

Consequently, Germany modified its Cold War attitude to European
defence co-operation during the Maastricht negotiations. It was willing to
adopt a more proactive approach, even to the extent of risking misunderstandings with the US. It pursued a dual strategy of maintaining and
reforming NATO while unifying Western Europe with an emphasis on
the establishment of a common foreign and security policy which would
eventually include the area of defence. Though NATO had to remain the
bedrock of German security, there was broad consensus that a reformed
NATO had to become a more European organisation (Hyde-Price 1992:
163). Bonn now played the role of an active interlocutor and mediator
between Washington and Paris, believing that European integration would
not antagonise the US. Germany's new stance, however, caused transatlantic irritation in the run-up to the Maastricht Treaty (Menon *et al.*
1992: 98–118). Many of the debates which now emerged among the allies
had been explored earlier (Wallace 1984: 251–61). This time, however,
Germany believed that the 'Atlanticist' and 'European' approaches could
be reconciled.

The traditional dilemma of 'Europeanisation' was illustrated by transatlantic quarrels over the Eurocorps. Shortly after Bonn strengthened its
Atlantic ties through participation in NATO's Rapid Reaction Force, it
decided to advance a European defence identity via the creation of the
Eurocorps. Faced with worries in Washington, Bonn had constantly to
reassure the US that Franco–German initiatives would not undercut
NATO (Denison 1993: 123–6). Even so, the US administration responded
with hostility when it learnt about plans for the Eurocorps and the
envisaged role of the WEU in European security (Brenner and Williams
1992).

As mediator between Paris and Washington, Bonn came increasingly to be viewed as a volatile partner. In January 1993, however, France and Germany signed an agreement along with Supreme Headquarters Allied Powers Europe (SHAPE) to make the Eurocorps available to NATO and to put it under NATO's operational command, thus easing American concerns. It was decided that Germany would not withdraw any units from its NATO assignment. Instead, the agreement provided a 'bridge' for France to move closer to NATO, even if Paris would not admit this openly.

A breakthrough in reconciling European and Atlantic security options was achieved at the NATO summit of January 1994. Transatlantic disputes and misunderstandings were eased when President Bill Clinton explicitly emphasised US support for the development of a genuine European defence identity. It was decided to promote operational compatibility between NATO and the WEU, particularly by making NATO's means available to the WEU through the concept of Combined Joined Task Forces (CJTF) (Europe Documents 1994). The shift in US policy towards acceptance of 'Europeanisation' has increased Germany's room for manoeuvre in influencing developments relating to European security.

Germany has often been criticised in Western capitals for pursuing the impossible, for 'doing the splits'. The government, however, has maintained its belief that the WEU could be developed as both the defence arm of the European Union and the European pillar of a strengthened NATO. The Germans claimed that an effective European defence could be built only within an Atlantic framework. As Germany's Defence Minister, Volker Rühe, stated: 'European integration and a trusting transatlantic partnership do not preclude each other' (Rühe 1993:132). The German attitude required much diplomatic skill, and was largely successful at Maastricht and thereafter. In fact, the Maastricht compromise was essentially a symbiosis of the US and French positions. Nevertheless, Bonn, unlike more Atlanticist states such as Britain, would have liked to see a stronger connection between the WEU and the EU.

More recent developments have underlined the German commitment to enhanced European defence capabilities. The 1994 Defence White Paper states that Germany has 'greater international responsibility' and that it has 'learnt the lessons of history and will thus continue to pursue a policy of active integration and broad international co-operation' (Federal Ministry of Defence 1994). Accordingly, as Timothy Garton Ash has argued, Germany pursued 'a symbolic act of profound significance' through the amendment of Article 23 of its constitution.

[T]he same Article 23 of the Basic Law under which unification had been achieved was amended in December 1992 so that the Federal Republic, instead of being open for 'other parts of Germany' to join, was now committed to the 'realisation of a united Europe' through the 'European Union'.

(Garton Ash 1993: 385)

In addition, the old and still valid Article 24,1 raises the possibility of transferring national sovereignty to a supranational level. Legal texts are reinforced by political rhetoric designed to allay concern about a possible nationalist resurgence in German foreign policy after unification – stressing that 'our vital national interests coincide with those of Europe altogether' (Kinkel 1994b: 336).

In sum, Bonn has proved increasingly willing to strengthen the EU's role by promoting a future defence component. Ironically, the project of European integration was largely designed to contain the Germans, not to foster their role in world affairs. Yet German support for European integration has often had the effect of enhancing, rather than reducing, German autonomy in defence matters.

CONSTRAINTS ON DEFENCE POLICY

Domestic pressures

The development of Germany's military policy has been profoundly affected by the legacy of the non-military past. Any visible assertiveness has been taboo since 1945. Hence, Germans developed a largely amilitary strategic culture which deeply influenced security thinking. The use of the German military for purposes other than national defence is difficult to legitimise with a public which still experiences feelings of guilt. Many Germans, particularly to the left of the political spectrum, concluded from the World Wars that the use of force is immoral under any circumstances – a belief arguably strengthened by the supposed 'civilising' effects on the German public of the country's social market economy (Hyde-Price 1992: 156). During the Cold War, however, when the only conceivable scenario for military action was a direct and massive attack against the national territory, a broad consensus existed (periodically broken by issues such as INF) which maintained the government's relative autonomy from domestic pressures.

The German political class maintained a reserved, if not hostile, attitude towards external military engagements, justifying it on a clause in the constitution which prohibited such actions. This prohibition was eventually lifted by the Constitutional Court in 1994. But in the immediate aftermath of 1989 German reservations about out-of-area missions were actually heightened by the multiplication of regional clashes. Even the Chancellor, who on many occasions had demanded that Germany assume greater responsibility for international stability, stated in early 1993 that:

there are places in Europe where it is out of the question for German divisions to be sent, because there are people still alive who have a very concrete experience [of the Second World War] and all the horrors connected with it.

(Mortimer 1993)

Such a restrictive attitude had the potential to jeopardise the scope and coherence of a future European defence identity. Josef Joffe noted that, if this view were to be accepted, the only place in Europe where German troops could be deployed would be Sweden (Mortimer 1993). At the end of 1995, with Germany committing troops and planes for the IFOR operation in Bosnia, the stance of the Chancellor, Helmut Kohl, was modified. This was due to international pressure on Germany to participate in international peacekeeping missions together with the ruling of the Constitutional Court.

The Chancellor's argument was also reflected in the 'principles of participation' the Foreign Minister, Klaus Kinkel, outlined in October 1994 for German out-of-area activities. The second of these states that 'Germany will never undertake peace missions alone', while the sixth spells out that German participation must not exacerbate a conflict. 'This could be the case, above all, in areas where there is still strong animosity dating back to the period of German occupation during the Second World War' (Kinkel 1994a: 7). Such strictures are clearly open to interpretation. Nevertheless, they are meaningful because they highlight the intellectual climate in which the new German security policy is being formulated.

Germany has clearly taken a number of steps to pursue a more active and responsible security policy.[1] The political battle to create a domestic consensus around Germany's future military role is, however, still raging and the outcome is uncertain (Noelle-Neumann 1995: 6). Opinion polls have suggested that the pacifist tendency among the German public is fading and that a more pragmatic approach to defence is likely to prevail in the long term (Köcher 1993; Asmus 1993). However, modifying Philip Gordon's assessment (1994: 241) 'that the normalisation of German foreign policy has already begun', Franz-Josef Meiers (1995: 82) argued in mid-1995 that 'Germany is still far from being a "normal" international actor'. The political class has, for example, repeatedly shied away from a national public debate about the priorities of its foreign and security policy (Noelle-Neumann 1995: 12). Moreover, a public opinion survey demonstrates that support for military engagement exists in principle, but that it declines sharply when specific scenarios are put to Germans (Asmus 1995: 28–31). Nevertheless, the author of this study considers that there has been a 'geopolitical maturation' in Germany.

Whilst, in terms of domestic pressures, the government's room for manoeuvre was only mildly constrained during the Cold War, this changed after unification with the growing interest of the public and political parties in foreign affairs. The government had to include the public in its strategic planning as controversial debates emerged around bloody regional conflicts and the need to redefine Germany's role in the international arena. The question of out-of-area commitments was ultimately solved by the Constitutional Court and not by the politicians. The creation of a broad domestic consensus had still to be established, despite Volker Rühe's somewhat over-optimistic statement, in early 1996, that 'in only a few years, a new consensus about the central tasks of German security policy, the mission and role of the armed forces, has developed' (Rühe 1996). Nevertheless, one might conclude that the glass was half full rather than half empty. Germany was increasingly adapting to the new military realities, despite the fact that domestic constraints remained powerful.

International pressures

The international system

The constraints on German defence policy imposed by domestic pressures came into clear focus with the end of the Cold War and the debates this spawned. Yet, paradoxically, three of the international constraints on policy during the superpower confrontation were dramatically weakened by its termination. First, the geographical position of the Federal Republic had acted as a crucial constraint on German military policy, lest the country become the battlefield for an East–West nuclear or conventional confrontation. Since 1989, however, the country has been entirely surrounded by allies and friends, and no longer finds itself in the position of a front-line state. Today, Germany's central location helps equip it to shape the future of East–West relations significantly by facilitating the development of a new European security structure. Geography is, thus, no longer a constraint but has, instead, provided Bonn with the opportunity to use its political weight to shape European affairs more actively.

Second, under bipolarity, the government's capacity to act was largely determined by the superpower relationship. In addition, fluctuations in the balance of power among the key Western actors, particularly the US and France, also constrained its room for manoeuvre. William Paterson described Bonn's Cold War status as follows:

> The feature that distinguishes the Federal Republic from other states has been the absolute centrality of foreign policy, reflecting the Federal Republic's genesis as more a foreign policy in search of a state than a state in search of a foreign policy. The division of Germany meant that the Federal Republic was centrally preoccupied with the external environment in its effort to bring about reunification.
>
> (Paterson 1994: 127)

Third, it was precisely the goal of unification and the Federal Republic's responsibility *vis-à-vis* East Germany which further constrained the government's capacity to act. With unification, Germany ceased to be a revisionist country and thus enjoyed enhanced freedom of action.

Moreover, Germany's step-by-step approach to achieving international emancipation and greater autonomy was mirrored in the legal field. Germany's accession to NATO and the WEU led to an enhancement of Germany's status but also to a number of restrictions. On the one hand, Germany was to be integrated within NATO as an equal partner. On the other, the WEU was partly aimed at preventing an 'equal' rearmament of the Federal Republic, thus constraining Bonn's autonomy. Whereas all member countries undertook to restrict or give up altogether the production of certain types of weapons, the toughest restrictions were those placed on Bonn (Cahen 1989: 3). In addition, Germany was forbidden to produce ABC weapons. The Western allies also reserved their rights in respect to the Federal Republic and Berlin with the signing of the Paris Agreements.[2] However, this formal restriction of sovereignty increasingly lost its impact as the Cold War progressed.

Since unification, Germany's autonomy has grown constantly. The legal constraints on the country were removed with the conclusion of the 'Two-Plus-Four Treaty', with the exception of Germany's (voluntary) renunciation of ABC weapons production. Germany is now, to all intents and purposes, a fully sovereign country. In sum, constraints on national autonomy decreased as the perception of threats diminished, and in recognition of its new geo-strategic position and increased political weight. The changed nature of the international system has therefore profoundly enhanced Germany's autonomy, allowing it, in principle, considerably more freedom of movement than under the crushing weight of the Cold War.

NATO

Since the 1950s, Bonn's security policy has been characterised by deep military integration within the Atlantic Alliance. Considering where Germany started from after the Second World War, an alternative to integration did not exist. In essence, NATO itself was Germany's defence policy, since the defence of Germany formed the core of the common defence, a fact most clearly illustrated by the Bundeswehr, whose decentralised structure was symbolised by the absence of a general staff. In contrast to their British and French counterparts, German generals could plan military strategy only within NATO. In the event of war, operational command over all combat units of the armed forces would have been transferred to NATO. Thus, German conventional forces, while the largest, were also the most integrated in Western Europe.

Moreover, the Federal Republic was the only country in Europe within which large numbers of troops from allied states were stationed, while Germany did not station troops outside its territory. In this sense,

Germany did not have to face up to awkward policy choices. NATO provided all the answers. The strategy of 'forward defence' and the nuclear guarantee were the two main elements of Germany's defence which linked its fate and security to that of its Western allies.

The impact of integration within NATO during the Cold War was not straightforward. The loss of autonomy suffered through Alliance integration, though striking, was acceptable, since unilateral military action was never a viable option given both the self-imposed legal constraints on extra-European military activity and the scale of the threat within Europe. The gain in influence derived from NATO membership was particularly important in relation to Germany's two major European allies, France and Britain. Compared to Paris and London, Bonn enjoyed fewer foreign policy options, particularly since nuclear status constitutes an essential asset for the conduct of an autonomous defence policy. However, through its deep integration in the Alliance, Germany has been able steadily to increase its influence over the two European nuclear powers. Germany's desire to bring France closer to NATO has thus also acquired a power-political dimension. Bonn aims to increase its influence on Paris by constraining French autonomy through further integration (Sauder 1995: 163).

When Germany's geo-strategic position altered after unification, the pressure to maintain Alliance commitments under any circumstances decreased. Integration in NATO became less a question of survival and more a long-term insurance policy. Bonn opted convincingly and promptly in favour of continuity by remaining fully committed to its military integration in NATO.

Four examples serve to illustrate why the scope and quality of the Bundeswehr's integration and capabilities have prevented the Federal Republic from conducting a more autonomous defence policy, even since 1989. First, the deep integration of the German military in multinational units (such as NATO's Rapid Reaction Corps), as well as the continued and deepened integration of its territorial forces in NATO, clearly demonstrates the limits of a national defence policy in the classical sense.

Second, the government does not have the military means to conduct unilateral power politics in the security and defence area. Germany possesses only a relatively small army of 340,000 men. Moreover, the Bundeswehr is ill-equipped for military activities apart from the defence of its territory since its forces were structured according to the needs of Nato's central front. No significant sea- or air-lift capacity is available to the army. It also lacks experience in projecting substantial forces abroad; its 'invasion capabilities' are very limited.

A third constraint on the possibility of a more autonomous policy is the Defence Ministry's decision that a general staff will not be established for the Bundeswehr. Instead, a so-called Heeresführungskommando (Army Operations Command) was created which established complicated command structures to co-ordinate centrally the three independent services. This new centre will lack the core function of a general staff, namely 'full command'. The establishment of a general staff with comprehensive competencies will remain a taboo for some time to come. Germany continues to have the only defence force in the world without a general staff (Feldmeyer 1995a and 1995b).

Finally, Germany lacks the financial means to promote significantly its own autonomy either in the area of national defence or in that of a more independent European defence structure. Huge investments would be necessary to develop, for example, intelligence and air-lift capabilities which could function independently of the US. Germany's relative military autonomy can only be seen and measured through its influence within the Alliance.

Thus, although pressures emanating from the international system were substantially reduced (including the removal of legal constraints on German sovereignty), the constraints imposed on national autonomy by the Atlantic Alliance remained in place and showed no signs of weakening. Moreover, it should not be forgotten that, despite the increased margin of manoeuvre Germany enjoyed as a result of the end of the Cold War, it was precisely over the issue of most relevance to security policy in the 1990s – out-of-area missions – that the new domestic constraints on policy were most keenly felt.

THE EUROPEAN UNION AND DEFENCE AUTONOMY

As illustrated earlier, German interest in the creation of European defence structures was manifest after the end of the Cold War. Developments in Europe, in turn, impacted on the evolution of defence policy.

First, defence-related initiatives at the European level have served to legitimise discussions of defence matters in the domestic political arena. A paradox in German debates was the inconsistency between, on the one hand, a relatively pacifist society, which militated against an active German military role, and, on the other, the logic of further European integration, which was widely backed by the German public and suggested that a credible political union would need a military dimension to reinforce its political authority. An emphasis on the latter by political leaders helped to limit the constraining effect of a relatively pacifist society on discussions about a more active German military role. Indeed, given German public acceptance of the aim of European integration, the prospect of a common European defence along federalist lines was held out as a means of influencing the domestic climate on defence and the debate on German forces out-of-area (Jopp 1994: 9).

In several instances, Europe was explicitly used as a justification for specific initiatives in the defence sphere. A crucial example of this was the out-of-area debate, where members of the administration argued in favour of German participation in crisis management activities. A dispute took place not only between the government and the opposition, but also within the governing coalition. During the prolonged arguments, the Chancellor made an implicit link between an out-of-area capability and European integration. Speaking of his vision of a Europe which would speak with a single voice, he added that 'a European defence was one of the crucial aims of the common initiative taken by François Mitterrand and myself with the creation of the Eurocorps.' He further stated: 'Those who refuse the development of a European defence identity – this sentence has to be underlined – oppose, in the final analysis, the political unification of Europe.' (Kohl 1994: 136)

According to the Christian Democrats, 'the vital issue' in the out-of-area dispute was 'to pave the way for unrestricted German participation in a common European defence' (Lamers 1993). The Defence Minister, Volker Rühe, summed up the 'Europe argument' by stating in the German Bundestag:

> If we make mistakes, we do not make them only for ourselves. Due to the particular role and location of Germany, a special role [*Sonderrolle*] would make Europe incapable of acting. What is at stake is that we should not think nationally in a narrow way, but that we grasp that it will not only be a mistake for Germany if we refuse ourselves, but that we hinder others from developing a European capability to act.
>
> (Rühe 1994a: 5)

While the Social Democrats advocated giving the UN a power monopoly to be written into the German constitution, the Christian Democrat (CDU) foreign affairs spokesman, Karl Lamers, insisted that 'Germany cannot deny the community of its European partners the same solidarity which it is willing to grant the United Nations.' (Lamers 1992: 3). Moreover, the Bundeswehr had made military plans in December 1992, the so-called defence policy guidelines, based on Germany's participation in out-of-area operations. This policy accorded with the Eurocorps agreement and the WEU Petersberg Declaration which granted the organisation an out-of-area role. Thus, the government had created facts which parliamentarians had to recognise. References to Europe and the decisions already taken certainly played a role in persuading the FDP to find common ground with the CDU/CSU in an agreement of 13 January 1993. The coalition agreed to change the constitution in order to allow German peacemaking missions in any collective framework, be it the UN, NATO or the WEU. Eventually, the Constitutional Court gave the widely expected permissive interpretation of the Basic Law on 12 July 1994. This ruling allowed German forces to take part in combat action under various security organisations.

Similarly, when Germany found itself under considerable pressure from its partners not to withdraw its personnel from surveillance aircraft over Bosnia, Volker Rühe praised the degree of integration in the AWACS fleet, saying it represented important progress in European construction which Germany should not question, if it did not want to risk undermining both European and NATO integration (Rühe 1994b: 43).

Furthermore, both European and Atlantic multinational forces serve as useful legitimisation for out-of-area activities. Neither the ARRC nor the Eurocorps could function effectively without German participation. The same applies to the two newly-created US–German corps in Ulm and Frankfurt as well as the Dutch–German corps in Münster and the German–Danish corps in Rendsburg.

Similarly, European initiatives may serve German interests as far as its defence industry and arms procurement are concerned. There are three reasons why Germany has a particular interest in Europeanisation and harmonisation in this area. First, the competitiveness of the German defence industry is shrinking. Whereas the government has traditionally been cautious about interfering in Germany's private defence market, the industries of other West European countries have benefited from heavily subsidised national armaments projects. Second, the room for future investments has been reduced as a consequence of cuts in the defence budget. Finally, Germany continues to have the most restrictive arms export rules. Between 1992 and 1994, 98.8 per cent of German exports went to NATO and Scandinavian countries, whereas Britain exported 76 per cent and France 50 per cent of its arms to developing regions. Thus, there is a huge market to which Germany cannot deliver because of its self-imposed policy (Rode 1995: 4–5). This is particularly painful since the preservation of a national industrial defence base is crucial for the country's ability to participate in European arms co-operation and, more generally, a future European defence.

The 1994 Defence White Paper thus points to the fact that all European states have fewer resources at their disposal and states that 'this situation demands common solutions more urgently than ever before.' (Federal Ministry of Defence 1994: 95). Volker Rühe even asked European governments to 'buy European' rather than to 'buy American'. Only a common and consolidated European market for armaments would provide the possibility to remain competitive *vis-à-vis* the US, hence German proposals for the creation of a European Armaments Agency (Presse, 1995: 41). For the German defence industry, Europeanisation has become an important vehicle to promote its interests – it may even become a question of survival. In some senses, the European opportunities offered are enhanced by changes in the international constraints confronting Germany. During the Cold War, Germany's emphasis on heavy weapons, shaped by the needs of the central front, were significantly different from the British and French focus on lighter and cheaper weapons for out-of-area activities. This is changing since 'equipping the reaction forces has priority' in the future, as the new White Paper soberly states (Federal Ministry of Defence 1994: 99). Practically all investments will be made to allow German participation in crisis management under the auspices of the UN, NATO or the WEU.

While in many instances acting as a means of reinforcing autonomy by allowing the state more effectively to deal with domestic constraints, or to further German interests, developments at the European level have also sometimes acted as a constraint on policy. The increasing security links between West European states, whilst potentially useful in the case of, for example, procurement and arms production, were profoundly embarrassing and potentially volatile in the context of public opinion when Paris raised the prospect in September 1995 of a possible Europeanisation of the French nuclear force.

A second example of unpleasant European pressure was in the summer of 1995, when it became apparent that multinational units could also entail commitments and invite pressures to take action in a crisis. When France proposed deploying the Eurocorps to implement a peace plan for Bosnia, the German government was very reluctant. Yet a German officer, General Helge Hansen, at the time NATO's CINCENT, warned that Bonn, which had actively promoted multinational structures, was in danger not only of losing credibility but also of indirectly encouraging a re-nationalisation of allied defence structures (Inacker 1995).

Third, initiatives to increase Germany's international weight through the acquisition of a permanent membership of the UN Security Council also ran up against European-level constraints. As early as September 1993, the German Foreign Minister pointed out in a speech at the UN that 'Germany is prepared to assume responsibility as a permanent member' of the UN Security Council (Kinkel 1993). However, in a debate among German security experts the claim was criticised as being premature on the grounds of European considerations (Wagner 1993: 533–40). One argument was that Germany's position on the Security Council could weaken the influence of a future common European security policy. Karl Lamers favoured a common EU representation in the UN Security Council over a national German one. Germany should seek a seat unilaterally only if this endeavour should fail (Lamers 1992a and 1993a).

CONCLUSIONS

In assessing the impact of the EU on German defence policy, it is crucial to distinguish between the extremes of autonomy and dependence, on one hand, and sovereignty and integration, on the other. Integration does not necessarily lead to a loss of autonomy or of influence. Indeed, it can create new opportunities for action as well as increase the impact of that action on others. This is precisely what has happened in the German case. For a superpower such as the US, the path of integration followed by

Germany would have led to an increase in dependence. Germany, however, a medium sized power with a very distinct history and geographic location, has often seemed to gain in autonomy and influence through integration. In particular, just as France has viewed European economic and monetary union (EMU) as a means of preventing German monetary policy from taking on a dangerously nationalistic character, Germany has viewed European co-operative schemes in the defence realm as a means of gaining influence over its militarily more active and independent European partners.

Pressures emanating from the European level coexisted with wider international and domestic pressures. In many cases, it was these other, alternative pressures which exercised the overriding impact on defence policy. The move towards participation in out-of-area activities, for example, was in the first instance due to pressures from NATO and the UN. Those two organisations were probably much more in the minds of both the politicians and the public. More fundamentally, it was only the relaxation of the international constraints associated with the Cold War that made recent German European initiatives conceivable at all. Moreover, the Alliance continues to exert a huge influence over defence policy.

However, the European level has asserted a stronger influence since the old external Cold War determinants of German security policy shifted and the process of European unification has continued. With the disappearance of an overriding threat and US encouragement to further integrate in defence matters, Bonn is more willing than ever to promote a distinct European security and defence identity. Germany did not become less Atlanticist but, compared to the days of the Cold War, the government developed a new determination to work towards a genuine European security and defence capability within the framework of NATO. At the same time, the US increasingly views it as being in its own interest that Europeans develop their own defence structures. The old dispute between Atlantic and European designs for European security has eased significantly.

Europe also represented a useful means of circumventing domestic pressure. This was particularly true during the out-of-area debate and the interrelated political squabbles over the Maastricht Treaty and the creation of the Eurocorps. The progress made by the EU/CFSP, the WEU and Eurocorps was used by the government as a vehicle to influence the domestic debate – a debate which was dominated by Germany's reluctant attitude towards military engagement. The government aimed to externalise internal conflicts about Germany's participation in combat missions in order to ease societal strains and to foster the achievement of its goals. The fact that further European political integration would inevitably have to comprise the area of defence provided a powerful argument for the government. European calls for action within CFSP and the WEU frameworks helped the government to establish its autonomy on the out-of-area issue and in its defence policy more generally. This autonomy was a prerequisite for fully asserting German influence in integrated Atlantic and European structures. That the government was able to use European pressures for its purposes was due to the fact that European consider- ations have been internalised both by the public and the politicians in Germany.

It is relatively easy to see why Germany has pursued with determination the policy of encouraging enhanced European defence integration in recent years. For a country unusually affected by anti-military public sentiments derived from the Second World War and which has already become accustomed to far-reaching integration of its military forces, such integration can often provide enhanced, rather than reduced, autonomy. It is no surprise, then, that German officials are willing to speak of the symbiosis between German and European interests. It will be interesting to see how Germany manages – possibly through well-calculated use of the EU – to reconcile its increased external room for manoeuvre as well as growing international expectations with the relatively low internal preparedness to take ever greater international responsibility.

NOTES

1 By 1995, Germany had: cleared the way to take part in international combat missions out of NATO area; pledged Tornados for a possible UN pull-out operation in Bosnia; actively contributed to the operational readiness of the Eurocorps which was made available for out-of-area missions; claimed a perma- nent seat in the UN Security Council; taken part in the UNOSOM mission to Somalia with armed forces; deployed minesweepers in the Persian Gulf; sent 2,000 German troops to Iran in order to assist in relief efforts to threatened Kurds; participated in air-lift operations to supply Sarajevo with food and medical equipment; supervised the arms embargo on Serbia with officers in the mixed units of the AWACS airborne surveillance; participated with sanitation and medical officers in the UN mission in Cambodia; and decided to restructure the Bundeswehr according to the needs of international crisis management.
2 Paradoxically, whilst reducing the autonomy of the state in defence matters, this restriction served German interests in that it served to stabilise the country. The legal reservations served Bonn's goal of unification and guaranteed the security and freedom of Berlin (Haftendorn 1993: 51). Moreover, the stationing of allied troops provided the necessary protection in case of military aggression.

REFERENCES

Asmus, R. D. (1993) 'Germany's Geopolitical Maturation. Strategy and Public Opinion After the Wall', Santa Monica, CA, *Rand Issue Paper*, February.
—— (1995) 'Germany's Geopolitical Maturation: Public Opinion and Security Policy in 1994', Santa Monica, CA, Rand, January.
Brenner, M. and Williams, P. (1992) 'Europe and the United States: US security policy toward Europe in the 1990s', Konrad Adenauer Foundation, Internal Studies, no. 36.
Cahen, A. (1989) *The Western European Union and Nato*, London: Brassey's.

Denison, A. (1993) 'Amerika und das Eurokorps', *Europäische Sicherheit*, no. 3, pp. 123–6.

Europe Documents (1991) 'Political Union: Franco–German initiative on foreign, security, and defence policy', 1738, 18 October.

—— (1994) 'NATO Declaration of the Heads of State', 1867, 12 January.

Federal Ministry of Defence (1994) White Paper 1994, Bonn.

Feldmeyer, K. (1995a) 'Bundeswehr erhält Führungszentrum', *Frankfurter Allgemeine Zeitung*, 3 January.

—— (1995b) 'Die schwierige Normalität', *Frankfurter Allgemeine Zeitung*, 12 January.

Garton Ash, T. (1993) *In Europe's Name. Europe and the Divided Continent*, London: Jonathan Cape.

Gordon, P. H. (1994) 'Berlin's Difficulties. The Normalization of German Foreign Policy', *Orbis*, Vol. 38, No. 1, pp. 225–43.

Haftendorn, H. (1993) 'Im Anfang waren die Aliierten. Die alliierten Vorbehaltsrechte als Rahmenbedingungen des außenpolitischen Handelns der Bundesrepublik Deutschland', in Hans-Hermann Hartwich and Göttrich Wewer (eds), *Regieren in der Bundesrepublik V*, Opladen: Leske & Budrich.

Hyde-Price, A. (1992) 'Uncertainties of security policy', in Gordon Smith (*et al.*), *Developments in German Politics*, Macmillan: London.

Inacker, M. J. (1995) 'Nichtbeteiligung an Bündnis-Einsätzen bringt Deutschland um Glaubwürdigkeit', *Welt am Sonntag*, 1 October.

Jopp, M. (1994) 'The strategic implications of European integration', *Adelphi Paper*, 290, London: IISS/Brassey's.

Kinkel, K. (1993) Speech given at the UN on 29 September, in Das Auswärtige Amt, *Mitteilung für die Presse*, no. 1116/93, 29 September.

—— (1994a) 'Peacekeeping missions: Germany can now play its part', *NATO Review*, 5, October.

—— (1994b) 'Deutschland in Europa. Zu den Zielen der deutschen Präsidentschaft in der Europäischen Union', *Europa Archiv*, 12.

Köcher, R. (1993) 'Breite Mehrheit für Blauhelmeinsätze deutscher Soldaten', *Frankfurter Allgemeine Zeitung*, 11 February.

Kohl, H. (1994) 'Europäische Sicherheit und die Rolle Deutschlands', speech given at the Wehrkundetagung in Munich, 5 February; reprinted in *Bulletin*, No. 5, 16 February.

Lamers, K. (1992a) 'Lamers: Keine Bedingungen an die UN', *Frankfurter Allgemeine Zeitung*, 15 August.

—— (1992b) 'Zehn Bemerkungen zu den Aussenpolitischen Erfahrungen des Wiedervereinigten Deutschlands und zur Diskussion über sein Aussenpolitisches Selbstverständnis', Bonn, 25 August.

—— (1993a) 'Lamers widerspricht Kinkels UN Politik', *Frankfurter Allgemeine Zeitung*, 11 February.

—— (1993b) Statement on behalf of the CDU/CSU faction, *Pressedienst* der CDU/CSU Fraktion, Bonn, 8 August.

Meiers, F.-J. (1995) 'Germany: the reluctant power', *Survival*, 37/3.

Menon, A., Forster A. and Wallace, W. (1992) 'A common European defence?', *Survival*, 34/3.

Mortimer, E. (1993) 'Ready, willing but still unable', *Financial Times*, 10 February.

Nölle-Neumann, E. (1995) 'Öffentliche Meinung und Außenpolitik. Die fehlende Debatte in Deutschland', *Internationale Politik*, Vol. 50, No. 8.

Paterson, W. E. (1994) 'The Chancellor and foreign policy', in Stephen Padgett (ed.), *Adenauer to Kohl. The Development of the German Chancellorship*, London: Hurst.

Presse-und Informationsamt der Bundesregierung (1995) 'BM der Verteidigung

Rühe zu Beschaffungsprojekten der Bundeswehr', *Stichworte zur Sicherheitspolitik*, no. 5, May.

Rode, J. (1995) Der Deutsche Rüstungsexport 1992–1994, unpublished manuscript, Ebenhausen, August.

Rühe, V. (1993) 'Shaping Euro–Atlantic policies: a grand strategy for a new era', *Survival*, 35/2.

—— (1994a) speech in the Bundestag on the occasion of a debate on the Constitutional Court ruling of 12 July, 1994, reprinted in *Das Parlament*, 5 August.

—— (1994b) 'Europa im Umbruch – neue Aufgaben für die Bundeswehr', speech given in Ludwigsburg on 6 May, 1994, reprinted in Presse und Informationsamt der Bundesregierung, *Stichworte zur Sicherheitspolitik*, no. 6, June.

—— (1996) 'Mut zur Verantwortung', *Frankfurter Allgemeine Zeitung*, 9 February.

Sauder, A. (1995) *Souveränität und Integration. Französische und deutsche Konzeptionen europäischer Sicherheit nach dem Ende des Kalten Krieges (1990–1993)*, Baden-Baden: Nomos.

Stratmann, K.-P. (1992) 'The future of West European security and defence co-operation – German Perspectives' in Peter Schmidt (ed.), *In the Midst of Change: On the Development of West European Security and Defence Co-operation*, Baden-Baden: Nomos.

Wagner, W. (1993) 'Der ständige Sitz im Sicherheitsrat', *Europa Archiv*, 19.

Wallace, W. (1984) 'European defence co-operation: the reopening debate', *Survival*, 36/6.

4 Italy

Filippo Andreatta and Christopher Hill

Italian foreign policy has been little written about outside Italy. Even inside the country it has been the preserve of a narrow range of specialists, most of whom have preferred an historical method to the theoretically-based approach of policy analysis. The same judgements apply *a fortiori* to the study of defence policy, where even Italian writing is fairly sparse. Work which discusses both defence issues and the European Union dimension has barely begun, so there is a natural gap in the literature which this chapter may help to fill. It seeks to do so by placing Rome's view of European defence co-operation in the context of Italian defence policy trends since 1945; changing international pressures after 1985; and the domestic political environment. Only with this background analysis is it possible to understand the dilemmas which have confronted govern-ments in Rome (although so far they have largely averted their eyes) arising out of their support in principle for European defence integration and their inability in practice to contribute much towards it.

This uncomfortable stance has specific cultural roots, in particular Italy's lack of a strong and independent military tradition as well as a reaction against Mussolini's obsession with putting this right by asserting a strength which the country simply did not have. Like Goldilocks, Italy has gone from too much porridge to too little (Rosecrance 1995). In doing so it has displayed the force of two competing theoretical perspectives.

The first, which we can call the *strategic explanation*, points to the fact that any country confronted with a threat such as that posed by the Cold War has a choice of means on how to cope with it. As Waltz has pointed out, these are either forms of external balancing (such as alliances) or forms of internal balancing (rearmament). Given that a more independent 'internal' policy (such as that pursued by France after the Second World War) might have widened the profound domestic political divide between left and right, and given that resource and administrative weaknesses meant in practice that choice was in any case limited, Italy chose the former. Moreover Italy's geopolitical position was less vulnerable in a Cold War centred on Germany, and Rome could therefore allow itself a degree of free-riding in terms of military preparedness. The NATO umbrella and the relatively light pressure for defence expenditure meant that guns did not get in the way of butter as, it could be argued, they did in Britain and to a lesser extent in France. From this viewpoint, Italy responded rationally to its external situation and took advantage of willing allies to leave its defence sector undeveloped (Posen 1984: 239).

The second theoretical perspective can be termed the *domestic explanation*, and this emphasises the lack of state autonomy in Italy. Far from being a unitary actor, Italy is in this sense the victim of extensive bureaucratic politics and of sub-rational log-rolling among political factions (Snyder 1991: Ch. 1; Allison 1971; Steinbruner 1974). Once its place in the Western camp had been settled, Italy fell prey to a virtual breakdown in rational state practice. The result was that policy tended to be more the product of domestic brokerage and a precarious political balance than of any deliberate decision making. On this view, any success in defence policy was ascribed largely to good fortune and to external circumstances.

A mix of these two perspectives is necessary for a satisfactory explanation of Italian defence policy since 1945. In the late 1940s and early 1950s the strategic explanation is more appropriate. Italy could do little to affect the emerging Cold War one way or the other, while at the same time it desperately needed domestic reconstruction. Later, however, domestic factors became increasingly important, not least because of the continuity provided by the strategic choices of the early post-war period. Yet, by the late 1980s, decision making on defence, as on many issues, was paralysed. Moreover, the First Republic was entering a crisis, the end of the Cold War brought the structural problems of the Italian state out into the open.[1] Italy has not, so far, been able to adapt its defence posture to the changed international environment. In particular, the shift in threat-perception from the East to the South (however exaggerated) has left the country potentially on the frontier of a new arc of crisis. In these circumstances, free-riding is much less rational, and could leave Italy unprepared for the future. On the other hand, the Italian state, which is paradoxically both weak and highly distinctive, as well as being very difficult to shift, makes it improbable that any kind of strategic decision can be made in the near future. All the country's political energies are currently taken up with reforming the electoral and pensions systems. The last thing most party leaders want is to add a foreign policy distraction. They naturally fall back on the cover of a common European approach. Italy is one of the most enthusiastic supporters of a Common Foreign and Security Policy, and (in time) of a common European defence.

Defence policy should, in Clausewitzian terms, be the handmaiden of foreign policy. Political debate and goal formulation should precede the working out of the relatively technical question of how military capabilities can help to achieve the security and other more proactive aims of a particular state. Of course it is often difficult to distinguish clearly between ends and means, between foreign policy and defence. Moreover when it is possible, then the tail can often wag the dog; the nature of available capabilities all too easily determines the ends which are thought desirable. Thus for Rome the lack of national capabilities naturally makes the European option desirable, independent of its merit.

Italy has favoured multilateral solutions since 1949. But, whereas in the European Community Italy soon gained the confidence to promote integration, convincing itself that the national and the 'communautaire' were synonymous, in the area of defence it has had very little choice. The perceived need for the shield (economic as well as military) provided by the United States and Nato both simplified and paralysed decision-making on defence; the parameters were set, the primary burden lay elsewhere, and Italy saw no reason to rock the boat or to prepare against an uncertain future. Since 1985 and the arrival of Mikhail Gorbachev, these happy certainties have been under threat. Not surprisingly, at least for those aware of the cognitive, bureaucratic and political obstacles to adaptive change in all states, Italy's response to shifts in the environment has largely been more of the same. As we shall see below, whatever the theoretical arguments for and against radical change in Italy's defence doctrines and postures, the policy system itself has shown little sign of debating them, let alone of self-transformation. This is true in relation to both the end of the Cold War and the gradual emergence of a European security identity which preceded it. Even where the will to change might have existed, the Italian political system has not had the capability to pursue it, and has perforce fallen in (with the brief exception of the Berlusconi government's reflex nationalism in 1994–5) behind Franco–German plans.

TRENDS IN ITALIAN DEFENCE POLICY SINCE 1945

Italian defence policy has been low-profile and paid scant attention to the technical preparedness of the armed forces. Italy has preferred to rely on international alliances for its protection rather than face the financial costs and the strains on its delicate political system that a higher national profile would entail. The government was quite happy to surrender sovereignty to international organisations if this meant removing defence from the political debate. Apart from being an apt strategy for a civilian power – which is part of Italy's self-image – it has allowed the country to become a consumer more than producer of security. It has exploited its international commitments to legitimise defence activity domestically, while it has justified its minimal commitments to international bodies on the grounds of internal weaknesses.

However, the foundations of this policy have been shaken with the end of the Cold War. Italy's allies – especially the United States – are no longer irretrievably involved in its defence now that global tensions have calmed. Furthermore, the capability of the international institutional network to deal with lower-intensity conflicts is in doubt without the glue once provided by the Soviet threat and by American leadership, as the Bosnian debacle has sadly shown. Italy must therefore consider whether or not it should take more responsibility for its own defence, given that it is geopolitically exposed – as a Mediterranean bridge between Europe and the Middle East – to the regional conflicts which have followed the end of bipolarity. A thorough debate on the efficiency of the armed forces and on Italy's contribution to international organisations cannot responsibly be postponed much longer.

In the post-war period, Italian defence policy has been deeply affected by the country's structural weaknesses. At the international level, Italy lay vulnerably close to the Iron Curtain, with Yugoslavia occupying part of its pre-1939 territory in Istria and with Soviet troops in neighbouring Austria. At the domestic level, the scars of the War and the economic weakness of the country were compounded by the presence of the largest communist party outside the Soviet bloc, and the legacy of the virtual civil war between 1943–5, when allied landings had made possible partisan insurgency against Mussolini and his German ally.

The choice in favour of NATO made in 1948 by the Prime Minister, Alcide De Gasperi – who was able to count on only a narrow margin of support once the communist party had been expelled from the governing coalition in 1947 because opposition to NATO was not uncommon even in government circles – was therefore taken for a variety of reasons. First, Nato was to be an alliance to protect Italy from the Eastern threat. Second, Nato promised Italy a way to regain sovereignty and prestige as a founding member of an important international organisation only a few years after it had signed a peace treaty as a loser in the Second World War. Third, Nato membership helped anchor Italy in the Western camp and – through Marshall aid among other things – ensured the liberal development of the country's economic and social institutions (Scoppola 1991: 209–50).

In the 1950s the governing centrist coalition (1948–63) completed the positioning of Italy inside the Western camp, in the face of fierce domestic opposition, particularly from the left. Most commentators agree that Italy imperceptibly took a lower profile after the NATO decision of 1948. However foreign and defence policies were still important elements in Italian politics in the 1950s. The low-profile period really began with the centre-left governments of the 1960s. Italy was an enthusiastic supporter of European integration both during the European Defence Community episode and at the signing of the Treaty of Rome. The European dimension was intended to complement rather than to replace a close security relationship with the United States through NATO (as was demonstrated by the stationing of Jupiter missiles on Italian soil in 1957), and it was actively encouraged by Washington. In this period the Trieste dispute was also resolved on a basis satisfactory to Italy – at least, so it seemed at the time (Seton-Watson 1991: 346).[2]

Once these difficult but fundamental choices had been made the government preferred not to provoke a showdown with the communist-dominated opposition over such delicate matters. The 1960s were therefore a period of quiet in which the new centre-left coalition (1963–76) concentrated principally on domestic needs and on the creation of an 'economic miracle'. It is also important to remember that the public welcomed a low profile in foreign policy, given the memories of fascism and its combination of bombast and declining effectiveness. These domestic and economic goals were facilitated by the absence of major threats during this period: the Mediterranean was still a Western lake; Italy, unlike Britain and France, had no overseas empire to defend or painfully relinquish; while the exit of Albania and Yugoslavia from the Soviet bloc, and the withdrawal of the Red Army from Austria, pushed the Iron Curtain eastwards. Unlike Germany, Greece, Turkey and Norway, Italy after 1955 had no contiguous frontier with Soviet-bloc countries. While the question of loyalty to NATO and to the EEC was never put to the test, Italy was able to avoid dramatic debates on defence matters. The unchangeability of Italy's international position (the US, for its part, would not have welcomed any change) ensured that issues of security were kept out of public debate.

The 1970s marked a turning-point for Italian defence policy because some of the constraints had relaxed. First, the domestic opposition had moderated its opposition to NATO. The Socialist Party (PSI) had already endorsed NATO when it entered the government in the 1960s. Now the Communist Party (PCI) also modified its stance as a prelude to its support of the government in the period of 'National Solidarity' (1976–9). In 1976 the Communist leader Enrico Berlinguer declared in a famous interview with the *Corriere della Sera* that socialism was safer under the umbrella of NATO than outside it. In 1977 the PCI even endorsed a parliamentary resolution praising Italian membership of the Atlantic Alliance (Manzella 1984: 474–81; Romano 1995).

Second, the new-found consensus could also count on Italy's remarkable economic performance which boosted the country's prestige and eventually ensured it a place in the G7 from its birth in 1975.

Third, a new generation of politicians who had grown up in the 1960s had come to the fore with fewer preconceptions about Italy's role in the world and about the utility of military power than the generation of Giulio Andreotti. They were less cautious. Finally, changing circumstances in the Mediterranean highlighted Italy's particular geopolitical location and invited a more active role in an area which had come to the fore of international politics through a superpower naval build-up, the Greek–Turkish dispute, the renewal of the Arab–Israel conflict and the oil crisis.

From the end of the 1970s, therefore, Italy took a new direction in its

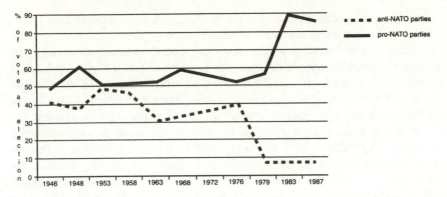

Source: Roberto Cartocci: Eletori in Italia (Bologna: il Mulino, 1990)
* Pro-Nato parties are the government parties between 1948 and 1963 (DC, PLI, PRI, PSDI), the PSI after 1963 and the PCI after 1977. The anti-Nato parties remaining are the MSi and the far-left parties.

Figure 4.1 Italian support for Nato, 1946–87

security policy (IAI 1979–92). But the new course has been characterised by a degree of schizophrenia (Seton-Watson: 354–8). On the one hand, the Atlantic and European foundations of defence policy have never moved. At critical junctures the Italian government has always preferred solidarity to the image of a maverick (Furlong 1994: 260). In 1978–9, during the debate on Intermediate-range Nuclear Forces (INF), Italian support (over strong domestic opposition) was essential to the decision to plan the deployment of Pershing and Cruise missiles. Italian support was essential because Germany's acceptance of INF was conditional on their acceptance by another major continental state. Since France was hardly a candidate, Italy was the only possibility. In 1980 Italy took the unprecedented step of guaranteeing Maltese neutrality, and between 1982–4 Italian troops participated in the ill-fated multinational force in the Lebanon (Caligaris 1983). At the same time Italy supported the Montebello resolution to modernise Short-range Nuclear Forces (SNF) and in 1987 it participated in the Western naval task force in the Gulf. In 1988, when Spain rejected the prospect of American F-16s at the Torrejon air-base, Italy offered to relocate them on its soil, in order to avoid weakening the Alliance's southern flank (Price 1989).

On the other hand, the government placated its internal opposition and those who wanted a more distinctive Italian policy with some paradoxical gestures. Most notable was the critique of American policy (especially over the Middle East) and the sustained commercial and diplomatic relations with Soviet-bloc countries and with anti-Western governments in the Mediterranean and Levant (in particular Libya, Algeria and Iraq). This strand of policy culminated in the Sigonella episode of October 1985 in which Italian security forces had an armed confrontation with an American special forces team trying to capture the Palestinians who had hijacked the cruise liner Achille Lauro, and who had then fallen into the hands of the Italians in Sicily (Pieson 1986). Even when two Libyan Scuds hit Italian shores at Lampedusa in retaliation for the American bombing of Tripoli in 1986, Italian protests to Washington were more vocal than those to Libya (Gray and Miggione 1987). As one view has it, by its unquestioning loyalty to the Alliance Italy bought itself the freedom to take divergent positions on less vital matters. This is what Sergio Romano calls 'microgaullism' (Romano 1993: 64–5).

THE CONDITION OF THE ARMED FORCES

In general, Italy has met its NATO commitments on paper. In practice it has had to rely on the protection offered by its alliance network and in particular by the United States, since some basic technical problems in its own defence establishment have never been solved (Jean 1994). Strategic deterrents ensured that for the most part these deficiencies would not be put to the test. While the size of the Italian armed forces is comparable to that of its main European partners, its quality is certainly not up to standard. Italy's per capita spending on defence has been persistently lower than that of its main partners. Spending is even lower if one takes into account the fact that a large proportion of the budget is allocated to the Carabinieri, whose function is internal order. On the military side, equipment is inadequate and training is poor. Italy has managed to ensure its security while not paying the full economic and political costs that this entailed.

The fact that defence matters have not been subjected to public debate for much of the post-war period and the lack of practical tests for the efficiency of the armed forces have both contributed to the lack of accountability of defence planning. Military bureaucrats have never had to be responsible for the quality of defence preparations and standards have, accordingly, been low.

During the changes of the last decade, successive Defence Ministers have attempted a rationalisation of the armed forces, but they have had only limited success.[3] In 1985, Defence Minister Spadolini issued a White Book which envisaged a thorough defence review. In the document, a reorganisation of the armed forces was sketched out in line with five 'missions': defence of the north eastern border, defence of sea lanes, defence of air space, territorial defence and humanitarian and peace-keeping duties. Given the new international situation, it was felt that Italian planning should also take into account operations outside the traditional NATO framework, namely beyond the first mission (Ministry of Defence 1985; Caligaris and Santoro 1987: 52–102; Cremasco 1987).

Unfortunately, reform has been frustrated by inter-service rivalry. Italian defence has traditionally been dominated by the army. However, in the 1980s the roles of the navy and of the air force gained in importance both through procurement requirements and the need to prepare for Mediterranean contingencies. The army's share of the defence budget shrank from the mid-1970s to the mid-1980s from over 50 per cent to 40 per cent. Instead of truly integrating and rationalising military efforts, the reorganisation implied by the five missions has been used by the services as an opportunity to fight for increased budget allocations, with each service in effective control of particular missions.[4]

A further reorganisation was prompted by the end of the Cold War. The end of bipolar confrontation meant the end of the primacy of European continental preoccupations and the emergence of out-of-area questions. The latter arose partly from the erosion of superpower discipline over regional clients. For Italy, this meant improving the quality of its armed forces. The principal military scenario involved small, quite conceivable wars rather than the one big (unlikely) war as Italy's geopolitical location left it abutting a new arc of instability running from Morocco to the Balkans, through the Middle East and the Caucasus. Rather than maintaining a large army useful for both strategic deterrence and as a bargaining chip at NATO summits, Italian planning had now to envisage smaller but more efficient forces which might become involved in real fighting. These were the considerations behind the 'new model of defence' initiated by Mino Martinazzoli when he was Defence Minister and updated by Virginio Rognoni and Salvo Ando (CEMISS 1990).

The new model was a compromise between the demands of the various services and between two different and opposing ideas on how to organise the armed forces. Consequently, Italian defence policy has so far not been able to overcome its technical impasse and adapt itself appropriately to the new international situation.

The Italian armed forces had traditionally relied on the 'nation in arms' idea based on conscription and a large number of mobilised forces and reserves geared to the defence of national territory. This was because planning focused on the contingency of a large European war and because it was thought that a conscript army would be a more credible pillar of democracy than its professional counterpart. With democracy consolidated and the need to establish a more efficient force, pressure mounted for a professional army on the British model. This concept embraced the notion of a smaller number of fighting units being trained and equipped for power projection in regional conflicts – while the fact that these units would be composed of volunteers might, in the event of casualties, make them more expendable in the eyes of the public.

In the event, the new model did not amount to a clear choice between

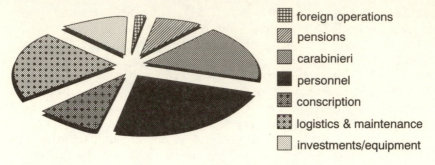

Defence Budget 1994	%	*in bn Lira*
foreign operations	1.35	355
pensions	7.55	1978
carabinieri	20.43	5352
personnel	25.48	6677
conscription	9.66	2530
logistics & maintenance	20.99	5500
investments/equipment	14.53	3808
total	100	26200

Source: Italian Ministry of Defence, 1994

Figure 4.2 Italian defence budget, 1994

the two ideas. The result was a hybrid monster which did not fulfil the objectives of the reorganisation. In its latest version, the army was to be organised into eight active brigades; conscription was not abandoned but was to be shortened, thereby reducing the training of soldiers; all-volunteer units were to be set up but had not been formed because of difficulty in finding suitable candidates and because of the need to detail some professionals to support conscript units. The difficulty in finding volunteers derived from low pay, competition from the law enforcement agencies and the absence of a military tradition in the economically depressed areas. Funds were simply insufficient to sustain a mixed model.

The size of the army was still too large given the relatively low defence budget, and quality therefore suffered. While the army was probably capable of low-intensity peacekeeping operations – as demonstrated in Somalia, Albania and Mozambique – serious doubts could be raised over its capacity to perform in a more extensive conflict. For this reason, the Italian contribution to the Gulf War included only naval and air force units in which the proportion of professionals was much higher.

Similar considerations applied in the area of equipment. It is significant that Italy was the only country (with Portugal) which, under the CFE agreement, had been allocated a higher ceiling for tanks than its current forces. Inter-service rivalry did not allow an integrated overall approach in this respect. For example, the navy fought hard to establish a fleet air arm to be able to protect its ships while out of home waters. However, the need to accommodate the other services as well meant that insufficient funds were allocated to the project. The result was that the navy had only one Garibaldi class helicopter carrier built in 1983 equipped with V-STOL Harrier aircraft. This meant that no air cover was available when the carrier was undergoing maintenance.

Some responsibility for this fragmented situation rests with procurement policy. The processes sketched above and the pressures from the arms industry produced an erratic course of policy evolution. There seemed to be no overall strategy. The lack of clear objectives and an *ad hoc* policy risked creating a situation in which equipment was not up to standard while national industry might not achieve the critical mass needed to survive.

In the case of systems of command, control, communications and intelligence (C^3I), Italy has chosen to collaborate in a pan-Western framework, given the pivotal role of American technology. In other fields, Italy chose the European dimension, as in the case of the European Fighter Aircraft (EFA) venture. In yet others, Italy took the route of trying to preserve a national industry. While in some instances this last choice produced positive results, as in the case of Italian combat helicopters which are among the best in the world, in others it promoted anachronism. The Italian purchase of Ariete tanks has left the country with an obsolete line of tanks equipped with 1980s technology. In general, the Italian armed forces do not purchase wholly foreign-made equipment, in order to please domestic industry. One of the reasons for the close relationship between the Defence Ministry and private industry is that many officers are offered seats in board rooms when they retire.

FOREIGN POLICY AND DEFENCE POLICY: THE CHANGING EUROPEAN CONTEXT

For most of the post-war period Italy has been able to allow the major plank of its defence policy, the NATO alliance, to determine its foreign policy – with the occasional divergence at the margins. Its enthusiasm, from the late 1940s, for the process of European integration did not seem to conflict with defence policy once ambitions for a European Defence Community had been set to one side after 1954. The United States actively favoured European integration and, for its part, the European Economic Community (EEC) seemed to have little capability in the area of classical foreign policy, even after the inauguration of European Political Co-operation (EPC) in 1970. Accordingly, the tensions inside the Italian political class – between those who wanted a stronger Europe as a means of strengthening NATO and those who saw it as a means of emancipation from US hegemony – seemed unlikely to come to a head.

In the early 1980s, however, a combination of the logic of EPC, which sought persistently to strengthen the European Community's capacity to exert international political influence, and concerns about a deteriorating relationship between the superpowers, led to the revival of the Western European Union (WEU) as a serious forum for European caucusing on defence, and to its steady convergence with EPC as means of expressing the long-awaited 'European identity' in world affairs. 'The Declaration of European Identity' of December 1973 had talked of Europe helping to promote its own security. But little had been done at the time, except for the collective diplomacy of the first phase of the negotiations for the Conference on Security and Co-operation in Europe (CSCE). Italy strongly promoted the 1984 revival and has consistently supported European security co-operation since, seeing no necessary contradiction in its equally strong support for the Atlantic Alliance.

With time, however, Italy has found it increasingly difficult to avoid the contradictions inherent in this posture. The country has participated willingly in ventures which have seriously angered the United States, such as the Venice Declaration of 1980 on the Middle East, the Central American initiative of 1984 and various quarrels in the General Agreement on Tariffs and Trade (GATT). Until policy changed in 1994, Italy had consistently supported French reservations about the GATT Uruguay Round. The allies in general have compartmentalised the various strands of their relationship surprisingly well. But Washington's impatience with Alliance-wide consultations and solidarity has seemed to grow in proportion to European states' determination to pursue their own distinctive interests and values. This has been evident, to Rome's embarrassment, in cases such as the Strategic Defence Initiative (SDI), and the harder line taken in Co-ordinating Committee on Multilateral Export Controls (CoCom) during the mid-1980s, and more recently in Bosnia, where Italy has been excluded from the Contact Group of Britain, France, Germany, Russia and the United States (Bonvicini 1996). For its part, Italy was sufficiently aware of the tensions just below the surface to stay out of the Franco–German Brigade and EuroCorps initiatives which seemed to threaten NATO's primacy in military affairs. It also joined with Britain during the endgame of the Maastricht negotiations in responding to US concerns over the possible convergence in the Treaty of the EU and the WEU. The Anglo–Italian Initiative of late 1991 succeeded in making the WEU, at least for the purposes of the Treaty, a bridge between NATO and the EU, rather than the defence arm of the latter. The Berlusconi government, which was elected in March 1994, only five months after the Maastricht Treaty become effective, articulated this preference even more strongly as it shied away from the Euro-enthusiasm of its predecessors.

Gianni Bonvicini wrote in 1983 that

Italy is strongly aware of the risks inherent in a strictly national security policy and has therefore solicited European solidarity at the military level [as well]. So far, however, the response has been partial and limited, and does not provide the cover Italy is looking for and needs.

(Bonvicini 1983: 81)

Since those remarks were made, and more particularly since 1991, the response has been much greater, with the Single European Act directing Member States to work together, 'where appropriate', on the 'technological and industrial conditions necessary for their security' (Article 30, 6b). Moreover the Treaty of Maastricht has taken matters much further forward by not only linking the WEU explicitly to the Common Foreign and Security Policy (CFSP) but also by breaking a forty-year taboo on referring to the possibility, 'in time', of a common European defence. The WEU itself, in its 'Platform' of October 1987, had talked of 'pursuing European integration including security and defence' by, *inter alia*, ensuring that 'the level of each country's contribution to the common defence adequately reflects its capabilities' and that policies on extra-European crises were concerted 'in so far as they may affect our security interests' (Cahen 1989: 91–6).

With such developments Italy has found itself in some respects hoist by its own petard. For one thing Italians have found it comfortable to

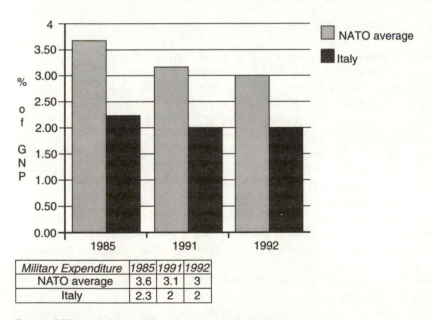

Military Expenditure	1985	1991	1992
NATO average	3.6	3.1	3
Italy	2.3	2	2

Source: Military Balance 1993–4 (London: IISS, 1993)

Figure 4.3 Defence expenditure as per cent of GDP: Nato average (exc. Italy) and Italy

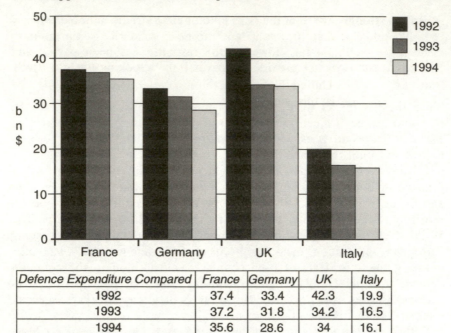

Defence Expenditure Compared	France	Germany	UK	Italy
1992	37.4	33.4	42.3	19.9
1993	37.2	31.8	34.2	16.5
1994	35.6	28.6	34	16.1

Source: Military Balance 1994–5 (London: IISS, 1994)

Figure 4.4 Defence expenditure of major European countries, 1992–4

spend a lower proportion of their GDP on defence than comparable Western states (Ilari 1992: 73–7). And when attempts have been made to spend more, circumstances have conspired against them. The Rognoni Report of 26 November 1991 recommended to Parliament a 'new defence model', requiring modernisation and a 27 per cent real increase in military expenditure to pay for it. Not surprisingly, the spread of 'peace dividend' ideas, together with the chronic public expenditure problems of the Italian government, soon put paid to this idea. Moreover, for all the increase in 'politico-military' operations out-of-area, such as naval activity in the Gulf in 1987 and 1991, the use of armed force abroad creates major political problems and logistical embarrassments – witness the humiliating experience in Somalia in 1992–3. Finally, Italy's lack of significant national military capability, together with the not uncommon view at home that pacifism is 'not a tactical choice but an assertion of identity' (Furlong 1994: 173) makes its governments very cautious about straying from the skirts of the United States.

The national path in foreign or defence policy barely seems an option for Italy, despite the increased activism of the twenty years to 1996. The situation in the Balkans, where NATO planes fly from Italian bases, WEU frigates patrol the Adriatic and Serbia (fancifully) threatens Rome with

Scud missiles against Rimini, together with Italy's exclusion from Bosnian peacekeeping or Contact group diplomacy, epitomises the weakness of the Italian position. Where Italy does act, as in Mozambique, Somalia or the Gulf, it will only do so where 'cover' can be provided by the authority of the United Nations, and on a relatively small scale (see Table 4.1). Nor is this simply part of a general move back towards multilateralism in the post-war years. As Carlo M. Santoro points out, in the midst of a general argument designed to show that Italy is finally claiming its rightful status as a middle power, '*i diversi interventi sono sempre stati abilmente travestiti sotto le sembianze di azioni di pace*',[5] as in Beirut, when Italian transports and warships were painted white '*quasi a far credere si trattasse di truppe dell'Onu, anche quando la bandiera delle Nazioni Unite non sventolava a riva del nostro Comando*'[6] (Santoro 1991: 213).

Table 4.1 Italian Participation in Multinational Operations, 1991–3

Multinational operations	Location	Italian participation
United Nations		
UNTSO	Palestine	8
UNMOGIP	Kashmir	5
UNIFIL	Lebanon	49
ONUSAL	El Salvador	10
UNIKOM	Iraq	6
MINURSO	W. Sahara	6
UNTAC	Cambodia	75
ONUMOZ	Mozambique	1,100
UNOSOM II	Somalia	2,500
Other		
MFQ	Sinai	80
SHARP GUARD	Adriatic	2 naval units
ECMM	former Yugoslavia	85
Italian-only operations		
Pellicano	Albania	650

Source: Military Balance 1993–4 (London: IISS, 1993)

Nor have bilateral relations provided a half-way house for Italy. Where the French and the Germans have moved some way towards creating a small core of European defence integration, and have been joined by the Dutch and the Spanish, and where the British have special naval relations with Portugal and the Netherlands (as well as substantial ties to the Pentagon), Italy has little outside its very asymmetrical relationship with the USA. The various instances of Anglo–Italian co-operation, limited to pure diplomacy and trumpeted in the two years to 1996, are signs of desperation in both countries, which are excluded from the Paris–Bonn axis. In terms of armament joint ventures Italy has participated in the

Tornado and the SP-70 self-propelled 155mm gun projects, and was a key player in both of the competing helicopter consortiums which hoped to buy the Westland company in 1986. But problems with these programmes meant that there has been no transformational effect on either the content or framework of Italy's defence policy making.

THE DOMESTIC ENVIRONMENT AND DECISION MAKING

The basic characteristics of the Italian situation have also been affected by the decision-making process. It is indicative of the low priority ascribed to defence that the constitutional issues concerning the chain of command in times of crisis have not yet been resolved (Manzella 1984: 477–93). The Constitution gives command of the armed forces (art. 87) to the (largely symbolic) figure of the President of the Republic. However, the responsibility for directing policy belongs to the President of the Council (art. 95). Yet it must be remembered that the whole Council of Ministers is collectively responsible for implementation and that in Italy the President of the Council is traditionally only *primus inter pares*. In the absence of a new constitution, this remained true even for Silvio Berlusconi, entering power as a 'presidential' Prime Minister on the back of television publicity, and leaving it in January 1994 as yet another broken-backed coalition leader.

The Constitution explicitly calls for the establishment of a Supreme Defence Council (art. 87) chaired by the President of the Republic and including all relevant ministers and bureaucrats. However, even this co-ordinating mechanism cannot be the ultimate locus of decision making since its functions are not specified and are restricted only to consultation. It is therefore unclear which institution is ultimately responsible for decisions about war and peace.[7]

Between 1986 and 1988, President Cossiga tried to raise the question of the chain of command by sending letters to four consecutive Prime Ministers (Craxi, Fanfani, Goria and De Mita). However, by 1996 the only response had been the establishment in February 1986 of a crisis management unit, with strictly technical duties, in the Prime Minister's office (Silvestri 1990). The question of the exact responsibility of the various constitutional bodies is still very much open (Caligaris and Santoro 1987: 150–215).

The Italian political system is dominated by political parties. The lack of a single majority party and the consequent need for coalition governments (still the case despite the new predominantly first-past-the-post electoral system) reduces the autonomy of the executive branch and leaves crucial decisions in the hands of party leaders, while parliamentary groups are characterised by a strict discipline. This means that most decisions are reached by a skilful but slow process of bargaining and consensus building among parties and that inter-departmental rivalries sometimes take place for party political reasons rather than because of substantive differences over policies.

Defence matters, except for the trades union problems involving personnel, have not traditionally been subject to much parliamentary scrutiny and have therefore been immune from what can be a cumbersome process. Parliament and the parties have left the relevant ministers with considerable autonomy. Ministers in turn have allowed the services much freedom of action. They are only co-ordinated and represented by a Chief of the Defence Staff. Inter-party bargaining tended not to take place on defence, either because the decision was so important (as in the cases of NATO and INF) that cleavages were clearer and deeper than in other areas, or because the issues in question were considered unimportant and could therefore be delegated to the Ministry of Defence.

Since the end of the 1970s, however, with the higher profile of foreign and defence policy, Parliament has increasingly involved itself in security affairs even when – as in the case of participation in peacekeeping operations – it is not constitutionally required to do so. Such involvement has been sporadic and largely reactive. As a general rule, the centre-left coalition ruling Italy until 1994 managed to stick together on foreign policy, despite opposition from the communist left and some pressure from Catholic pacifism within the largest party, the Christian Democrats.

A few debates have also stirred up public opinion, generally dormant on such matters. This has been the case especially when Italy has had a dispute with the United States, as for example in the Sigonella episode and over the United Nations operation in Somalia. In Unosom II Italy and the US were the major participants and had a lively argument about the amount of force necessary for the mission's success. Even when public opinion is intensely concerned, however, the government has retained much freedom of action. In 1987, 63.6 per cent of respondents to a poll (Silvestri 1990: 193) declared themselves against sending naval units to the Gulf. Nevertheless, the government sent a task force and kept it there for more than a year. Similarly, public opinion was sceptical of Italian participation in the international coalition during the Gulf War. On 15 January 1991 62 per cent of Italians were against military intervention. After the war around the same proportion approved (Schmidt 1994: 28). Here again, the government was able to make a contribution – albeit small – without significant repercussions (Ilari 1986). Yet another significant example is the acceptance of US F-16s of the 401st wing in 1988, which occurred after polls indicated that 78 per cent of the public were opposed to American bases in Italy.

The influence of the public is low because of its general lack of interest, interrupted episodically by emotional outbursts. The government has also done little to encourage an open and educated debate on defence. This situation has had drawbacks. The government's freedom of action is not based on a sound consensus – as for example in France – but on a political vacuum. This means that the government feels it enjoys only a conditional mandate which may be revoked at any moment. A certain amount of caution is consequently dictated by the unpredictable reactions of the public. This is one reason why no Italian land forces have been sent to a combat zone in the last fifty years.

CONCLUSION

The central question on Italian defence policy is how a weak state copes with the most crucial state functions: providing security and defence. An historical view of the post-war period shows that Italian governments have managed to ensure the country's security at relatively low cost. By joining the NATO alliance, and through skilful diplomacy and some good fortune, Italy has been physically protected without suffering an excessive burden on its economy and precarious political system. The government has used international commitments to justify, in the domestic political arena, difficult and divisive decisions. Italians have generally deferred the need to situate the country within a set of durable multilateral institutions, even if membership of Western clubs has done little to challenge domestic political and institutional stagnation and has to some extent reinforced it.

In its post-war weakness, Italy willingly compromised elements of its sovereignty in order to avoid a domestic political crisis. At the same time, at the international level, it exploited its domestic weaknesses to excuse its low military spending and the adoption of some of its more individualistic foreign policy positions. Italian public opinion has often been more radical or pacifist than elsewhere within the Alliance (*The Economist* 21 February 1987), with consequences for official stances on such issues as the Middle East. But it has not affected the fundamental commitment to NATO, as expressed through such decisions as that to accept Cruise missiles.

However, this diplomatic skill has not been matched by the quality of Italy's armed forces, whose standards – in both training and equipment – are below those of its major partners. The economic and political costs of developing a more efficient military instrument were thought to outweigh the benefits. This may have been admissible during the static international system of the Cold War, when strategic deterrence made it unlikely that armed forces would be used. In the more volatile contemporary international system, however, the technical deficiencies and the lack of an adequate debate over defence policy could have much more serious consequences. Consequently Italian foreign policy is undermined by its lack of the supporting capabilities that Britain and France, for example, still possess. Italy's political weight is, consequently, not equivalent to its economic standing.

For this reason the first two governments after the Cold War, those of Amato and Ciampi, responded in two new ways to the challenges of the external environment. First, Italy's defence budget did not shrink by as much as those of other European countries, despite the wish to cash in the peace dividend. Moreover, the reform of the armed forces has been generally accelerated – although the idea of forming some all-volunteer units for out-of-area operations has been postponed due to the difficulties in finding enough suitable candidates.

Second, in the 1992–4 period Italy tried to develop a new political approach to its changed domestic and international situation. Acknowledging the fact that the country will not in the near future possess the resources to face a major threat alone, the government has tried both to strengthen those international institutions which can protect it and to increase Italy's weight in them. Now that Italy's geopolitical position is no longer so important in the East–West equation (even if it is correspondingly more important in Euro–Arab relations), it has to achieve a more credible profile in alliance diplomacy. Participation in UN activities has, therefore, grown exponentially (including substantial contributions to such difficult missions as those to Somalia and Mozambique), as has its willingness to help elsewhere, as over Albania and the WEU enforcement of sanctions against Serbia. Furthermore the Farnesina has launched a campaign for the reform of the Security Council to give more weight to middle-ranking powers such as Italy. Rome was concerned over the US wish to see Germany and Japan become permanent members of the Security Council. After an ill-fated attempt by Foreign Minister De Michelis to achieve a permanent seat for the EC as a whole, Italy proposed at the end of 1993 that a special class of semi-permanent members should be created – comprising Germany and Japan but also Italy, Brazil and India, among others. These states would sit in the Security Council on a rotating basis. The proposal is still under consideration.

The elections of 27 March 1994 were held under a new electoral law and the results were initially hailed by many as enabling major changes. The traditional parties have almost disappeared because of their inability to tackle urgent economic problems, their involvement in corruption and even their alleged ties to organised crime (Scoppola 1991: 395–438). The election was won by a new coalition which employed a new rhetoric appealing for a thorough renovation of the political system. The mainly majoritarian electoral system which was introduced seemed to allow the new coalition government to make the brave reforms the country needed, in the area of defence as elsewhere.

Yet high expectations could lead to disillusion and the early signs are not encouraging. The structural weaknesses of the Italian political system have not been overcome and, in some respects, they have worsened. The governing coalition led by Silvio Berlusconi was heterogeneous and paralysed by internal divisions. Defence reform was inhibited by the preoccupation with unresolved domestic problems – such as scandals, and ineffective policies on the budget deficit – and by the government's obsession with short-term issues affecting opinion polls. After the fall of Berlusconi, there was a brief respite under the technocratic government led by Lamberto Dini. Yet there was a high level of uncertainty in Italian politics and a further series of realignments looked likely.

Moreover, the ideological orientation and the lack of international experience of most of the new political parties – which belong to none of Europe's traditional groupings and so lack institutional ties to parties in other countries – undermine Italy's credibility abroad. While one of the major parties in the Berlusconi Coalition, the regionalist Lega Nord, wants to review Italy's status as a single state and therefore looks relentlessly inwards, another, the neofascist National Alliance, does not hide its doubts about international integration and has encouraged a nationalist attitude towards the European Union. The Foreign Minister in the Berlusconi government of March 1994–January 1995, Antonio Martino (of Forza Italia, Berlusconi's own party) became an ally of the anti-integrationist British government within the EU (Romano 1995: 68).

Domestic politics absorbs most of the government's attention and the debate on the reforms needed to restructure the Italian armed forces is inadequate. It is therefore impossible to build a consensus behind them. It is not a coincidence that the 1994 budget made deep cuts in defence which, because there was no bold policy to reform personnel allocation, affected mainly the procurement of equipment. Moreover, Berlusconi's government seemed to have reverted to a more passive and indecisive approach in Italy's main foreign policy arena, Europe. Significant examples are the delay in 1994 in the nomination of Italy's EU Commissioners, the abandonment of efforts to revitalise the CSCE, and lack of involvement in Eurocorps. NATO might have been sufficient insurance in the static world of the Cold War. But, in the volatile contemporary situation, Italy's lack of credible armed forces and its inability to achieve a stable and respected role for its foreign policy could prove dangerous. Not only is Italy threatened with the spillover of regional conflicts, but it could also be affected by some of their less orthodox consequences, such as terrorism, environmental damage, refugees and the proliferation of weapons of mass destruction.

Conversely, Italy's inability to join wholeheartedly in with Franco–German moves towards a common European defence community undermines the multilateralism on which Italy has relied in the economic and political spheres. Italy has been a good European, but as in other areas of co-operation, more in name than in substance. The actual evolution of European foreign and security policy has found Rome unable to do more than applaud from the sidelines. But the time for choice over the level of its defence capabilities and contributions to a joint European effort is fast approaching. The alternative to clear decision may be crisis. Italy needs a serious public debate on the direction and scope of its foreign and defence policies. In this, it is hardly alone. But unlike some other members of the EU, there are depressingly few signs of one getting under way.

NOTES

1 The view that the end of the Cold War precipitated a crisis in those of Italy's institutions created during the Cold War is common. For a powerful counter argument, focusing on an endogenous crisis, see Stefano Guzzini, EUI Working Paper, 1994.
2 Resentments about the status of Istria remained only just beneath the surface, particularly in Friuli–Venezia–Giulia. These were not wholly assuaged by the Treaty of Osimo in 1975, and burst into the open again after the election of the Berlusconi government in March 1994. The question of the rights of Italians still left in the republics of former Yugoslavia remained an unresolved issue between the Berlusconi government and the new Slovenian Republic.
3 The first attempt at reorganisation was with three provisional laws (one for each of the services) at the end of the 1970s. However, these laws were more concerned with procurement than with a strategic reassessment. The army used the reorganisation to purchase a Leopard-1 line of tanks; the air force to equip itself with Tornados and the navy to acquire the Garibaldi heli-carrier.
4 Missions 1 and 4 became shorthand for army funds, while mission 2 and mission 3 were jargon for navy and air force funds, respectively. The reorganisation also established an ambitious Rapid Intervention Force on the model of the French *Force d'Action Rapide* (FAR). In practice, the FoIR never took off.
5 'the various actions have always been ably disguided as peace operations'.
6 'almost as if to make people think they were UN troops, even when the United Nations flag was not flying over our HQ'.
7 The War Powers Law, which dates back to 1938 when Italy was still a monarchy (R.d. 1415/1938), is also unclear on the exact status of the various institutions making up the state.

REFERENCES

Allison, G. T. (1971) *Essence of Decision: Explaining the Cuban Missile Crisis*, Boston: Little, Brown.
Bonvicini, G. (1983) 'Italy: an integrationist perspective', in Christopher Hill (ed.), *National Foreign Policies and European Political Co-operation*, London: Allen and Unwin.
—— (1996) 'Regional reassertion: the dilemmas of Italy', in Christopher Hill (ed.), *The Actors in Europe's Foreign Policy*, London: Routledge.
Cahen, A. (1989) The Platform on European Security Interests, The Hague, 27 October 1987, III.a.4, reproduced in Cahen, A., *The Western European Union and NATO: Building a European Defence Identity within the Context of Atlantic Solidarity*, London: Brassey's, Brassey's Atlantic Commentaries No. 2, pp. 91–6.
Caligaris, L. and Santoro, C. M. (1987) *Obiettivo Difesa*, Bologna.
Caligaris, L. (1983) 'Italian defence policy: problems and prospects' in *Survival*, vol. 25, no. 2.
CEMISS (1990) *Nuove concezioni del modello difensivo italiano*, Rome.
Corbetta, P. and Leonardi, R. (1989) *Politica in Italia*, Bologna.
Cremasco, M. (1987) 'Italy: a new definition of security?' in Kelleher, C. M., and Mattox, G. A., *Evolving European Defence Policies*, Lexington, MA: Free Press.
Furlong, P. (1994) *Modern Italy*, London: Routledge.

Gray L., and Miggione, P. 'L'incidente di Lampedusa e la politica italiana di difesa', in Corbetta and Leonardi, *op. cit.* (1987 edition).

Guzzini, S. (1994) 'The implosion of clientelistic Italy in the 1990s: a study of "peaceful change" in comparative political economy', EUI Working Paper SPS No 94/12, European University Institute, Florence.

Ilari, V. (December 1992) 'Il nuovo modello di difesa italiano', *Relazioni Internazionali*, LVI.

—— (1986) 'Storia politica del movimento pacifista in Italia', in Jean, C. (ed.), *Sicurezza e Difesa*, Milan.

Istituto Affari Internazionali (IAI), *L'Italia nella Politica Internazionale*, Milan, Yearbooks 1979–1992.

Jean, C. (ed.) (1994) *Storia delle Forze Armate in Italia 1945–1975*, Milan.

Manzella, A. (December 1984) 'Il processo decisionale nella political estera italiana', in *Quaderni Costituzionali*.

Ministry of Defence (1985) *Libro Bianco della Difesa*, Rome.

Pieson, F. J. 'La political estera italiana: il caso Achille Lauro', in Corbetta and Leonardi (eds), *op. cit.*, 1986 edition.

Posen, B. R. (1984) *The Sources of Military Doctrine: France, Britain and Germany Between the Wars*, Ithaca, NY: Cornell University Press.

Price, E. D. (1989) 'La Scelta della base per gli F-16 ed il ruolo dell'Italia nella NATO' in Corbetta P. and Leonardi R. (eds), *op. cit.*

Romano, S. (1993) *Guida alla politica estera italiana*, Milan.

—— (1995) *La politica estera italiana: un bilancio e qualche prospettiva*, Bologna: Il Mulino.

Rosecrance, R. (Spring 1995) 'Overextension, vulnerability and conflict: the "goldilocks problem" in international strategy', *International Security*, Vol. 19, no. 4.

Santoro, C. M. (1991) *La Politica Estera di Una Media Potenza: L'Italia dall'Unita ad Oggi*, Bologna: Il Mulino.

Schmidt, K. (1994) *Collective Western European Resort to Armed Force: Lessons from the Danish, Italian and British Experiences in the Gulf and former Yugoslavia*, Copenhagen: Danish Institute of International Studies.

Scoppola, P. (1991) *La Repubblica dei Partiti 1945–1990*, Bologna.

Seton-Watson, C. (1991) 'La Politica estera della Repubblica Italiana', in Bosworth R. J. B. and Romano S. (eds), *La Politica Estera Italiana*, Bologna.

Silvestri, S. (1990) 'L'Italia: partner fedele ma di basso profilo', in Caligaris L. (ed.), *La Difesa Europea: Proposte e Sfide*, Milan.

Snyder, J. (1991) *Myths of Empire: Domestic Politics and International Ambition*, Ithaca, NY: Cornell University Press.

Steinbruner, J. D. (1974) *The Cybernetic Theory of Decision: New Dimensions in Political Analysis*, Princeton, NJ: Princeton University Press.

5 The Netherlands

Alfred van Staden

INTRODUCTION

Among the countries of Western Europe, the Netherlands is one of those with a weak military tradition. This is reflected in the relatively low social esteem the military profession has held throughout the ages in Dutch society. Perhaps an exception should be made for the Dutch navy, which managed to preserve the memories of its glorious sea wars against England in the seventeenth century. It is always hazardous to speculate about the roots of national tradition. But the modest social position of the nobility, the strong orientation towards international trade as well as a dislike of virulent patriotism and heroism among the ruling merchant–magistrates (*regenten*) seem to be relevant to the mainly civilian character of Dutch political culture. In addition, the policy of neutrality (which lasted over a century to the Second World War) constituted a fertile breeding ground for anti-war attitudes. This policy was successful in the sense that the Netherlands managed to stay outside the major European quarrels of the nineteenth and early twentieth centuries. Unlike, for instance, its southern neighbour, Belgium, it was not attacked by Germany in 1914.

In Dutch society, neutrality was presented as part of a lofty national mission; it was described as a beacon in a world of darkness. The Netherlands began to see itself as a champion of international law (building on the illustrious reputation of the seventeenth-century Dutch scholar Hugo Grotius) and posed as a moral example to other nations. Religious influences (namely Calvinism and Mennonism) provided the moral underpinnings of Dutch foreign policy, which expressed a holier-than-thou attitude (not unlike Nehru's non-aligned India of the 1950s and 1960s). But neutrality was in fact hardly more than a response to geopolitical reality: the rival powers Germany and Great Britain would not allow each other to control the large estuaries of Holland and Zealand (the two western provinces of the Netherlands) which were obviously of great strategic importance. The Dutch could of course have sought a 'natural' alliance (as it has been called by some Dutch historians) with

Great Britain (van Sas 1985) but it was widely felt that it would be unable to protect the Netherlands against a military threat from the East, namely Germany. On the other hand, aligning with Germany did not make sense because the strong German land forces could not safeguard Dutch colonies in the East Indies from the ambitions of strong maritime powers such as Great Britain and – from the late nineteenth century onward – Japan (Voorhoeve 1979: 42–97).

Until the Second World War the Dutch defence posture was overwhelmingly static; it was a pure specimen of what would later be labelled 'non-provocative defence'. The army lacked the capacity to carry out large-scale manoeuvres, as it was concentrated in fortified positions behind natural water barriers (the famous *Hollandse waterlinie*). One of the consequences of deliberately rejecting a posture of forward defence was that a large part of the country would be sacrificed to the enemy at the outbreak of war; only the western part (the political and economic centre) would be defended. The preservation of the territorial integrity of the Netherlands during the First World War seemed to justify the foundations of this national defence strategy. The Dutch government at the time succeeded in maintaining a delicate balancing act between the warring parties.

The brutal German violation of Dutch neutrality in May 1940 dealt a severe blow to the collective Dutch psyche. It was ruefully acknowledged by politicians and opinion leaders alike that a foreign policy which had tried to keep the country aloof from the conflict between would-be aggressors and likely victims had turned out to be an exercise in self-delusion. Pacifist sentiments, which had prevailed not only in the leftist Dutch labour movement but also in some sections of the bourgeoisie, were discredited. During the years of German occupation the handful of Dutchmen who had the foresight to think about the nation's international future once the occupation ended were unanimous in their belief that it was imperative to base post-war Dutch security policy on radical new principles. Eelco van Kleffens, who continued to serve as Foreign Minister in the London-based Dutch government in exile, voiced ideas about regional security co-operation among the Western nations which in many respects anticipated the creation of the Atlantic Alliance in 1949. Thus, for example, at the end of 1943, addressing his fellow countrymen in a radio broadcast to the occupied Netherlands, he called for the establishment in the West, after the defeat of Nazi Germany, of

> a strong formation in which America with Canada and the other British dominions would function as an arsenal, Great Britain as a base (particularly for the air force) and the Western parts of the European continent – I refer to Holland, Belgium and France – as bridgehead.
>
> (Wiebes and Zeeman 1993: 71)

After the war it would take four years before a Western alliance led by the United States could be established. The United States put its trust in the new United Nations Organisation as a universal guarantor of security. For want of an alternative the Netherlands followed suit, whilst seeking to cultivate its image as a law-abiding country and as a promoter of the rule of law in international relations. In light of this pretension, it was ironical (to say the least) that the Dutch government was punished twice by the Security Council for the so-called police actions it undertook in 1947 and 1948 to maintain law and order in the East Indian colony, then being set alight by the powerful forces of Indonesian nationalism. About 130,000 Dutch troops (many of them trained in Great Britain and the United States) were involved in campaigns to pacify the rebellious colony.

During the Korean War (1950–3), Dutch military units went into combat as they joined other pro-Western forces under UN command to repel communist aggression. At a later stage, Dutch troops became entangled in armed incidents during the confrontation with Indonesia over the status of Western New Guinea (1960–2), formerly part of the Dutch colonial empire and claimed by Indonesia since its independence in 1949. More recently, in quite a different political setting, Dutch military personnel have participated in six or seven UN peacekeeping operations. These include UNAVEM II in Angola, UNTAC in Cambodia, UNOMSA in South Africa, and UNAMIH in Haiti and UNPROFOR I and II in the former Yugoslavia. Although the total number of Dutch troops deployed in these operations never exceeded about 3,500, their participation reflected the prominent role UN peacekeeping has taken in Dutch defence policy since the end of the Cold War. Although unmistakably driven by humanitarian impulses, the Netherlands also tried to use this participation as a vehicle for enhancing international prestige.[1]

This chapter will analyse the main lines of post-war Dutch defence policy, with a view to ascertaining to what extent the quest for European security and defence co-operation may be considered an important factor in Dutch defence planning and whether the Netherlands can maintain an autonomous defence posture. What have been Dutch military priorities and objectives? The focus will then fall on post-Cold War defence reviews setting out plans for a drastic restructuring of the Dutch armed forces. Finally, the prospects for maintaining autonomous Dutch armed forces will be analysed.

THE EVOLUTION OF POST-WAR DEFENCE POLICY

Dutch defence policy during the Cold War was somewhat predictable in that it followed the pattern of national integration into the common transatlantic defence structure. The United States was seen as the linchpin of that structure and there was no suggestion of a need for European alternatives. Domestic political debates were about familiar themes: the size of the defence budget, the length of military service, the purchase of major weapons systems and, initially, about the role of the navy.

By the end of the 1940s, when the Dutch government was compelled by outside pressures to transfer its sovereignty over the East Indies to the newly-formed Republic of Indonesia, the Dutch army had to be converted from an overseas counter-insurgency force to a military organisation capable of making a credible contribution to Western efforts to resist the perceived Soviet threat. An important issue was what priority to accord to the defence of Western European territory. A commitment had already been made to build two cruisers. The Dutch navy objected to the defence plans of the then Western Union (the Brussels Treaty Organisation), as endorsed by Field Marshal Montgomery. These suggested that, in view of the vast Western naval forces already available, there was no need for a Dutch ocean-going fleet and that, for this reason, the Dutch navy could confine itself to building minesweepers. The navy argued that the plans in question did not take into account the overriding need to protect the sea lanes and those of the Dutch merchant fleet in particular. The Dutch government refused to give in to the pressure from the navy. It told the navy it could order some minesweepers, but that it should be patient with respect to other orders, especially its request for six destroyers and four submarines. At the same time the decision was taken to develop a field army of three divisions (later expanded to five), whilst the air force was allowed to operate twenty-one squadrons (provided that US aid was received) (Honig 1993: 15–16).

The signing of the North Atlantic Treaty (and the entry of the United States into the defence of Europe) aroused the hope that the ambitions of the Dutch navy could be fulfilled. Indeed the treaty area of the new alliance, extending over the northern part of the Atlantic, provided a new theatre of operations. However, the first results of allied planning (in early 1950) were not encouraging for the Dutch navy. Neither the Americans nor the British envisaged any substantial role for Dutch naval vessels on the open seas; they saw the mission of the Dutch navy being limited to coastal defence in the North Sea. An important consideration for the Dutch government was the promise by the United States to secure the maritime lifelines of the Netherlands in return for a tangible Dutch land and air contribution to NATO. In the Spring of 1950, the government drew the conclusion that, for the Netherlands to become a credible partner in the Western Pact, the build-up of the army must be the first priority. On the other hand, the government was inclined to share the view of those who held that the navy was better organised and more efficient than the other services and that it could generate employment opportunities for Dutch shipyards (Honig 1993: 18).

Paradoxically, the surplus of naval capacity in the hands of the main maritime powers, namely the United States and Great Britain, as a result of their huge Second World War expansion strengthened the bargaining position of the Dutch navy. The two maritime powers were unreceptive to the Dutch government's idea that they take over the Dutch navy's three most expensive capital ships (the carrier and cruisers under construction) to enable the Dutch to economise on operational costs. The reason was clear: both powers were themselves engaged in a struggle to maintain their large fleets. Moreover, they were convinced of their own ability to build the best cruisers. Additionally (and quite ironically), although American military planners wanted the Dutch to boost the strength of their army and air force, the US military assistance programme to the Netherlands provided for significant naval capabilities. Thus, in June 1950, the first two of six destroyers were transferred to the Dutch navy, to be followed by, among other things, two submarines in 1953.

The criteria employed by the US administration in allotting military aid to its European allies also played into the Dutch navy's hands. The principal criterion was derived from a judgement of whether national defence efforts were instrumental to NATO's military strength. As most Dutch maritime activity was not undertaken for allied missions, the Netherlands risked receiving substantially less aid than if a large part of the navy was assigned to NATO duties. Hence, to reap some benefit from keeping the carrier and the two cruisers, the Dutch government was forced to make the case for an Atlantic role for its naval units. At the end of the day, the Netherlands was fairly successful in persuading NATO's military authorities to accept the Dutch claim, even though it was officially stipulated that the Dutch navy's tasks in the Atlantic were to remain secondary and that the priority continued to lie in the North Sea (Honig 1993: 22). The official stipulation notwithstanding, the operational plans worked out later by NATO's naval command (SACLANT) commissioned the greater part of the Dutch navy for anti-submarine warfare in the northern Atlantic where the Soviet naval threat was presumed to be greatest.

A second interesting episode was the negotiations for the formation of the European Defence Community (EDC) which started in Paris in February 1951. Initially, the Netherlands was not enthusiastic about the Pleven Plan. Whereas Italy, West Germany and the Benelux countries accepted the French invitation to take part in the negotiations, the Netherlands took the same line as Great Britain, Norway and Denmark and sent only observers. The Dutch government, in contrast to the federalist reputation it was later to gain, expressed its fear that the transfer of supreme military authority to a European body would undercut national sovereignty and put a heavy financial burden on the nation. It also doubted the realism of trying to forge six different national armies into a single unit. These official reactions disguised the government's actual position, which was a dislike of continental European defence co-operation. After all, the country was quite willing to accept NATO proposals which had similar implications for sovereignty. When, in October 1951, the Americans decided to endorse the EDC proposal and the negotiations seemed to be making real progress, the Netherlands joined as a full participant and even became a staunch supporter of EDC. The government, however, was not driven by the idealism of the federalists, who had strong influence in the Dutch parliament and believed EDC would be the germ of a politically united Europe. On the contrary, it repeatedly stressed the importance of incorporating EDC into NATO. The emphasis on the Atlantic Alliance can be seen as an early indication of the priority of NATO over European integration implicit in post-war Dutch foreign policy (Voorhoeve 1979: 110).

From the early 1950s until the end of the Cold War, two major defence reforms took place in the Netherlands. In 1960 a programme for 'mechanisation and motorisation' was adopted. This transformed the Dutch army from a five-division force (which relied heavily on mobilisation capacities) to a three-division force consisting of two combat-ready (active duty) divisions and one mobilisable (reserve) division. The reorganisation implied a reduction in manpower, particularly in the number of conscripts, and the procurement of new equipment intended to turn the army into a more mobile force (Siccama 1985: 128). The second restructuring in the era of East–West confrontation occurred in the mid-1970s when the left-of-centre Den Uyl cabinet decided to cut back on military spending. Although the overall structure of the army was maintained, the number of combat-ready battalions was considerably reduced. For over 30 years, in an effort to stifle inter-service feuds, the financial appropriation over the services remained fixed: the army was to receive half the defence budget, the navy and the air force a quarter each.

Reviewing the whole Cold War period, it is hard to avoid the impression that the military contribution of the Netherlands to NATO was relatively high. Relative to the other smaller NATO allies, the percentage of national income the Netherlands spent on defence was the highest. More generally, the Netherlands did not want to look like a free-rider; it attempted to develop a reputation for keeping its promises while carrying out its military obligations in good faith (van Staden 1989: 99–100). Until the late 1960s, defence efforts could easily be justified to parliament by simply referring to NATO requirements. After that the Dutch contribution to NATO became more politicised (that is to say, it became an issue in domestic political strife), but the appeal to Atlantic solidarity remained a powerful weapon in the hands of any Dutch government. Even in the early 1980s when widespread opposition in Dutch society to the deployment of cruise missiles gave rise, in allied political circles, to complaints about 'hollanditis' and neutralist fever (Laqueur 1981: 19–26), the substantial Dutch contribution to conventional NATO capabilities was not challenged by influential domestic groups.

The question therefore is: why has the Dutch defence effort been so sustained? One explanation suggests that successive Dutch governments were very responsive to the demands of NATO and its leading power, the United States. The underlying argument is that the Netherlands deliberately sought to play the role of faithful ally and that, consequently, a substantial defence contribution with a conscientious fulfilment of commitments was one of the main features of Dutch Alliance behaviour. The strong reliance of the country on the US, the great trust in the American (nuclear) security guarantees and the rejection of independent European security arrangements were determined not only by fear of Soviet aggression but by considerations of intra-Alliance bargaining which affected the Netherlands' interests as a small state. The Dutch hoped to capitalise on their reputation for loyalty to the Alliance by developing American support for the containment of the regional ambitions of the larger Western European nations, first and foremost of France which it suspected of striving for regional leadership (van Staden 1995: 39–43).

This explanation has been criticised by the Dutch defence analyst Jan Willem Honig. He has argued that, in accounting for the Dutch defence performance, the perspective of bureaucratic politics would be more rewarding than assuming any deliberate compliance with Alliance demands. He contends that the decisive influence on the substance of Dutch defence policy lay neither with NATO nor with the makers of Dutch foreign policy but rather with the national armed services.

> The Alliance does not possess the power nor the institutional framework to effectively control or steer allied defense policies. What is more, the mistaken perception of the importance of foreign policy and the way NATO functions enhances rather than constrains national military independence.
>
> (Honig 1993: 4)

Honig tries to demonstrate the consistent and continuous success of the services in building up and maintaining relatively large Dutch military forces.

On the face of it, there seems to be a wide gulf between the two explanations. On reflection, however, the difference is less significant than it would appear. While Honig certainly has a point in claiming that the composition, make-up and missions of the Dutch armed forces were affected to a large degree by inter-service rivalries and pressures on the part of the military establishment, he fails to give a convincing explanation for the overall level of military spending and the general military commitments of the Netherlands to NATO (for instance the readiness to accept American nuclear weapons on its territory and to provide Dutch forces with those weapons). Indeed in other smaller NATO countries, too, the services enjoyed a great deal of bureaucratic autonomy and, equally, they had the opportunity to benefit from the intricacies of military planning, but they did not maintain the same level of defence efforts as their Dutch counterparts. This suggests that the political aspiration of being a faithful ally in NATO did play an important part in the military contribution of the Netherlands. Among the political leaders it created, almost as a matter of course, a sympathetic understanding for the demands made by the services.

Earlier, a passing reference was made to the Dutch rejection of independent European security arrangements. One may wonder how the Dutch have tried to reconcile their generally perceived support for a federal Europe with a suspicious attitude towards European integration efforts in the defence field. A plausible answer is that the Netherlands has used the principle of supranationality (which underlies the concept of federalism) both as a goal and as an instrument or a political weapon (Kwast-van Duursen 1991: 42–59). It was used as an authentic goal as far as economic co-operation (the internal market, common agricultural policy, etc.) was concerned. In the domain of low politics, tight European integration was clearly in the Dutch interest. However, aware of the fact that the large majority of European countries would not allow foreign and defence policy to come under the authority of the European Community (with the European Commission playing a major role), the demand for supranationality was used as a tactical manoeuvre to thwart co-operation in that field while achieving the strategic objective of preserving NATO's exclusive responsibility for Western defence. This interpretation, again challenging the official motives behind Dutch European policies, was supported by Susanne Bodenheimer in her analysis of the Dutch reaction to the French proposals of the early 1960s to establish a Political Union dealing with foreign policy (and in time defence) collaboration, the so-called Fouchet negotiations. She claims that, given the basic opposition of the Netherlands to any 'high politics' arrangements among the EC member states, Dutch support for a supranationally-orientated revision clause which the French would not accept 'was motivated as much by a desire to prevent any agreement on a permanent Union as by a preference for supranational institutions' (Bodenheimer 1967: 159). She concludes that the essential criterion in Dutch calculations to assess schemes for European political co-operation 'is the preservation of the Atlantic Alliance'. She says: 'This is not merely one aspect of Dutch policy: it is the fundamental element' (Bodenheimer 1967: 160–1). The Dutch attitude reveals how the process of European integration can be used by states to further their own ends. The following section will indicate that the attitude has not fundamentally changed twenty years later, as new attempts are made to achieve a Political Union among the EC members.

THE DUTCH DEFENCE POSTURE AFTER THE END OF THE COLD WAR

As in most other Western countries, the collapse of the communist regimes in Eastern Europe and the subsequent disintegration of the Soviet Union did not fail to affect the size and structure of the Dutch armed forces. The disappearance of the massive military threat from the Warsaw Pact brought about, on the domestic front, political efforts to slash the defence budget and to cash the so-called peace dividend. Those efforts have proved very successful in that between 1990 and 1994 the level of expenditure decreased by over 20 per cent in real terms.[2] Since the publication of the Defence White Paper (*Defensienota*) of March 1991, the armed forces have been in a process of radical and continuous restructuring. The reform plans, as set out in this policy document, reduced the strength of the Dutch army by about one third; the plans were followed by even more drastic reorganisation measures announced in the so-called Priorities Review (*Prioriteitennota*) of January 1993.

The main lines of the latter may be summarised as follows:

1 The total personnel strength of the armed forces (military and civilian) would be reduced from a previous peace-time level of 130,000 to 70,000 by the end of 1997.[3]
2 Instead of an army of ten brigades (six combat-ready and four mobilisable), a much smaller army of five brigades (three combat-ready and two mobilisable) was to be established. To enhance the flexibility and mobility of the new army, the creation of one air-mobile brigade (to be equipped with both transport and armed helicopters) was announced.
3 The number of naval frigates would fall from nineteen to sixteen; the number of submarines from six to four.
4 The effective number of F-16 fighter squadrons would be reduced from eight (144 aircraft) to six (108).[4]
5 National military service or conscription was to be abolished; as of January 1998, the Dutch armed forces would consist of volunteers only.

It is difficult to argue that these far-reaching decisions reflected clear policy priorities apart from the strong commitment made to United Nations peacekeeping. The Dutch government took the view that in the new post-Cold War security environment the armed forces should be able to contribute to no less than four UN operations simultaneously. Many politicians on the left of the Dutch political spectrum considered the implementation of missions undertaken by the world organisation the main rationale for the Dutch armed forces. By contrast, right-wing politicians began to criticise official policies because the balance of interest was said to tilt too far from traditional NATO tasks to new UN missions.

The formation of the social–liberal Kok cabinet in August 1994,[5] after the parliamentary elections in May which brought heavy losses for the Christian Democrats, led to new cutbacks on the defence budget. In a lengthy letter to parliament in November 1994 (*Novemberbrief*) the new Minister of Defence, Joris Voorhoeve, announced a further reduction of the overhead and logistic sector of the defence apparatus (largely by harmonising parts of the three services and by cutting the civilian defence staff); the delay of several weapons programmes (notably the purchase of expensive armed helicopters); and the decision to advance the abolition date of conscription. Additional savings were sought through increased international co-operation.

In these policy documents and in other government statements many references were made to the need to promote European defence co-operation. This is all the more remarkable since the Netherlands, as a consequence of its outspoken Atlanticist orientation, had previously been wary of exclusively European ventures which it felt could easily undermine the cohesion of NATO. Thus, for example, the Dutch government supported Britain in its opposition to the development of a European defence component outside NATO structures in the early 1990s (van Staden 1994: 152). According to Alfred Pijpers, the then Foreign Minister, Van den Broek, visited Washington in order to reinforce the Dutch position in the negotiations, particularly on joint Franco–German proposals. He rightly notes that the Dutch stance in negotiations in the early 1990s did recall some memories of the political clashes during the Fouchet negotiations of the early 1960s (Pijpers 1996: 253). In the same spirit, the Dutch refused to participate in the Eurocorps as it was not integrated into the military organisation of the Alliance.[6] At the same time, however, the government agreed with strengthening the position of the Western European Union. Emphasising the dual role of WEU in both advancing the security dimension of European integration and developing the European pillar of NATO, the Netherlands took the view that the organisation should focus on common European action in regions outside the NATO treaty area. In that context, the Netherlands encouraged the idea of establishing a European intervention force (Defence White Paper 1991: 27). Moreover, over the past twenty years the Dutch have vigorously made the case, especially in the Eurogroup and in the Independent European Programme Group, for closer European collaboration in the field of defence procurement. The repeated Dutch plea for withdrawing Article 223 from the Treaty of Rome (exonerating the rules of free competition in the area of the production and trade of military material) met with firm resistance, particularly from France and Britain, which were eager to protect their national defence industries.[7]

A major reason for Dutch foreign policy, and indirectly Dutch defence policy, moving in a European direction was a change in the position of the United States. Though the Bush administration had actually discouraged attempts at European defence co-operation as it feared Europe might gang up against Washington, President Clinton took a more positive stance on this matter by wholeheartedly supporting the development of a European security and defence identity. At the same time, Dutch policy makers had come to realise that the United States, widely depicted as a power in relative decline preoccupied with domestic troubles, was no longer willing to bear the brunt in regional European conflicts where vital American interests were not at stake. This view was especially prevalent among spokesmen of the political left and centre who pleaded for closer collaboration with continental European nations. Inside the Dutch government apparatus, slightly different views existed in the Ministry of Foreign Affairs and the Ministry of Defence. Unlike the pattern of bureaucratic preferences in Great Britain, the Dutch Foreign Ministry used to be strongly Atlanticist whereas the Dutch Defence Ministry, perhaps under the influence of a group of uncommitted civil servants who sought to enhance the political profile of their ministry, had more pro-European leanings. However, those moderately different orientations were to lose a great deal of their political relevance after the Brussels NATO summit of early 1994, when the Americans made a strong public case for the concept of Combined Joint Task Forces (CJTFs).

CJTFs were aimed at creating European military units separable but not separate from the allied command structure. At the same time, it was envisaged that NATO facilities could be made available to autonomous European military operations in the future. American blessing allowed the Dutch Foreign Ministry to believe that CJTFs could strengthen WEU without undermining NATO. The Foreign Minister, Hans van Mierlo, commended the concept as the most cost-effective way to enhance WEU's operational capabilities. Expressing the view that Europe should take a larger share of responsibility for its own security and the security of its allies, he said the implementation of CJTFs was necessary not only to give a credible operational role to WEU and NATO itself, but also for the development of a more balanced relationship between the two organisations (van Mierlo 1995: 9). Further Dutch support for the strengthening of WEU was likely at the Intergovernmental Conference (IGC) which was still ongoing in 1997. Whilst in the short term the Netherlands did favour (mainly on practical grounds) the integration of WEU into EU's second pillar (dealing with a common foreign and security policy), the government turned out to be more sympathetic to the idea as a long-range perspective.[8]

Characteristic of the new look to Dutch defence policy of the mid-1990s is the following statement:

> On both sides of the Atlantic it is realised, more than ever, that the European allies must jointly bear a greater responsibility for peace and security. The Alliance is well served by this, as was also recognised by the NATO Summit of January 1994. A common foreign and security

policy and eventually a common defence policy are, moreover, essential components of the process of political unification in Europe. The interests and ideas in the field of security policy of the countries of the European Union are gradually converging. Against this background the Netherlands opts for more intensive European defence co-operation. As a consequence, our armed forces will be interwoven increasingly with those of our neighbours.

(National Budget 1995: 7)

Mere rhetoric? No. Indeed, the Dutch government proved very committed to pursuing the goal of bi-nationalisation or multi-nationalisation of European armed forces. Until the 1990s, apart from general operational co-operation in the allied military structure, only parts of the Dutch marine corps were closely integrated with units of the British marine corps in the UK/NL amphibious force (brigade size) assigned to the defence of NATO's northern flank. But since then the situation has changed radically. The most important change was the creation of a joint Dutch–German army corps in August 1995. Although the German government also aimed at the formation of one or more binational corps with the United States, the level of integration of the Dutch–German corps is without precedent in the NATO structure. All senior command and staff posts are occupied by Dutch and German officers on an equal footing and on a rotational basis. The need to establish common support units has also been agreed. The plan has gained wide public support in the Netherlands, notwithstanding occasional anti-German sentiments in Dutch society, rooted in cultivated memories of the Second World War and in a sort of David-vs-Goliath complex evident in many small–great power relationships. These sentiments sharply contrast, however, with the basic agreement between the Dutch and the German governments on most international issues and the future course of European integration in particular. Also, in view of the close economic ties between the two countries, influential Dutch opinion makers have recently pleaded for a stronger political orientation of the Netherlands towards its eastern neighbour, the strongest political and economic power of Western and Central Europe (van Staden 1995: 43–51).

In addition to the formation of the Dutch–German corps the Netherlands government also decided to assign the country's air-mobile brigade for participation in NATO's so-called Multinational Division, which is part of the rapid reaction forces of the Alliance.[9] As for naval forces, the Netherlands and Belgium reached an agreement to realise maximum co-operation short of a formal merger between the navies of the two countries; in January 1995 a joint Dutch–Belgian operational staff started its duties in the Dutch naval base of Den Helder. In view of the traditional orientation of the Dutch navy towards Great Britain, it may seem rather surprising that the Netherlands also sought closer co-operation with

Germany in the field of naval patrol and air surveillance largely related to anti-submarine warfare. Furthermore, the Netherlands has entered into consultations with Belgium to look into the possibilities of expanding common training and maintenance programmes as well as other forms of co-operation between the two countries' air forces. The Dutch government has also promised to contribute to European defence procurement programmes. An interesting test of Dutch intentions in this area was the purchase of armed helicopters for which both American and European options were available. This purchase involved a number of bureaucratic skirmishes. The Ministry of Defence was, on operational grounds, in favour of the AH-64 *Apache* helicopter built by McDonnell Douglas, whereas, for reasons of European industrial policy, the Ministry of Economic Affairs tilted towards the multipurpose version of the *Tigre* made by the Franco–German Eurocopter consortium. After several delays the Dutch cabinet eventually sided with the Ministry of Defence in April 1995, making clear that it did not favour European arms at any price.[10]

It is one thing to point out that the Dutch government believes that more intensive European defence co-operation is necessary for Europe to take greater responsibility for its own security. It is another, however, to suggest that the co-operative defence ventures the Netherlands has undertaken with neighbouring countries can be regarded as a deliberate adjustment of national objectives to goals associated with European integration. The shrinking defence budget, almost as inevitable as the profound changes in the European security landscape, forced the government to find savings. Yet the perspective of a common European security and defence policy made the pooling of national resources with other countries a far more attractive and politically viable option than unilaterally terminating defence tasks.

In some instances the Dutch government simply has no alternative but to seek closer international co-operation. Dutch land forces are a case in point. Because the size of those forces was reduced to hardly more than one division, the Netherlands was no longer able to maintain a full army corps as it did in the Cold War. So the more sceptical observer may be inclined to look upon the integrated Dutch–German corps, widely advertised as a model of international military co-operation, as a fine example of how to make a political virtue out of financial necessity.

In sum, recent changes in Dutch defence policy and to the shape of the Dutch armed forces should be interpreted as a reaction mainly to shifting international circumstances as well as to shrinking resources. The reorientation of defence policy from its traditional Atlanticist leanings to Europe was dictated less by European zeal than by a lack of alternatives. One might speak, in this context, of Europe *faute de mieux*. Yet the solutions contemplated by the Dutch government to the problem of how to maintain a substantial defence effort under increasing budgetary constraints have been substantially affected by recent opportunities for

European defence co-operation as well as by the government's commitment to promote that endeavour. The collaborative agreements that the government has recently concluded with some of its European partners may be signs of an incipient European 'defence culture' in the Netherlands.

THE FUTURE OF DUTCH DEFENCE POLICY

Can one imagine such a thing as a national or autonomous defence policy for a small state like the Netherlands in the years ahead? The answer is not without ambiguity.

What is meant, under present circumstances, by national defence policy? It may refer to three different situations: the power or ability to embark unilaterally on military action; the authority to decide on participation in multilateral military action; and the possession of independent defence capabilities. National (or autonomous) defence policy in the first sense has, in the Dutch context, long lost any substance. There is widespread agreement in Dutch society that, if any significant action by Dutch military units takes place, it should do so only in the framework of existing international organisations (UN, OSCE, NATO or WEU) or within *ad hoc* coalitions of 'the able and willing'. Military expeditions such as Britain staged during the Falklands crisis or France conducted in Chad several times have become unmanageable for a country the size of the Netherlands. Indeed, apart from the protection of the Dutch Antilles (Dutch overseas territories in the West Indies holding a form of dominion status), it is difficult to think of any contingency which might require the unilateral intervention of Dutch military forces.[11]

But there certainly is still life for an autonomous Dutch defence policy in the second sense – of retaining the authority to decide on participation in multilateral military action. In spite of its reputation for being an ardent supporter of supranational authority in international relations, the Netherlands is no more willing than any other European country to sacrifice its national sovereignty in matters of life and death. In other words, even in the framework of an evolving common European defence policy, it is inconceivable that the Dutch would accept any system of majority rule that might oblige them to take part in military operations against their will outside the treaty area of NATO or WEU. Like successive Dutch governments, the Dutch parliament is also opposed to relinquishing its say in decisions to send Dutch troops to international trouble spots. In June 1994 the Netherlands became the first UN member state to commit military units to the so-called UN Stand-by Arrangements System (UNSAS), as called for by the then Secretary General Boutros Boutros-Ghali. However, in line with the prevailing attitude in the country, the agreement with the United Nations contained a provision making participation by the Netherlands in any UN operation subject to prior parliamentary consent.

The prospect of building an integrated European defence community is still very remote. Such a community presupposes the identification of common European security interests as well as the formulation of a common European strategy for dealing with international contingencies. In spite of the current efforts by, for instance, the WEU Planning Staff and regular meetings of WEU member states' Chiefs of Staff to co-ordinate national views, experience in the Gulf War, former Yugoslavia and also Somalia give little cause for optimism in this regard (Martin and Roper 1995).

The larger European countries are divided by different national priorities and by different perceptions of their national interest. Thus, for example, France, as always subject to *inquiétudes allemandes*, seems to be paralysed by fear of Germany's growing power. But France cannot regress into narrow chauvinism; it must be willing to sacrifice enough sovereignty to keep European co-operation credible in German eyes. Additional problems arise from the fact that, unlike the monolithic and massive threat of the past which touched upon the security of each European country in the same degree, current sources of instability do not affect all countries equally and, consequently, their reactions vary. Whereas France worries about the rise of fundamentalism in North Africa, Germany is preoccupied with sources of instability in Eastern Europe and therefore advocates rapid eastward expansion of the European Union. Although the constitutional inhibitions on German military units outside NATO's treaty area have been removed by the ruling of the German Constitutional Court in the summer of 1994, the German government, at least for the time being, is likely to remain wary of having German soldiers participate in common European combat actions. Great Britain still oscillates between full engagement in Europe and its (putative) special relationship with the United States. The British government seems to assume that the fate of Germany hardly concerns its security. For its part, the United States itself is no longer willing to bear the brunt in any European conflict, although it remains committed to European security to the extent that it is in its vital interest to forestall any attempt at hegemony by one of the European powers (Joffe 1995: 94–117). The West European powers, having relied on American military protection for a long time, have unfortunately lost – to borrow Stanley Hoffmann's words – 'their habit of external military action' (Hoffmann 1994: 9–10).

This analysis, which presumes the enduring influence of national history and geography, is not exhaustive, but one wonders how many new demonstrations of European impotence (and public scorn for that matter) will be necessary to overcome considerations of national prestige and short-sighted calculations of self-interest. Given the formidable obstacles to establishing a fully-fledged European defence community, the Netherlands is likely to uphold independent defence capabilities for the foreseeable future. The question is, however, whether the Netherlands can afford to maintain an army which, as far as its structure, composition and missions are concerned, resembles the armies of the larger European countries. Several Dutch defence analysts have taken issue with the tendency to maintain a wide array of defence tasks in spite of declining resources. A case in point is the small Dutch submarine fleet which currently consists of only four submarines but which nevertheless requires relatively big overheads. But even in a country like the Netherlands, with few industrial interests in the defence sector, sweeping reform proposals to concentrate on a limited number of tasks and to discontinue complete services are bound to trigger vehement bureaucratic resistance. As the army, air force and navy are eager to defend their autonomy, the authority of the inter-service Defence Staff is limited to the co-ordination of military planning.

At some stage in the future Dutch defence planners will be compelled to reappraise the concept of the comprehensive army and to set real priorities. If the economic criteria of comparative advantage were to govern the allocation of Dutch defence resources, a stronger emphasis on naval forces would result. Not only are those forces the most prestigious component of the Dutch defence structure but they are probably also the most professional by international standards. A co-operative arrangement between, for instance, Germany, Belgium and the Netherlands whereby the first exploited its strength in land forces, the second specialised in air force capabilities and the Netherlands concentrated on naval forces, may seem a utopian thought today, but it could become a test for the viability of European defence co-operation. An increasing division of responsibilities between the defence forces of the European countries is the only practicable way to deal effectively with mounting budgetary pressures.

CONCLUSION

Under the influence of the diminishing involvement of the United States in the security of Europe and the expansion of European integration beyond low politics, Dutch defence policy is more focused on security co-operation among the countries of Western Europe than some years ago when such co-operation was thought to erode the Western alliance. The Dutch government has come to recognise that the long-range commitment of America to NATO may be put at risk if the European allies refuse to pool their forces and bear a larger share of the joint transatlantic defence burden. Typical of the new political landscape is the paradox that closer European defence co-operation strengthens, rather than weakens, the Atlantic Alliance – a familiar theme in the Dutch debate about Western defence.

The major reasons for the subordination of national defence planning to the needs of European defence integration have been economic. Budgetary constraints caused by post-Cold War relaxation and competing welfare state claims have provided the main motivations for the recent Dutch quest for collaborative agreements with surrounding countries. Reduced financial resources are also bound to force Dutch policy makers to reconsider their ambitious plans to burden a relatively small army with a wide range of missions. Role or task specialisation will probably be the catchphrases in future defence planning. The impact of budget savings at the present level on the composition of the armed forces of the larger European countries may be less far-reaching than on the forces of smaller states. It would appear, however, that the larger countries, too, can no longer afford to disregard savings from pooling national resources with other countries. New developments in international political economy have called into question the ability of states in general to remain autonomous in the defence sphere. Indeed the accumulated effects of the enormous rise in fixed capital costs, accelerated obsolescence, and increased production risks have caused rapidly escalating costs in weapons production and procurement. One is prompted to conclude that, on the whole, leaner defence budgets are likely to become a good companion along the road to European defence co-operation.

NOTES

1 For this reason it was a great disappointment to the Dutch government that it was not admitted to the international contact group dealing with the Bosnian crisis. It gave rise to complaints in the style of 'no taxation without representation'.

2 Projections towards the end of the 1990s show a total decrease of more than 25 per cent. The percentage of GNP spent by the Netherlands on military expenditure will sink from about 3 per cent at the end of the 1980s to about 2 per cent in the years to come.

3 To be expanded to 110,000 during war.

4 The pre-1991 number was 10 squadrons (180 fighters).

5 The cabinet was composed of ministers from three political parties, namely the Labour Party of the Prime Minister, Wim Kok, the free-market liberal VVD party of the parliamentary floor leader, Frits Bolkestein, and the radical liberal D66 party of the deputy Prime Minister, Hans van Mierlo, who was also Minister of Foreign Affairs.

6 The corps was also joined by Belgium and Spain.

7 The Article allows 'any member state to take such measures as it considers necessary for the protection of the essential interests of its security which are connected with the production or trade in arms, ammunition and war material'.

8 See the Netherlands government's policy memorandum specially prepared for the debate in the Dutch parliament on the forthcoming IGC, *Common European foreign, security and defence policy: towards stronger external action by the European Union*, 28 March 1995.

9 The Multinational Division is composed of Belgian, British and German brigades. The division is also answerable to the WEU.

10 The purchase amounted to Fl1.3 billion (about $700 million).

11 Some time ago there were rumours about US pressure on the Dutch govern-

ment to take military action against drug trafficking in the former Dutch colony of Suriname.

REFERENCES

Bodenheimer, S. (1967) *Political Union: A Microcosm of European Politics 1960–1966*, Leiden: A. W. Sijthoff.

van den Bos, B. (1992) *Can Atlanticism Survive? The Netherlands and the New Role of Security Institutions*, The Hague: Netherlands Institute of International Relations Clingendael: Martinus Nijhoff.

Hoffmann, S. (1994) 'Europe's identity crisis revisited', *Daedalus* 123, 2: 9–10.

Honig, J. W. (1993) *Defense Policy in the North Atlantic Alliance. The Case of the Netherlands*, Westport, Connecticut/London: Praeger.

Joffe, J. (1995) ' "Bismarck" or "Britain"? Toward an American Grand Strategy after Bipolarity', *International Security* XIX,4: 94–117.

Kwast-van Duursen, M. (1991) 'Nederland en een federaal Europa: kleine landen-politiek of ideaal van buitenlands beleid', in Ph.P. Everts (ed.) *Nederland in een veranderende wereld. De toekomst van het buitenlands beleid*, Assen: Van Gorcum.

Laqueur, W. (1981) 'Hollanditis: A new stage in European neutralism', *Commentary*, 19–26.

Lower House of the Netherlands Parliament (Staten-Generaal) (1991) 'Restructuring and reduction: the Dutch army in a changing world', *Defence White Paper*, 21991, 2–3.

—— (1995) *European Foreign, Security and Defence Policy: Towards Stronger External Action by the European Union*, 24128, 1–2, forthcoming.

—— (1995) *National Budget 1995, Explanatory Memorandum*, 23900.

Martin, L., Roper, J. (eds) (1995) *Towards a Common Defence Policy*, Paris, Institute of Security Studies of WEU.

van Mierlo, H. (1995) 'The WEU and NATO: prospects for a more balanced relationship', *NATO Review*, 9.

Pijpers, A. (1996) 'The Netherlands and the CFSP: The Weakening pull of Atlanticism?', in C. Hill (ed.) *Actors in Europe's Foreign Policy*, London: Routledge.

van Sas, N. C. F. (1985) *Onze natuurlijkste bondgenoot. Nederland, Engeland en Europa, 1813–1831*, Groningen: Wolters-Noordhoff.

Siccama, J. G. (1985) 'The Netherlands depillarized: security policy in a new domestic context', in G. Flynn (ed.) *NATO's Northern Allies. The National Security Policies of Belgium, Denmark, the Netherlands, and Norway*, London and Sydney: Croom Helm.

van Staden, A. (1989) 'The changing role of the Netherlands in the Atlantic Alliance', in H. Daalder and G. A. Irwin (eds) *Politics in the Netherlands. How Much Change?*, London: Frank Cass.

—— (1994) 'After Maastricht: Explaining the movement towards a Common European Defence Policy', in W. Carlsnaes and S. Smith (eds) *European Foreign Policy. The EC and Changing Perspectives in Europe*, London: Sage Publications.

—— (1995) 'Small state strategies in alliances. The case of the Netherlands', *Co-operation and Conflict* XXX, 1:39–43.

Voorhoeve, J. J. C. (1979) *Peace, Profits and Principles. A Study of Dutch Foreign Policy*, The Hague: Netherlands Institute of International Relations Clingendael: Martinus Nijhoff.

Wiebes, C. and Zeeman, B. (1993) *Belgium, the Netherlands and Alliances, 1940–1949*, Leiden: Leiden University Press.

6 The United Kingdom

David Chuter

This chapter sets out to explain British attitudes to the possibility of European defence integration in the light of historical and cultural factors, and to examine what scope there may be for these attitudes to change. It describes how the British view of European defence integration differs from the European norm and why, uniquely, such integration would be regarded in London as more of a threat than an opportunity. It tries to account for, rather than defend or criticise, this view. The chapter is necessarily conditioned by the author's experience as a government official, involved, in a minor capacity, in some of these issues, although the views expressed here are entirely personal and unofficial.

The chapter takes as its point of departure the fact that pressures towards European integration in the defence field have made virtually no impact on the conduct of British policy in recent decades. Governments and formers of opinion have, of course, been obliged to take note of these pressures, but the responses have never exceeded a reactive shading of statements or a modification of some nuances of policy. There has been no substantial change of mind. Here, it is important to make a distinction (to which I return in looking ahead at the end of the chapter), between defence *co-operation* in Europe, which the British have historically been prepared to contemplate, and *integration*, which they have not. The instinctive British preference, in all areas, for pragmatic co-operation, whose worth is assessed on a case-by-case basis, partly explains this, as does the traditional mistrust of a large state for an integrated structure where its freedom of action is more limited. The latter view is, of course, shared by the French, in the defence and security area, even though they have always been keener on strengthened European co-operation than have the British. Their continued preference for co-operative and inter-governmental, rather than integrated, defence solutions has, in this one case, strengthened the British position.

The British aversion to integration (or anything more than the most *ad hoc* co-operation), is of long standing. Under the stress of the First World War, the British agreed to the formation of an integrated military structure in France, under the leadership of the French Marshal Foch.

But attempts by Briand, the French Prime Minister, to continue these close connections after the War were rebuffed. Briand and Lloyd George met several times in the early 1920s, but there was a complete mismatch between the French desire for a wide and ambitious alliance, ultimately involving other European nations, and British wariness of anything except limited co-operation in specific cases (*DBFP*, I, 15/110 and 19/10). Subsequent French proposals became more elaborate, culminating in the presentation, at the 1932 Geneva Disarmament Conference, of plans for an international army. Sir John Simon, then Foreign Secretary, roundly dismissed all such schemes, asserting that Britain could never accept 'any plan which involved the creation of a super-state' (*DBFP*, II 3/45).

The British were subsequently to stay outside the ill-fated European Defence Community (in spite of American pressure to become involved), limiting themselves to mild encouragement of others. The supra-national, integrated aspects of the EDC were anathema to London, but, even here, the British were ready to co-operate with the eventual organisation, to the point where, in 1952, Eden offered to negotiate a fifty-year mutual security treaty. This was part of what was known as the 'Eden Plan', designed to build bridges between the (integrated) six, and 'those European countries who preferred intergovernmental co-operation' (Young 1993). By the time of the 1962 Fouchet Plan, an unenthusiastic British response to yet another proposal for an organised European defence surprised nobody.

Given this history of coolness to European defence integration, the discussion of the British case cannot proceed as it would with almost any other European country. Whilst scattered favourable references in the political debate to the possibility of closer European co-operation in defence can occasionally be found, especially during the early 1970s, their influence on actual British behaviour has been small. Rather, it seems more useful to examine the sources of this British attitude, to see whether they are deeply ingrained, and so unlikely to change, or whether they are of recent origin, and so capable of modification.

A suitable place to begin is with the words 'Europe', 'Defence' and 'Integration'. 'Europe' first. Physical and intellectual separation from Europe itself has always been a problem. British governments have always tried to avoid the domination of the continent by any single power or ruler, and have chosen allies, or paid subsidies, to try to prevent it. Although Britain cannot help but have been a major player in Europe – and especially in the defence area – the nation has never had the military capability to dominate the continent forcibly, and, because of cultural and philosophical differences, has not offered itself, and is not sought out by others, to be a leader and example, as the French conceive themselves to be. But if British leadership of Europe is for these reasons not credible, then the leadership of Europe by any other nation is felt to be dangerous, and to be prevented. A united Europe, in other words, always carries the risk of being a Europe united against Britain.

Generally, also, the fear has had an ideological component: the dread of domination by an alien ideology. For much of modern history it was catholicism, subsequently it was democracy (or at least the principles of republicanism and popular sovereignty), more recently it was communism, today it is something described (quite erroneously) as 'federalism'. All these ideologies have a common thread running through them: they are foreign-produced, intellectual rather than pragmatic, antipathetic to traditional British concerns, and potentially disruptive of the social order at home. The necessity of combating them naturally dictates a choice of allies: successively, protestants, monarchists and anti-communists. Indeed, there are some indications that it was the ideological effect of the Reformation which encouraged the view that Britain was isolated and different: disparaging references to 'The Continent' were already being made in Shakespeare's lifetime.[1]

Thus, the British have always feared that an organised Europe will be a Europe organised by somebody else, according to alien principles. Indeed, the more organised Europe becomes, the more the British position will weaken, assuming that the rules which will be adopted for common use are likely to be those which the majority of states find natural and sensible, and Britain is therefore likely to be excluded from this majority, and even to be in a minority of one. No European state can stand alone against a consensus forever. If this assessment is correct, then it could be further argued that British interests are therefore best served by resistance to the concept of the development of Europe as a whole, or, more realistically, attempting to delay it as long as possible and to limit its field of application. This is especially the case with defence. By contrast, *ad hoc* co-operation can be carried out without fixed sets of rules, and is therefore safer.

In theory, of course, it may be possible for the British to acquire habits of thought and behaviour from their European partners, and so bridge the gap a little and reduce their isolation. But the possibility of any wider assimilation of European attitudes is remote: even those who flatter themselves that they understand something of the mind-set of their European colleagues do not claim actually to share all of it. So long as our cultural norms, our education system and our political culture, remain essentially as they are (and they show few signs of significant change), we are unlikely ever to find ourselves sharing the same point of departure as our neighbours. I am not suggesting that these British characteristics stand in opposition to a single, homogeneous European alternative everywhere shared, but rather that the culture, education systems and political culture of our European partners are considerably closer to each other (for historical reasons), than we are to any of them.

The second term I propose to explore is 'Defence': a case where, in addition to the general conceptual differences outlined above, there are also a host of practical differences which separate the British experience, and concept, of defence from those of its neighbours. Because moves towards integration elsewhere in Europe have deep roots in a collective history and an experience of war which the British do not share, the very different British experience has helped to insulate us from sharing these pressures or even understanding them for the most part. Being an island, Britain has never had to concern itself with the defence of the territory from a conventional attack in the sense that a nation with land borders has had to. Such a threat would only come about if control of the sea had been forfeited, and this the British were always able to prevent.

In addition, the army, still the subject of distrust after the experience of Cromwell's generals, was not, as it habitually was elsewhere, the guardian of the nation, nor did it have the practical and symbolic role of safeguarding the frontiers. In Britain these roles were carried out, in a rather different way, by the navy. As a result, the political position of the army was totally different from that elsewhere. Although the Royal Navy had a position which in some senses was the equivalent of that of European armies, it would have never been able to convert this into political influence even had it wanted to, given that most of it was in distant waters at any one time, and that, in any case, there are certain practical difficulties in mounting a *coup d'état* with ships.

The army itself was generally deployed, in small pockets, in distant parts of the world. The requirements of a successful commander, with forces often of brigade size or less, were personal courage, leadership and initiative, awareness of the ground and skill in small-unit tactics, rather than the kind of wider acquaintance with the theory of war and the use of massive forces which his French or German opposite number would be expected to have. Interestingly, the British reaction to defeats in the early years of the Second World War was not to try to study and promulgate theoretical lessons appropriate to the massive forces they were by then using, but to take refuge in the proliferation of small groups – commandos, special forces, bomber crew – where the traditional virtues of courage, initiative, etc., could come into play, and to put many of the best brains into scientific research and intelligence analysis. This habit of mind survived until modern times. The operational level of warfare, appropriate to the handling of large forces, was, indeed, not formally taught in the British Army until 1988.

A corollary of the distance at which Britain's battles were fought is that defeat was seldom dangerous, and never terminal. Because of the inviolability of the islands themselves, defeat in battle might imply the loss of territory or of allies, but not of the nation itself. The British were the one combatant in Europe in 1914–18 and in 1939–40 which, if defeated, had somewhere else to go, and it is not surprising that, in each case, the French feared that they would do exactly that. Likewise, given the difficulty of an invasion of the islands themselves, the British had a great deal of choice in how they conducted the War, and where. To this extent, most of Britain's wars have been elective: the common European experience of finding that one is at war because the enemy has crossed the frontiers was impossible.

There is simply no point of contact between this concept of defence and the continental one, which has featured conscription, rapid mobilisation, the command and control of huge forces and the likelihood of a decisive battle of colossal proportions, upon which the fate of nations would hang. Even in the days of NATO solidarity on the Central Front, it was obvious that the war the British were planning to fight would, in its totality, be a different war from that of its continental allies: a large part of the British ground forces, and most of its sea and air forces, were based not on the Central Front, but in the UK and elsewhere.

This kind of warfare has a number of important political consequences. The first is the general lack of any requirement for conscription in peacetime. As a result, Britain has not suffered the wrenching political conflicts over conscription which have been common in Europe. There is no concept of a 'Nation in Arms': except for the later years of the two World Wars, fighting has largely been confined to the professionals. The second is the difference in the objectives for which military units were employed. Although the Second World War was, in some degree, a war for national survival, it was untypical in being so. Typical British wars have been fought for territory, raw materials and the protection of trade routes. (Much military force was employed, of course, at levels well below what we would think of as a war.) This, combined with the professional nature of the combatants, gave the British a relaxed attitude to the concept of intervention in somebody else's country which, apart from France, is not really shared by any other European nation. Thus, the common suggestion in 1990–1 that the Gulf War was being fought to secure the oil supplies of the West was not greeted with the kind of horrified disavowal which was the case elsewhere, because such motives are comprehensible in terms of British history, and are widely regarded as acceptable. These attitudes are a product of history and geography rather than education or culture, and it is hard to see them changing.

The limited nature of traditional British objectives in war made small, highly-trained forces perfectly adequate. Often, the threat of force was enough: there might be only a single regular battalion for hundreds of miles, but British rule would be achieved by moral, rather than physical, ascendancy, over carefully-divided native rulers, many of whom would furnish contingents of soldiers for the Empire. Indeed, the highest expression of the application of British influence was the Resident, who would try to achieve such an intellectual and moral dominance over the local ruler that even the threat of military power never needed to be invoked. Whilst this situation no longer exists in reality, the mental habits it gave rise to have perhaps lasted longer.

The third consequence is the more technical, less political nature of defence as a concept. Defence of interests, of allies, or of trade routes has an entirely different political resonance from the all-out defence of the national territory from overwhelming attack. Defence, whilst serious, is a far more technical matter than is the case in nations (like the rest of Europe), where the loss of a war can imply the loss of the nation. Moreover, Britain has been historically one of the few countries which has been able to make a credible stab at defence of its territory. Through much of modern history only France and Germany (not necessarily at the same time) have been able to make similar claims. Most European nations (and indeed most nations) have never, in practice, been able to defend their sovereignty against a determined attack. This being so, they have adopted a concept of defence which is primarily political: essentially armed forces exist as an actualisation of the claim to sovereignty and independence, as a concrete sign of the state's willingness to act on the international stage, and as a sign of the importance placed on the maintenance of the physical boundaries of the state. Defence, in other words, is a subsidiary task deduced from the existence of the nation state, irrespective of enemies. It is this difference of view which has led to such confusion over the concept of European defence. European states, by and large, use this more political interpretation of defence as a starting-point, and take for granted that the European Union, like the nation-state, will not be truly sovereign – indeed will not truly exist – unless it has defence forces under its own control. It is sufficient, in this logic, that these forces should simply be, since just by existing they are a political statement and a symbol of Europe's new political status. The British, on the other hand, slaves to a tradition of pragmatism, and unable to conceive of armed forces as political symbols, are always asking what exactly it is that the European forces are going to do.

If one considers the two component parts of the European attitude – ideology and experience – it is clear that, in recent years, European experience has increasingly come to resemble that of the UK, especially in the disappearance of an identified threat and the likely obsolescence of conscript forces. But such patterns of history are slow to fade, and it will be a long time – certainly decades – before the full effects of these changes come to be felt in ideology, even assuming things continue as they are. Even then, memories of destructive European wars will not fade quickly on the continent, and with their memory will remain the impulse to integration as a prophylactic against a revival of dangerous nationalism. This kind of experience may, of course, be studied by the British, but can never be replicated: imaginative sympathy cannot reproduce the experience of defeat, occupation and devastation, nor the political consequences to which they give rise. We cannot bridge the gap between history as pageant (the British impression of history as successful wars, triumphant expansion, resistance to foreign invasion, absence of large-scale civil war), and history as trauma (the more general European experience). This gap in understanding extends even to the simplest form of (non-integrated) co-operation, such as that between Britain and France. It is common to say that these two countries have much in common and fulfil similar tasks, but that is only true at the superficial level. For example, each retains colonies, operates outside Europe and possesses nuclear weapons, but the political origins of these (and other) defence tasks, the way they are defined, the priority given to each and the way they fit into overall policy are all quite different.

Even in the pragmatic world of practical military co-operation, therefore, Britain has found it difficult to work with its European partners. Yet the really difficult obstacles lie in the different conceptions of what defence is about, as we have seen. This is one consequence of the completely different concepts of the organisation of government and policy making, which bedevil relations inside the European Union now. For example, the continental concept of administrative law (derived from French ideas), has no parallel in Britain, where there is, indeed, no legal basis for the existence of the civil service. More importantly, perhaps, and not ignoring the necessary pragmatism politics forces upon bureaucrats, it remains true that the thrust of the European administrative tradition, based on the French model, is towards the need to find the right answer to a given question, often from a detailed study of legal texts. On the other hand, the British tradition is one of studied ambiguity and a readiness to move from one pragmatic position to another as the detail of the argument changes. This is no doubt what one senior German diplomat meant when he complained at a meeting where I was present, that the British had 'no principles'.

Taking all this into account, it is not surprising that the British concept of defence is quite different from the European norm, and this is reflected, for example, in the physical organisation of defence and in the attitudes of those professionally involved in it. Traditionally, the armed forces, and especially the army, have been a profession: one of the typical careers for upper middle-class males, and one of the few acceptable pursuits for a gentleman. (The army, in particular, has always been seen as a profession or a career on the same level as the law, medicine or the city, but it is a career, not a vocation.)[2] The British concept of military professionalism is therefore a fairly narrow one, confined largely to the working day and directly comparable with that of professionals in other walks of life. There is little trace of the patriotic mystique and asceticism found in some other European countries. The armed forces demonstrate the traditional British preference for the bright, practical individual, strong on native wit, rather than the person who has studied a great deal. (Even today, for example, a technical background is rare at the highest levels, even in the air force). Officers are much less inclined than their European counterparts to develop an intellectual bent, and are much less involved with the political, social and economic aspects of defence than their continental counterparts, which can lead to poor communication and misunderstandings in dealings with them.

The reason why the armed forces cultivate this fairly narrow professionalism are only partly social. They also result from the fact that – almost alone in Europe – the British system has a large input by civilian officials. Defence policy, and the management of the defence programme and budget, as well as the entire political and Parliamentary side of the Ministry, are dominated by career civil servants. This arrangement seems normal to Anglo-Saxons, but differs greatly from European practice, where far fewer civilians are involved, and where there is a strict distinction between military questions (where the armed forces provide technical advice), and political-strategic questions, which are the preserve of the President or Prime Minister and the Foreign Ministry, and on which the military are not consulted. European delegations from Defence Ministries are generally military and will have far less freedom of manoeuvre than their (usually civilian) British counterparts. These bureaucratic variations flow, of course, from precisely the same difference of opinion about what constitutes defence. It will be clear that the two philosophies have considerable potential for conflict, and it was the experience of many (including the author) that these fundamentally different concepts were a major complicating factor in, for example, many of the discussions which surrounded and followed the Maastricht negotiations.

This narrower professionalism excludes much involvement with politics. In most European Defence Ministries, where uniformed personnel are the rule, senior officers cannot help becoming involved in political issues. In Britain, the military are content to leave this to the civilians and prefer to detach themselves from the political dimension. There is the paradox, therefore, that whilst those who work with the British military find them overwhelmingly conservative (and Conservative) in their views, they voluntarily abstain, during their career, from seeking to further their own political ideas. Indeed, the conservatism of most military officers is instinctive and social, rather than ideological, which is why, when they retire, they might become the Treasurer of a local Conservative Party, but, on past evidence, are most unlikely to go into politics as such.

I have already said much, implicitly, about integration, and it should not be surprising to learn that, as with most subjects, the British have no real attitude to integration as a concept, but a series of attitudes towards particular examples of it. Integration is best defined as a situation where there is an international bureaucracy which has the right of initiative, and a degree, at least, of influence over national governments, and where the intention is that nations move in a commonly-agreed direction. It is the opposite of the more traditional, inter-governmental approach, which proceeds by consensus and where the right of initiative is largely reserved to governments.

For the British (and they are not alone in this), the test is whether the philosophy and the practical operations of the integrated structure are consistent with their views and objectives or not. In the present NATO structure (unlike various European alternatives on offer at different dates), the British were able to get much of what they wanted. Thus, they were reasonably happy with post-war integration in defence (where American norms were dominant), but not in areas like social policy (where European norms were the rule), The first kind of integration largely delivers what the British want and strengthens their position, whereas the second proceeds from a set of beliefs which have not recently been dominant in British politics. It should be clear, in consequence, that, were defence integration no longer to proceed according to American rules but to change to something close to the social policy model, and its rules to be made in European fora much as those for social policy are made, the British might well have difficulties with it. Once more this would not be a judgement about whether integration was a good idea in principle, but about whether this example of it served British interests as they were perceived at the time.

This follows from the fact that international organisations do not simply happen: their structures, organisation and working methods are generally imitated from national models, depending on who the founding nations are and what the power relationships are between them. Organisations have what in a computer is called an 'operating system', an agreed set of rules about ethos and procedure. Ownership of (or influence on) the operating system is a powerful means of securing influence in the organis-ation. NATO, as we now have it, is almost entirely an organisation of Anglo-Saxon construction, and its operating system functions in an Anglo-Saxon way: there are good historical reasons for this.

In the panic which followed the outbreak of the Korean War in 1950, when it was expected that a similar attack in Europe would begin at any minute, the previous structure set up under the Washington Treaty, which was inter-governmental and largely political, was rapidly replaced by the NATO structure with which we are now familiar. The automatic choice of an American (Eisenhower) as Supreme Allied Commander in Europe (SACEUR), together with the massive influx of US forces, guaranteed that the Integrated Military Structure, as it developed, would be according to US models. Likewise, virtually all of the command appointments went to British or American officers: Germany was not then a member, and France, distracted by Indo-China, was still putting its European-based forces together. Although the number of non-Anglo-Saxon commanders was to increase as the years passed, the NATO staff system has remained dominated by US practices, and the working language has remained American English. Subsequently, the first Secretary General, Lord Ismay, structured the political side of the organisation after that of Whitehall, with which he was very familiar. Its ethos was, however, quite different from the European norm, and difficult for most European nations to understand and work with. Ismay's influence is still clear, and the British have managed to retain a disproportionate influence: the key post of Assistant Secretary General for Policy and Planning has been held by a senior official from the UK Ministry of Defence for as long as anyone can remember.

For the British, all this represented a sizeable opportunity. (They had, of course, been involved from the beginning in the secret talks which led to the Washington Treaty). It was not that British and US views and practices were identical: there were (and are) quite noticeable differences between the policy-making processes in the two countries. But the British and Americans were familiar with each other's procedures and personnel from the War, had many cultural similarities and had developed the habit of working together. The British had already evolved their basic principles for dealing with their large ally: quiet persuasion where possible, eventual acquiescence if the British view was not acceptable and, at all costs, the avoidance of direct conflict.

The differences between British and American practices often worked in the British interest. The Washington politico-military bureaucracy has always been large, fragmented and inflexible, and senior officials, appointed from outside with only a brief time to make their reputations, do not always find consensus easy. By contrast, the smaller and nippier British system, with its informal working practices and flexible hierarchies, considered itself (probably rightly) able to work much more quickly, and from assumptions, moreover, which would have been largely common to the two countries. Victory (or influence, at least) in these matters often goes to the side which produced the first piece of paper, and this was often the British.

All this put the British in a position which enabled them to retain (albeit mostly vicariously) a position of influence in the world to which they were not, in other respects, entitled. It is the result of a specific choice, made at the end of the Second World War, to try to retain a status as close as possible to that of a great power by finding a genuine great power to influence, and on whose coat tails to be pulled along.[3] It is a choice which is consistent with British historical experience, and with the indirect methods of operation which London has always favoured. It is a choice made easier by the ingrained pragmatism of the Whitehall machine, which can move rapidly from the defence of one position to the defence of another, including one which it previously opposed. And, although British officials would die rather than admit it, it is also a choice which perpetuates some aspects of the imperial mode of dealing with large nations whom you can never face down but can certainly hope to influence. Finally, it is also a choice which reflects the pragmatic Anglo-

Saxon preference for practical institutions. British officials frequently refer to NATO – and the operating system in general – as providing 'real defence', contrasting this with the more political, less functional, concepts on offer in the European context.

The importance of the Anglo-Saxon operating system goes well beyond the more relatively mundane matters of bureaucratic structure and working methods, important as they are. What we have here is also a book of rules for the treatment of topics related to European security. In this sense, NATO, and the whole Anglo-Saxon operating system, can be compared to a grammar superimposed on the otherwise chaotic vocabulary of events in the security area. This grammar said, until recently, that matters affecting European security would only be discussed in the presence of the United States, and only in a forum where that nation had the dominant voice. It said that European nations might not (except furtively) discuss these issues collectively among themselves. It said that the practical implementation of policy would be through an integrated, rather than inter-governmental structure, and a structure dominated by Anglo-Saxon concepts and personnel. Apparently arcane arguments about which acronym should take charge of a particular crisis – NATO, WEU, UN – are really arguments about the relative weight of the United States (and to some extent the UK), in the decision-making process.

We take this so much for granted that we are inclined to forget just how curious it has been, and how easily the grammar of European Security could have been differently constructed. Other models are easily conceivable, including one which has stalked the corridors of Europe for forty years – a European defence organisation with a treaty relationship with the United States. Such a development (which might now, finally, be on the way), would imply, of course, massive changes in power relationships, and, in particular, an effective end to British attempts to implement an agenda through the United States and the current NATO set-up. In turn, this leads to fears that defence arrangements in future, constructed according to different principles, will be less effective than those which exist at present. Indeed, looked at from London, there is a fear that any conceivable evolution in European defence integration will weaken the British position, since it will mean the loss of the force exerted, normally in the same direction as the British, by the United States. Although the current situation is not perfect, it is doubtful whether there is a realistic alternative which could leave Britain better placed, and better able to influence European defence in what it considers to be an effective and practical direction. So long as the large questions of European security are addressed in an institutional forum whose traditions, language and bureaucratic culture are all congenial to the British way of thinking, and so long as the chief determinant of Western policy is an ally with whom the British have a far closer relationship than other nations, then so long will the British position, and the British concept of what makes sensible defence, remain strong. Yet this judgement depends on a number of things remaining true, even leaving aside pressure to do more in Europe. In the tight, disciplined, bi-polar world of the Cold War, there was (or there was felt to be) enough common ground in interests and outlook between Britain and the United States to make a relationship such as I have described both possible and valuable. It is not clear that this will be true in the future: many will suggest that it has already begun to change. If the United States becomes less amenable to quiet British persuasion, or if the real interests of the two countries, in security matters, but also in the areas of trade and industrial policy, are felt to be diverging, then London will certainly begin to wonder whether the arrangements entered into during the last War now need to be looked at again.

In any event, the grammar of European security is observably changing. On the one hand, there is an increasing tendency for security matters to be treated in a European context. This is likely to increase as the United States disengages, both mentally and physically, from Europe and European questions. On the other hand, pressures for integration (or at least increased co-operation) in the defence field are steadily increasing, and more integration in the defence field is coming, as surely as it is coming everywhere else. The British response to this has been characteristic. In the Maastricht negotiations, and those on the future of the WEU which took place at the same time, British tactics – largely successful – were to limit, to the maximum extent possible, any move by the European Union into the security field, and to ensure that collective European defence issues were discussed in the WEU, an intergovernmental body and one with close links to NATO. So far, London has resisted the idea that a fundamental choice between Europe and the United States is inevitable, not least because the choice is not an equal one. A Britain which is part of a tight European grouping with which it is frequently at odds will decline relatively in its importance and in its ability to influence the debate, even if it is objectively an important player. Confronted by a less attractive future, the tendency will be to try to postpone it for as long as possible. In true British fashion, this will not be through some elaborate plan, but through a series of opportunistic moves and temporary expedients, all designed to put off the evil day, since who knows what might happen in the future.

In the light of the historical and cultural factors reviewed above, some preliminary comments can be made about the possibility of British moves in the direction of close European defence co-operation. First, and barring some ideological transformation which seems unlikely, the British will not make any such move with enthusiasm. The essential motivations for such enthusiasm – desire for Europe to balance the United States, commitment to the European *finalité*, judgement that Europe will not be sovereign until it can act in the defence field, concern to avoid future destructive wars – are not part of the British debate and never have been. Likewise, the argument that integration (or at least closer co-operation) in the defence field is a natural consequence of other elements of the European construction is greeted with hostility and incomprehension, because the British do not really share the holistic concept of a Europe developing in all areas which is common on the Continent. As always, British pragmatism is only interested in the merits of specific proposals. Yet the clear recognition of national self-interest has always been a characteristic of the British. It is interesting, therefore, to look briefly at the origin and management of a half-century of British closeness to the United States in defence issues, since this shows how and why a close relationship, not previously envisaged, can develop quickly on the basis of a perceived change in national interest, which in turn led to a change in policy.

The defence relationship (not the same as the 'special relationship'), was not born out of a sudden conversion to American norms and values. Indeed, the decision-making classes were from the start, and still are, frequently infuriated and resentful of US behaviour in the defence area. As early as 1942, for example, the British were profoundly annoyed by Roosevelt's insistence that De Gaulle should not be informed of the landings in French North Africa until after they had taken place, but they were reluctant to challenge the Americans openly (Thomas 1979: 141). The relative openness of the American system, the Freedom of Information Act, affirmative action and the dispersed nature of political power in Washington have all caused exasperation in London, as have any number of episodes of American insensitivity and bad tactics. Moreover, those who crafted the defence relationship originally, and those who have attempted to preserve it, did not necessarily find many aspects of American life or culture attractive. And indeed, although the defence relationship with America was not necessarily a political liability (except for such instances as the 1985 bombing of Libya), neither was it particularly popular outside the elite which managed it. It was a policy of pragmatic self-interest for the good of the nation, not a policy of sympathetic identification.

There are also reasons to think that the subordinate relationship with America might not have been everyone's original first choice. There was certainly a period in 1947–8 when a European alternative appeared possible. In the view of Bevin and some of his officials, it might have been possible to construct a European grouping, led by Britain, which would be a 'Third Force', allied with the United States, but politically independent of it. These plans came to nothing, and, even now, it is unclear what real support they had, and how far they could have been implemented (Young 1993: 12–18). Yet British ideas had little or nothing to do with moves towards European integration: if anything, they represented its antithesis. The idea was to preserve Britain's great power status by harnessing Europe to it, from a position where, given French problems and German demilitarisation, there would be no challenge to Britain's preeminence. A European security order constructed along these lines would not have been integrated, and would have been entirely innocent of any of the motives for European co-operation which Monnet and his colleagues took to be self-evident.

It is likely that any closer relationship with Europe will develop in a way which is consistent with these experiences: therefore, a change of perceived interest and a consequent change in policy, not a change in ideological orientation. Obviously, there is no single preponderant state in Europe like the United States, and therefore the British role in Europe will not be that of a faithful ally of a large nation. Moreover, political, military and economic power has shifted since 1947–8 to the point where Britain can no longer hope to play the dominant role in any European defence organisation (although it will still be very important). But the objective will be the same: to maximise British influence in the world by skilful manoeuvring within decision-making structures. Assuming it remains true that defence and security issues of importance to the UK are increasingly treated in European fora, it will be as important for the UK to be present and influential where these decisions are made as it will be to retain a major role in NATO for decisions which are made there. The current Anglo-Saxon operating system is already breaking down, and Britain will want to play a role in creating a new operating system where British interests are preserved as far as possible.

To this extent, there are obvious similarities with the British attitude towards economic and monetary integration but there is one important way in which the defence argument is quite different. In defence, as in few other areas of European co-operation, there is a non-integrated option, where the provisions of the Treaty of Rome do not apply and the Commission is not involved. The scope of possible co-operation in the 'defence' area is very large: from the control of integrated military forces at one extreme, to the co-ordination of positions in multilateral negotiation at the other. Whereas a European army (should there ever be one), would imply an integrated structure to support it, there are many lesser options for defence co-ordination (as there are not for economic co-ordination, for example), which would involve co-operation rather than integration. Attempts to co-ordinate national positions on security issues, *ad hoc* despatch of peacekeeping forces, outline planning for possible European military operations to be conducted by states willing at the time – all of these are possible forms of European defence, which would be acceptable to the UK because they seem pragmatically sensible. (Some, indeed, like the WEU planning cell in Brussels are already established, with UK support.) They are not, of course, integration in any real sense of the term, both because of their *ad hoc* flavour and because, for the British at least, they are unrelated to any warmth towards the general principle of European integration. The British were among the most powerful advocates, in the Political Union negotiations and the concurrent discussions on the future of the WEU, of confining European defence co-operation to the WEU, and allowing the Union only to discuss security issues without an explicit defence dimension. (This attitude, which carried the day, was largely shared by the French, for somewhat different reasons.) By preventing the setting up of integrated structures, and thus privileging the three or four states whose voices really count in European defence discussions, it preserved for the UK the maximum influence possible, as well as keeping the grammar of European defence closer to one which the British find intellectually congenial.

Once again, this attitude is based on the perception of national interest, not on any vision of what the future of Europe should be. And, as they have been in the past, the British will be happy to engage in *ad hoc* co-operation where it is in their interest to do so. Effective co-operation in Europe really implies co-operation with the French, as the only other power with a wide spectrum of defence capabilities and a global reach. This co-operation is understood to be based on expediency and mutual benefit, not the sudden philosophical conversion of one side or the other. Nothing has yet been said in the UK which implies a conversion to – or even a sympathetic understanding of – the ideologies and motivations which drive French and other European ministers to propose closer defence co-operation. There has, therefore, been no change in underlying British strategy in recent years and only a modest change in tactics. Now that independent great power status is not on offer any more, the British will continue to aim for arrangements which give them the support of other nations when they need it, whilst retaining the maximum freedom of manoeuvre. They will prefer case-by-case co-operation to anything more formalised, and shun integrated structures unless these structures are organised according to principles the British find attractive. This implies both an increasing readiness to work in European fora and with Europeans, and a continued aversion to extending European integration to the defence area. It will be clear from the historical and cultural factors surveyed that – in British eyes at least – there is no contradiction between these two positions.

NOTES

1 In a prefatory poem to the memoirs of a famous Elizabethan traveller, Thomas Coryat (1611), cited by John Hale, *The Civilisation of Europe in the Renaissance*, London, HarperCollins, 1993, p. 6.

2 A very different tradition from that in most parts of Europe. In France under the Third Republic, for example, the 'professions', such as lawyers, doctors and teachers (but not bankers), were pillars of the militantly secular, and mildly left-wing, Radical party, and bitter enemies of the (anti-Republican) army. Career choices then involved stark political choices as well.

3 The British had recognised, even during the War itself, that something of the sort would be necessary. This thinking was summed up most clearly in Sir Orme

Sargeant's famous 'stocktaking paper' written in July 1945, in which he argued that, whilst Britain should have its own policy, London should also try 'to persuade the United States to make it *their own* as well'. The text is in *Documents on British Policy Overseas*, Series I, Vol. I, No. 102. The emphasis is in the original.

REFERENCES

Documents on British Foreign Policy 1919–1939 (DBFP), First Series, Vol. 15, No. 110, and Vol. 19, No. 10.
DBFP Vol. 3, No. 45
Thomas, R. T. (1979) *Britain and Vichy: The Dilemma of Anglo-French Relations, 1940–42*, London: Macmillan, p. 141.
Young, J. W. (1993) *Britain and European Unity, 1945–1992*, London: Macmillan.

7 Arms procurement

Trevor Taylor

INTRODUCTION

Arms procurement is a subject of particular interest to students of European integration since in the Treaty of Rome it was specified as an area of government activity exempt from Community competence. However, the reasoning associated in integration theory with the concept of spillover suggests that quarantining any area of government activity from Community influence would be difficult, and indeed this exemption of defence procurement was never straightforward. By the early 1990s it was becoming ever more difficult for governments to justify treating defence equipment differently from other goods. Economic and military considerations placed significant pressures on efforts to maintain defence procurement as an activity isolated from Community business.

Defence procurement is concerned with the purchase of goods and services for the armed forces and the defence ministry which oversees them. Some such goods and services have a clear military nature, for instance a new combat aircraft, while others involve civil goods also needed in the military sector, such as food, medicines and housing. An intermediate category comprises basically civil goods which are amended to a lesser or greater degree for military use. Many militarised trucks and computers fall into this category. Narrowly, defence procurement issues concern the rules and practices by which purchases are executed, including the purchasing agency. More broadly, however, defence procurement must pay attention to supply as well as to the demand side, that is to such questions as the structure and capabilities of the industry which provides the goods to be bought. In broad terms the member states have excluded the European Community/European Union from the demand side of specialised defence equipment, but the Commission has acquired some influence over the procurement rules of civil goods by defence ministries and over the structure and capabilities of industrial suppliers.

ARTICLE 223 AND ITS IMPLEMENTATION

The crucial article of the Treaty of Rome as far as procurement was concerned was 223, which reads as follows:

1. The provisions of this Treaty shall not preclude the application of the following rules:
   (a) No member shall be obliged to supply information the disclosure of which it considers contrary to the essential interests of its security;
   (b) Any member state may take such measures as it considers necessary for the protection of the essential interests of its security which are connected with the production or trade in arms, munitions and war material; such measures shall not adversely affect the conditions of competition in the common market regarding products which are not intended for specifically military purposes.
2. During the first year after the entry into force of this Treaty, the Council shall, acting unanimously, draw up a list of products to which the provisions of paragraph 1 (b) shall apply.
3. The Council may, acting unanimously on a proposal from the Commission, make changes in this list.

This article had a clear focus on defence equipment but was rather open ended in its implications. Thus paragraph one of the article has been used to justify the denial of the Commission's right to investigate the merger of purely defence companies.

Several reasons explain the inclusion of Article 223. When European integration through defence had been attempted through the European Defence Community (EDC) proposal in the early 1950s, the French 1954 veto of the EDC Treaty caused the effort to collapse. The lesson was that defence was too close to the core of sovereignty and so should be set aside from the Rome Treaty. There was also a sense that European security and defence were the prime responsibilities of NATO rather than any European body. Indeed, the amendment to the Western European Union Treaty in 1955 (which brought about the admission of Germany to the WEU and NATO) made clear that the WEU would be subservient to NATO: the WEU was not to duplicate tasks being performed in NATO. Finally, there was and is the consideration that there were areas of governmental activity where member states did not want to see the Commission having a role. Defence procurement was a leading candidate: governments wanted to be able to choose defence equipment without being restrained by the European Community. To a significant extent, this preference remains in place, but there is also a further consideration. Governments became aware that, if they had a single market in defence equipment in the EC/EU, they would also need a common arms export policy – to prevent EU governments with more relaxed arms export poli-cies from buying equipment from other EU states with tighter controls and then re-exporting with an appropriate price markup. Also, with a single market but without a common arms export policy, it would be likely in the long term that defence production would be concentrated by European defence firms in countries with the loosest policies for export beyond the Union.

In the early days of the European Community, implementation of Article 223 was facilitated by a 1958 agreement among member countries on a list of products to be covered by the article. Consensus on the list was facilitated by the involvement of the six states in a separate, non-Community body, the Co-ordinating Committee on Multilateral Export Controls (CoCom). The participants in Cocom in fact drew up three lists of goods whose export was to be controlled, with the aim of limiting the military strength of the Warsaw Treaty countries. These comprised the industrial list, covering dual-use goods, the international atomic energy list, covering nuclear equipment, and the munitions list, covering specialist defence goods and services. It was the last which bore a close resemblance to the Article 223 list.

The Article 223 list addressed the following headings, some in more detail than others:

portable and automatic firearms;
artillery, smoke, gas and flame-throwing weapons;
ammunition for such weapons;
bombs, torpedoes, rockets and guided missiles;
military fire-control equipment;
tanks and specialist fighting vehicles;
toxic or radioactive agents;
powders, explosives, and liquid or solid propellants;
warships and their specialist equipment;
aircraft or equipment for military use;
military electronic equipment;
camera equipment specially designed for military use;
other equipment and material (parachutes and parachute fabric, water purification plant specially designed for military use, and military command relay equipment); specialised parts and items of material included in this list insofar as they are of a military nature;
machines, equipment and items exclusively designed for the study, manufacture, testing and control of arms, munitions and apparatus of an exclusively military nature included in this list.

(Vredeling Report)

Significantly the Article 223 list steadily became devalued as no provision was made for its review or updating, and an increasing number of defence products became available which the list did not anticipate or cover in any detail. This gave national governments in the European Community growing leeway to interpret Article 223 as they saw fit. In principle – especially after the Single European Act of 1986 included water, transport, energy and telecommunications as areas where governments were expected to hold open competitions for contracts – ministries of defence in the EC were supposed to advertise their non-Article 223 needs and open up tenders to bids from throughout the Community. In practice, defence ministries remained free to decide for themselves which firms would compete for which of their contracts.

Although some consideration was given to abolishing Article 223, the Single European Act left it in place. Governments were keen on their freedom to control defence exports and place contracts with national suppliers. However, governments did indicate a desire to keep co-operative options open. In particular, Article Six (b) stressed the signatories' determination 'to maintain the technological and industrial conditions necessary for their security. They shall work to that end both at national level and, where appropriate, within the framework of the competent bodies' (*Single European Act* 1986).[1]

PRESSURES FOR OPEN COMPETITION

Long before the Act it was apparent that governmental insistence on keeping all aspects of defence procurement in national hands was causing severe problems.

First, because governments preferred their own national suppliers, they frequently had to pay more for their defence equipment. It was not just that in any given instance a national firm might be less competitive than a foreign company: structural problems also existed. With national firms producing mainly for national defence markets, research, development, production investment and other fixed costs had to be spread over a smaller number of units produced than if the output had been for the EC market as a whole.

Second, research efforts across Europe were being replicated unnecessarily because so many firms were involved in particular sectors. Some duplication would have been desirable to ensure competition, but in the Europe of the 1980s governments were often wasting money for the redevelopment of products which had already been worked on elsewhere in the Community.

On the supply side, preferential access to national markets did not encourage companies to pursue efficiency. Whilst the gains from export contracts beyond Europe were attractive and stimulated companies to keep their costs down, the winning of export contracts depended on many factors other than price and product quality: international political considerations as well as covert commission payments frequently played a role. Moreover, making companies dependent on export contracts for their survival scarcely encouraged arms export restraint. Rather, it promoted an attitude that anyone who could pay was an appropriate customer.

Not surprisingly, when defence contracts were not awarded to a national firm, they usually went instead to American companies enjoying the advantages of scale derived from their big domestic market. The intra-EC trade in arms remained small, while imports from the US were significant. The arms imported by the states of NATO Europe between 1979 and 1983 were worth $15.6 billion according to the US Arms Control and Disarmament Agency: $11.4 billion of this total (73 per cent) came from the US. The figures were even more striking for the major EC arms manufacturing states. The UK received 96 per cent of its $2.3 billion worth of arms imports and Germany 80 per cent of its $2.4 billion worth from the US. The situation in France was somewhat different, as it obtained just 51 per cent of its arms imports from the US, but since it imported only $350 million of arms in all, it had little impact on intra-European trade (US Arms Control and Disarmament Agency 1985: 132).

In short it was apparent that the lack of an open market in defence goods had significant negative effects in the EC, effects which were extensively covered in a 1986 report of industrialists commissioned by governments (Independent Study Team Report 1986).

COLLABORATION – AN ALTERNATIVE

In order to moderate the worst of these effects, governments strengthened their endorsement of collaborative arms projects. In such schemes, which first appeared in the late 1950s, governments generally agreed on a common requirement for a new piece of equipment, set up some joint agency to procure it, and awarded contracts for the development and production of the equipment to an *ad hoc* corporate entity linking several national firms. In the case of the *Tornado*, Britain, Germany and Italy agreed on a set of requirements for the new aircraft, established the NATO Multirole Aircraft Management Organisation (NAMMO) in Munich, and awarded contracts for development and production to Panavia, a consortium linking what are today British Aerospace, Daimler Benz Aerospace, and Alenia Aeronautica.

The economic virtues and weaknesses of collaboration have been extensively considered in academic and governmental literature.[2] The chief virtues are that it allows two or more states to share the development and other 'fixed' costs of a system rather than each having to fund a complete programme. In addition, production economies can be derived from supplying the joint demand of several armed forces: the demand of the three *Tornado* partners alone meant that over 800 aircraft could be built. Once a collaborative system is in service, the partners can also save money if they work together on logistics support (so that the ordering and storage of spares is a joint activity).

The weaknesses of collaboration stem mostly from the ease with which the virtues can be nullified. Organising development on a collaborative basis has to involve some delay and extra expense, if only the cost of international meetings. But the extra costs can become very significant if, for instance, one partner is given the lead on a part of a system where it has little expertise, or if important aspects of development are duplicated. For example, more Eurofighter prototypes are being built to develop the aircraft than would have been needed in a national programme, in order that all four partners can contribute to the flight test programme. Since governments and companies have also tended to see collaboration as a means of acquiring or maintaining system-wide expertise in areas where they cannot afford a national programme, collaborative developments have also been designed so that each partner acquires or retains a role in each element, even every sub-system and major component, in a project's development. In Eurofighter, there is not just a four-nation consortium to develop the engine, there is also a four-nation grouping for the undercarriage, the head-up display, and so on. At the production stage, there may be some unnecessary duplication to meet national demands. For instance, each of the three *Tornado* partners insisted on a final assembly line in their state (final assembly accounts for about 10 per cent of total aircraft production costs). Four production lines are still planned for Eurofighter although this number may yet be reduced to pull down costs.

A major problem in securing all the economic benefits of collaboration is that European partners have been unable to secure agreement to move away from the principle of *juste retour*, under which a country should carry out work on a project in proportion to its contribution to total costs. The traditional work-share/cost-share arrangement in a collaborative project is that, at the beginning, each partner indicates the size of its requirement for the piece of equipment. The partners then contribute to the costs in proportion to their share of the combined demand for the equipment. If a partner accounts for 40 per cent of the combined demand, it pays 40 per cent of the costs and is earmarked 40 per cent of development and production work, measured usually in manhours rather than value. The constraints of work-share arrangements invariably mean that some rather uncompetitive suppliers have to be awarded contracts, and expensive unnecessary multinational consortia formed for major components and sub-systems.

All in all, however, major European states have apparently concluded that collaboration, like democracy, constitutes a terrible system which is nonetheless better than the alternatives. When collaborative projects first began to be established from the late 1950s, governments often had to press reluctant national companies into accepting them. Increasingly, however, companies have recognised collaboration as a valued procurement route and have taken the lead in suggesting projects. Collaborative projects are proliferating in the 1990s, and have become prominent in both the naval area and aerospace. Britain, France and Italy are to develop the *Horizon* frigate whose air defence system will have some capability against missiles; Germany, the Netherlands and Spain are linked to the Trilateral Frigate Co-operation programme; Sweden, Denmark and Norway are working to establish a common submarine programme (part of a regional effort in northern Europe to increase procurement co-operation), and France, Belgium and Spain are to have a combined modernisation programme for their Tripartite minehunters which they developed and built together in the 1980s. In European aerospace, the Future Large Aircraft (FLA), which brings together France, Germany, Italy and probably the UK, is the largest emerging collaborative programme, although there are three collaborative helicopters in development (the Anglo–Italian EH.101, the Franco–German *Tiger*, and the Franco–German–Dutch–Italian *NH.90*) in addition to the Eurofighter combat aircraft.

From the perspective of European integration, a significant element has been that the US has not been a significant collaborative player. Its national defence market has been sufficiently large for economies of scale to be obtained for national projects and, even when collaboration has been tried, it has rarely been successful. This has been due to attitudinal problems among unenthusiastic US services, a reluctance on the part of Congress to give the long-term commitments needed, difficulties under US law about the transfer of technologies, and a refusal to entrust collaborative partners with the responsibility for re-export of US sub-systems. The consequence has been that, while many US systems have been sold to Europe and sometimes made under licence there (the *AV.8B* aircraft of the US and the UK and the US–Norwegian *Penguin* missile stand out as by far the most successful transatlantic collaborative efforts), collaboration has been largely a European matter. But, as the US defence budget comes under more pressure, this could change.

A further key characteristic of collaboration is that its implications for integration are limited. Almost all European military collaborative projects have been *ad hoc*. Although similar practices are used in many cases, each project has its own precise arrangements and nuances. A specific group of countries agree on a common requirement, and specific consortia of countries and companies emerge to develop and produce it. Intergovernmental arrangements dominate, with neither international management agencies nor multinational corporate arrangements developing much power or personality. In principle, a collaborative arrangement can lead to more lasting structures if follow-on projects can be set up among the same partners. This has happened in civil aerospace where a wide range of *Airbus* jet transports and *Ariane* launchers have

been developed over decades. In defence, however, such follow-on projects have been rare. The Euromissile consortium which developed and
produced the successful *Milan* and *HOT* anti-tank missiles along with the
Roland ground-to-air missile as its first generation projects, has taken
BAe on board. As Euromissile Dynamics, it is furthering the development
of the *Trigat* family of anti-tank weapons, but these have been slow to
progress and are not yet in production. Europe's most important follow-
on project by far is the Eurofighter consortium which has brought in
Construcciones Aeronauticas of Spain to the three companies and groups
which built the *Tornado*.

This is not to deny the political implications of a collaborative project.
These can be substantial since, in taking the collaborative route, a country
can be committing itself to two decades of working with another state or
states on what may be a key piece of equipment in its armed forces. The
emergence of projects such as the Anglo–French *Jaguar* in the 1960s and
the Multi role Combat Aircraft (which became *Tornado*) helped to tie
Britain to Europe in a tangible form before its membership of the European Community. However, at least until recently, collaboration by a
group of governments on one piece of equipment was not seen as obliging
them to co-operate on anything else in the future. The influence of the
pressures of 'spillover', under which co-operation in one field leads to
strong pressures to co-operate in others, was minimised in European co-
operative procurement by the stress on collaboration.

POST-COLD WAR PRESSURES

During the late 1970s and 1980s there was particular pressure on European governments to secure better value for money from their defence
spending so that conventional strength could carry a greater share of the
burden of deterring aggression by the Warsaw Pact states. Reliance on
the threat of early nuclear use became less acceptable in many states.
Since the Cold War ended, defence ministries have come under increased
financial pressure. Britain, which went furthest from the mid-1980s in
stressing the virtues of competition in procurement, maintained this
emphasis into the 1990s.

In broad terms co-operation in procurement offers the prospect that,
for a given budget, European governments will be able to operate larger
and better-equipped armed forces than would be possible if defence
development and production reverted to being a national undertaking. In
this regard, there are five specific issues which need to be addressed to
understand the conflicting pressures at work.

The first is that national projects become harder to justify the smaller
the number of weapons to be procured; since the late 1980s defence
budgets in Western Europe have been pushed down by a combination of
a reduced sense of threat, popular expectations of a peace dividend and

the need in a recession to cut public spending so as to reduce governmental budget deficits (as the national chapters in this volume make clear). Moreover, although the end of the Cold War made many governments review the sorts of equipment they would buy, in general there was no diminution in the technological sophistication demanded from military equipment by European governments. Like the US, Europeans were looking for technologically demanding systems which would collect and process massive amounts of information and deliver munitions accurately over hundreds of kilometres. By 1994, defence spending in NATO Europe was more than $70 billion a year less than might have been expected had the Cold War continued and defence been allocated the same share of GDP as during the Cold War.[3] In many states, particularly Germany, equipment spending was cut even more sharply than was defence spending overall.

With less money to spend, defence ministries feel under great pressure to use well what money they have. One option is to abandon national preference and to allow more or less global competition for major contracts. Britain is tempted to pursue this line and reluctant to endorse any principle of European preference. In such circumstances, UK companies are drawn to keep down their costs and prices as much as possible by incorporating off the shelf components and sub-systems, many of which are from overseas. The firm can then offer a 'British' bid which in reality has a significant foreign content. French companies, faced with louder demands from their government for lower prices, will be drawn down a similar route. Governments are often less worried about work-share in a national project than they are in a collaborative project.

Second, it would often be cheaper for European governments to buy their equipment from the United States, but for economic and strategic reasons they want to maintain significant defence industrial capabilities. Survival against American competition in European and world markets has become more difficult for European firms after the Cold War as US defence firms have restructured, consolidated and frequently enhanced their export efforts. The world demand for arms seems to have passed its peak and will not recover for some years (Grimmet 1994), and it is clear that US firms are winning the majority of orders (Kapstein 1994). In order to survive, European firms are under pressure to restructure and co-operate in ways not seriously contemplated during the Cold War. Arguably, they need to be able to achieve a significant scale of operations by being able to serve a single European market and to be able to structure themselves not in *ad hoc* collaborative consortia but as permanent transnational enterprises.

The rapid domination of European defence businesses by American firms remains an imminent possibility, especially if the Europeans do not restructure quickly. In 1995 US firms fought hard and successfully for important European contracts, such as the Dutch and British demand for an anti-tank helicopter and the British army's transport helicopter requirement. Lockheed will hope to sell more of its *C.1 3OJs* in and beyond Europe now that it has a small launch order for 25 aircraft from Britain. Although US firms are often ready to offer licensed production and extensive offset arrangements as part of their bids, European firms would lose the capacity to develop advanced new systems. Should the Eurofighter project collapse, it would be a major blow for industry in Europe and a massive boost for the US aerospace sector.

However, an uncompromising policy of European preference in defence procurement is unlikely to be compatible with a continued US commitment to Europe. Europeans have to buy US equipment when there is no European alternative so that, for instance, France is buying not only American *AWACs* but also *E.2C* airborne early warning aircraft (for the aircraft carrier *Charles de Gaulle*). Also they frequently have to take seriously, both on political and economic grounds, US bids for European requirements such as attack and transport helicopters. France would like to see an explicit policy of European preference adopted by EU states, but this is unlikely to be forthcoming from most governments: the Dutch–German–Spanish collaborative frigate will have American air-defence missiles, although France, Italy and the UK are working together on air defence for ships. In the longer term, Europeans would prefer collaboration between equals with the US but this is unlikely to occur while the obstacles which have hindered collaboration so far remain in place.

In addition to reduced defence budgets and increased American competition, a third factor affecting European procurement co-operation is the need for a common arms export policy given the European Union's aspiration to develop a common foreign and security policy and eventually a common defence. The Kuwait crisis, when the Western allies confronted an Iraq whose conventional and unconventional military potential owed much to European technology, highlighted the need for a common European approach and probably greater export restraint than had been the case in the past. As a consequence, a common policy on arms exports and non-proliferation was agreed early on as a desired element in a CFSP. That efforts to build such a common policy have not yet yielded great progress does not negate the consideration that a true CFSP must embrace arms exports. Also, there is the consideration that the need and potential of companies in Europe to export defence equipment will depend significantly on the co-operative arrangements for European procurement.

Fourth, the end of the Cold War has posed strategic questions for NATO governments about the role of their defence industries. It was obvious from the late 1980s that NATO would need smaller forces and a smaller industry to serve them. The European defence industry needed to be downsized and many cuts have already been introduced. None of the EU member states can afford to sustain comprehensive, modern, national defence industries. Reduced equipment budgets have served to highlight important questions for governments which go beyond unemployment considerations. Is a major threat to European security assumed to be gone forever, and if not what preparations need to be made in order that European states can restore their defence industrial output in the event of a major new threat to Europe emerging? In the US, government is increasingly drawn to the view that a strong 'civilian' industry is vital: from this, a defence industrial capacity for many goods could be reconstituted over a period of months and years as sources of hostility become clearer. Another question concerns the form of defence industry which needs to be maintained so that defence production and even weapons development can be made to surge in the event of a limited but serious crisis. On the last two occasions when British forces fought on any scale, the Falklands War and in the Gulf, they could do so only with industry making special efforts. European states, like the US, must decide whether they wish to maintain strict national autonomy, what provision if any they want to make for a surge production capability in some areas, how they are to address the reconstitution issue, and which states they are to accept as reliable suppliers in circumstances of crisis. Answers to all these issues will be reflected in individual procurement choices. Governments shape their defence industrial bases, not by edict, but by placing contracts.

Finally, there are developments in the civil sector to take into account, several of which predate the end of the Cold War. In particular, in the 1980s EC member states felt under pressure to enhance the competitiveness of their industries. Commercial and technological challenges from the US and Japan were clearly part of the motivation for the Single European Act of 1986 and other measures, such as the establishment and operation of EC research and development schemes such as ESPRIT (information technology) and BRITE/EURAM (industrial technologies and advanced materials) (Dinan 1994: 366–7). Given that technologies developed for the civil sector are increasingly of interest to the military and that the incidence of dual-use technology (and dual-use firms) is increasing, there are implications for the defence sector and procurement. For instance, insofar as the European Commission gained a veto over large mergers and acquisitions in the EC, it gained an influence over the possibilities for military competition in the EC since many firms have both a civil and a military character.

RECENT DEVELOPMENTS

In the light of these pressures and developments, governments have reluctantly sanctioned some degree of European integration in defence procurement. Because some defence ministry procurement involves products of a mainly civil character, and because many of Europe's 'defence' firms have extensive civilian interests, the EC/EU's concern with civil industry has given it some contact with defence. Some of the Commission's concerns with civil industry and technology have allowed it to exert an impact on the defence industrial sector. However, government wariness in this field has been great, and they have clearly restricted the extent to which defence procurement has gained an EU/EC dimension.

The Commission has been allowed to play four roles which have a direct or indirect impact on defence procurement. First, it administers the EU's framework scheme of research and development support, with at least some of the work involved having defence applications. The technological capacity of Western Europe's defence industrial base is to a small extent being shaped by European Union decisions.

Second, the Commission must give approval for major corporate mergers, even if they have a defence dimension. Interestingly, the UK government refused to allow the Commission to intervene in the competition between GEC and BAe to take over VSEL, arguing that it was a matter of UK security covered by Article 223. VSEL, however, is a rare example of a major company whose turnover is overwhelmingly in the defence area and which makes a highly sensitive product. The Commission was, however, given a chance to examine the planned merger of DASA and Thomson's armaments and missile propulsion businesses, which it approved.

The Commission has also been given some funds to alleviate unemployment in badly-hit areas, which has enabled it to get involved in some defence industrial conversion issues when failing defence firms or redundant military bases create employment in a region. Germany will get about 44 per cent of the EU's Ecu500 million Konver programme (*Jane's Defence Weekly* 11 February 1995).

Finally, the EU states agreed on a list of dual-use exports in the early 1990s and, after some investigation by the Commission, introduced a largely licence-free regime for such goods for trade within the Union in March 1995 (*Defense News* 9–15 January 1995, *Jane's Defence Weekly* 4 February 1995). While EU member governments have not wanted to give the Commission powers to investigate what sort of goods should be on the list, they have found it convenient to use the Commission as a body to examine the effectiveness of national export controls and to make quiet suggestions for their improvement. States with export control regimes of limited effectiveness seem to find it easier to take guidance from the Commission than from a fellow member state.

However, after a major argument in the mid-1980s concerning F-16 components, the Commission has not been allowed to require import duties to be imposed on either specialist defence or dual-use equipment which governments assert is for use in defence equipment; nor has the Commission been able to establish a standard practice for member governments regarding the imposition of value-added tax on defence equipment (Webb July 1989: 119–21; Taylor 1991: 144–9). The US objected to any tax on defence and the Commission withdrew its case. Moreover, governments remain free to fund the development of defence projects without external oversight. Given that many firms produce a range of civil and defence goods, this opens up the obvious possibility that governments can use defence payments to subsidise research and development in technological areas of considerable civil interest. Given that many firms, including nationalised or privately-owned companies, may issue only rather opaque accounts, there is also the possibility that defence funding will be abused in order to subsidise ailing civil elements in a civil and military goods firm. The Single European Act sought to control government subsidies for industry, but the EU has no control over payments to companies for defence work.

Thus the Commission's impact on defence procurement processes is real but not great. As noted above, the Single European Act and the Maastricht Treaty left in place Article 223 and the possibilities for its loose interpretation by national governments.

This does not mean that defence procurement has been left entirely in national hands. Governments instead have steered their co-operative efforts to bodies outside the EC/EU, especially the Western European Union. After the Maastricht Treaty, the WEU states incorporated the former Independent European Armaments Group into their organisation, so setting up the Western European Armaments Group. The Independent European Programme Group (IEPG) had been set up in 1976 by all the European NATO states except Iceland. It had sought to promote armaments co-operation but had had little success, particularly in its efforts to promote open competition. Under the IEPG, governments had become accustomed to discussing their future equipment procurement plans so that collaborative project possibilities could be identified at an early stage. But it had been more successful in identifying what would be helpful in the effort to gain value for money in defence procurement than it had been in actually securing changed procurement practice. Despite widespread recognition of the inefficiencies involved, a majority of EC/EU governments remained committed to the principle of *juste retour* in collaborative projects, and to restricting national competitions to preferred (usually national) suppliers. All European governments seemed to want at least balanced trade on their defence account and the so-called less developed defence industry states, such as Portugal and Greece, succeeded in having their calls for more defence work endorsed by the other states (Independent Study Team Report 1986).

In the WEAG, former IEPG members such as Norway and Turkey were treated as full members even though they were not full members of the WEU. In 1996 governments went further and established, as they had signalled at Maastricht they intended to do, a western European Armaments Agency. This Agency is to have a broad-ranging charter, which would mean governments could give it wide powers if they so chose. It is also to be responsible for some expenditure, namely the small Eureka programme launched in the mid-1980s after the US Strategic Defense Initiative. Eureka projects, however, were little concerned with ballistic missile defence. At the beginning at least, the Agency is to have few powers, being unable for instance to set down rules and practices for national procurement agencies, and its relationship with the Franco–German–Italian–British Armaments Organisation was also unclear. WEU governments were ready at most to set up an agency which, equipped with a broad charter, would have legal potential.

There were a range of functions which a European Armaments Agency could fill. Some opinion in the European Parliament apparently favoured the European procurement of all defence equipment on behalf of member states. This is simply not going to occur in the foreseeable future: despite the economies of scale which could be obtained, governments are not ready to concede such powers. However, a European Armaments Agency could generate and oversee binding agreements under which its members would agree to open up their national defence markets to WEU/WEAG-wide competition. The Commission has produced rules to address national government procurement in the civil sector, including the water, energy, transport and telecommunications sectors exposed to European competition by the Single European Act (Dinan 1994: 345–6; Webb July 1989: 114–15). The European Armaments Agency could adapt such rules for the defence sector.

Such an Agency, with a flexible structure, could fulfil procurement management functions with regard to collaborative development and production projects, having been given more power by participating governments than has in the past been given to bodies such as NAMMO, which managed the development and production of *Tornado*. More modestly, it could become the buying agency base for the logistic support of a range of collaborative projects. Most interestingly, it could serve as a buying agency for collectively operated WEU military goods: in the early 1990s the WEU states together set up an installation in Spain to train interpreters of satellite-generated data. This could serve as the first step in a collective WEU effort to establish space and groundbased facilities for global surveillance, early-warning and data processing.[4] A European Armaments Agency could act as the procuring body for a space effort. Other conceivable collective purchases, parallel to the *AWACs* fleet owned and operated by NATO, could cover an extended range airborne ground/battlefield surveillance system and/or an air transport fleet to facilitate WEU military interventions. In 1996, however, the Western European Armaments Agency was a body with only potential rather than actual rule-making or spending power.

Governments are well aware of the pressures for co-operation on them as regards defence procurement: an emphasis on national sovereignty and freedom of action leading to small-scale purchases is not an easy way to secure value for money and interoperable equipment. If a civilian single market makes sense in allowing governments to obtain good use of their resources and in stimulating improved performance by industry and business, there is no obvious reason why similar effects should not be felt also in the defence sector. Moreover it is hard to see how governments can expect to buy high technology goods from national firms when such technology is being developed often for the EU civil market as a whole by firms structured to serve that market. However, governments continue to resist the pressures formally to open up national defence markets in Europe and to deflect such pressures through collaborative arrangements burdened with *juste retour* restrictions.

In part this is because defence is seen intellectually as a rather fundamental element of sovereignty. But economic factors loom rather larger for most states when it comes to opening up defence markets. The countries which are most reluctant to open up their markets and to weaken the *juste retour* principle in collaboration are those which fear their industry may not compete successfully. Despite its position as the strongest civil industrial state in Europe, there are signs that the German government has such fears about its defence sector, especially in aerospace and electronics. Further co-operation in defence procurement would mean governments losing the ability to place defence contracts as a means of securing domestic employment, saving foreign exchange and boosting a country's technological capability. For some states and sectors, for instance Spanish and (increasingly) German aerospace, defence projects are seen as a way of strengthening national industry overall.

Even those countries which feel confident they can compete in a more open European arms market are wary, not least because they know it would mean a common arms export policy. There are states in the EU which favour rather more restrictive export policies than those operated currently by Britain and France, and the latter are understandably nervous that they might lose sales opportunities if other EU governments got a voice in their export policies. On exports, collaboration represents a satisfactory compromise, since collaborative projects tend to involve the practice that any partner may sell to any third state which it considers a reasonable and responsible customer.

Finally, there is the argument that, within the WEU and the EU, procurement co-operation must proceed at the pace of the slowest or most reluctant party since there is no provision for majority voting on the issue. This does not mean that co-operation cannot be attempted outside the institutions: after an initiative by the former British Chief of Defence Procurement, Peter Levene, Britain and France have had a rather lukewarm commitment for some years to open up their smaller defence contracts to companies in either country, and Germany, France,

Italy and the UK have set up a Joint Armaments Cooperation Organisation, in part to reduce the impact of *juste retour*.

A possibility over the next few years is that the demand side of defence
procurement will remain in only loosely-co-ordinated national hands but
that the supply side will be transformed: transnational mergers and joint
ventures may accelerate in Europe among high technology companies as
they seek to obtain efficiencies of scale and improved market access in
both civil and military fields. Siemens' partial acquisition of Plessey in the
UK in the late 1980s, though motivated mainly by Plessey's civil telecommunications business, made Siemens a major defence supplier in Britain.
By the mid-1990s, permanent transnational joint ventures were increasing
in Europe, with governments giving at least implicit blessing to such
important changes as DASA and Aerospatiale merging their helicopter
businesses into Eurocopter; GEC and Matra merging their civil and military space businesses as well as taking over BAe's space business; BAe
and Matra are to merge their missile businesses; GEC and Thomson-CSF
have put their sonar business into a joint venture; BAe and Giat intending
to merge their ammunition businesses; Pilkingtons is putting its defence
optics business into a joint venture with Thomson-CSF; and Thomson-
CSF and DASA may merge their armaments and missile propulsion
businesses into two joint ventures. The development of the defence multinational is proceeding, with Thomson-CSF having led the way with major
purchases from Philips in the Netherlands and the UK (Taylor 1990;
Brzoska and Lock 1992). A remarkable blend of transnational company
and collaboration occurred in the case of the *NH.90* helicopter, a collaborative project involving Germany, France, Italy and the Netherlands. By
1995, as the helicopter moved towards the end of development, the
responsible companies were Agusta (of Italy), Fokker (of the Netherlands
but taken over by DASA of Germany), and Eurocopter (the joint-venture
helicopter business of Aerospatiale of France and DASA of Germany).
Four governments were essentially dealing with two companies
(Eurocopter and Agusta). Governments clearly have to give permission
for these mergers and the defence dependencies they create. Governments
are increasingly if reluctantly realising the need for the 'Europeanisation'
of national businesses in many defence areas,[5] but they often shrink from
directing the precise linkages required: companies appear better placed
to make the appropriate technological and commercial judgements.

Such changes could have several implications for defence procurement.
First, governments would find themselves with a smaller number of hopefully more effective defence suppliers in Europe. Second, companies could
direct their restructuring, bearing in mind either or both of two criteria:
the impact of a merger or acquisition on market access or on overall
competitiveness. Conceivably, the defence industry could be restructured
in Europe so that governments could award contracts largely on the basis
of competition or other commercial criteria, and so that governments

kept a balance of trade on their defence account. It seems unlikely that this could be achieved by a process of national industrial specialisation. Instead multinational corporations would be required with research and development and production facilities operating across the EU. This, however, would mean the end of the national champion concept supported by governments over the past 30 years or so, and would make national controls on defence industries difficult. It would press governments to change their security clearance arrangements so that the free movement of labour within defence companies would be possible: countries would need to accept the security clearances of EU partners which currently they do not always do. Like civil enterprises, the emergence of genuinely European defence businesses would be facilitated by agreement on provision in law for a European company. As noted, there would also be a need for a common arms export policy.

The serious political and governmental control implications of the multinationalisation process in the defence area help to slow its progress in Europe. However, there are other obstacles. Many defence firms in Spain, France and Italy are state-owned, which makes their acquisition by a foreign firm impossible (although joint ventures are feasible). Many of these state-owned firms in the mid-1990s were also making large losses, as was DASA of Germany, which reduced their appeal as partners. Finally, there are sometimes domestic lobbies which are particularly anxious to protect jobs: French trade unions are notable for opposing defence industry restructuring because of the clear employment implications.

On balance, in 1996 it appeared that the restructuring of European defence businesses was proceeding more slowly than in the US and that European firms would often be overtaken by American competitors. While the Lockheed takeover of Marietta took only a few months, the merger of Matra's missile business with that of BAe has taken years to arrange.

A MODEST WAY FORWARD

This chapter concludes with some assertions, implied or noted earlier, about how governments might change their procurement practices in order to secure better value for money from their defence spending, but without sacrificing all national freedom of choice.

Most obviously, governments could moderate the *juste retour* principle so that more contracts within collaborative projects could be awarded according to competitive and commercial criteria. If governments were to agree to accept that their national companies might win only a reduced proportion, say 80 per cent, of the work which their share of orders of the finished product might suggest, many inefficient suppliers in collaborative arrangements could probably be excluded.

Second, governments could review the 1959 list of goods covered by

Article 223 of the Treaty of Rome. In connection with the effort to produce a common arms export policy, EU governments have already agreed on a list of goods to be considered as arms in connection with an arms embargo. They could agree to use that list, regularly updated, as the basis for exemption from single market regulations. In other words, governments would be obliged to open up their defence ministry needs to Union-wide competition for all goods save those defined as arms in an arms embargo policy. This would standardise and narrow the area where Article 223 distorted competition.

Third, the full members of the WEU should discuss cost-sharing principles which could be applied to any collectively procured equipment for joint use. They could either confirm that the principles behind the financing of the Torrejon satellite data interpretation centre are acceptable, or they could modify them. Associate and observer WEU members should not be asked to contribute to the procurement of such systems which, as noted, could cover such items as space-based reconnaissance and early warning assets, but full members should. Presently the European effort in space is being led by France, which has put up one *Spot* satellite and is now seeking collaborative support for its *Helios* programme. Italy and Spain have expressed varying degrees of interest and Germany may contribute something to *Helios* if it gets the lead on a collaborative radar satellite. The problem with this approach is that most of the smaller EU states will be contributing nothing and yet would expect use of the data from satellites in the event of crisis, while Britain will continue to rely on US information. Acting collectively and pooling their funding, WEU states could be expected to be able to procure a much more comprehensive space-based capability than would be the case if they proceeded in the *ad hoc* way which has dominated to date.

Fourth, governments could reduce the barriers to the development of multinational defence companies within Europe by privatising state-owned defence firms, changing personnel security clearance arrangements, advancing European company law, putting more effort into a common EU arms export policy, and so on. Such companies could acquire the flexibility to allocate defence development and production work on the basis of commercial, effective defence and balance of trade considerations. When Thomson-CSF took over Philips' naval radar business, despite having a radar business of its own in France, Thomson made the Netherlands the base for its activities in this area. Governments cannot direct work-shares and hope for cost-effective supply. Competing transnational companies could prove to be satisfactory suppliers, but would need to keep their political antennae constantly tuned to ensure that all states felt they generated a reasonable amount of employment and technological benefit in exchange for their defence spending.

The equipment and the sums involved in defence procurement mean it has a high political profile and European governments in the next decade will have a tricky series of ambitions to reconcile. They will want to sustain the European defence industry without paying an enormous premium for their equipment compared with buying it from the US. Ideally, they would like to strengthen European businesses so that they can compete effectively with US industry in world markets, while collaborating with American firms in expensive high technology areas, most notably ballistic missile defence, where the US, France and Germany are struggling to establish the MEADS programme and Britain is considering its position. They will need to avoid procuring equipment in such a protectionist manner that the US government takes offence because its firms are excluded. If, as the former British Defence Secretary, Malcolm Rifkind, preferred, there is increased emphasis on a broad-ranging Atlantic community as a foundation for NATO, transatlantic defence industry co-operation in the form of trade and/or collaboration will of necessity be part of that community. Europeans need to press ahead with co-operation in their national procurement programmes and practices so that they will be prepared for challenges and opportunities across the Atlantic.

NOTES

1 See also the provisions of Title VI of the Treaty.
2 See, for instance, *Vredeling Report*, Hartley 1983; Taylor 1982: 48–59; Draper 1990; Webb July 1989: 17–22; Taylor 1987; and Steer 1987: 143–86.
3 The $70 billion was calculated by the author using NATO data on the average share of GDP going to defence in the 1985–9 period and NATO Europe's GDP in 1993. Actual 1993 defence spending was subtracted from this hypothetical 'Cold War' defence budget.
4 *Defense News*, 21–7 November 1994 reports French views on a basic satellite network costing $6.6 billion and a full network costing $15.2 billion, comprising two optical satellites, two radar satellites and a data relay satellite.
5 See for instance Henri Conze's views (*Defense News* 3–9 October 1994; *Jane's Defence Weekly* 21 January 1995); UK procurement minister Roger Freeman reported in *Defense News* 19–25 December 1995; and Dutch National Armaments Director Jan Fledderus' views in *Jane's Defence Weekly* 19 November 1994.

REFERENCES

Brzoska, M. and Lock, P. (1992) *Restructuring of Arms Production in Western Europe*, Oxford: Oxford University Press for SIPRI.
Dinan, D. (1994) *Ever Closer Union: An introduction to the European Community*, Boulder, CO: Lynne Rienner.
Draper, A. G. (1990) *European Defence Equipment Collaboration: Britain's involvement 1957–87* London: Macmillan.
Grimmett, R. (July 1994) *Conventional Arms Transfers to the Third World, 1986–93*, Washington DC: Congressional Research Service, Library of Congress.
Hartley, K. (1983) *NATO Arms Collaboration* London: Allen & Unwin.
Independent Study Team Report (December 1986) *Towards a Stronger Europe*,

2, Enclosure 7, Annex A, Brussels: the Independent European Programme Group.

Kapstein, E. (1994) *Foreign Affairs* 30.

Single European Act (1986) Official Publications of the European Communities: Luxembourg.

Steer, M. C. (1987) 'The industrial implications of collaboration in defence', in Royal United Service Institute and Brassey's, *Defence Yearbook 1987*, London: Brassey's.

Taylor, T. (1982) *Defence, Technology and International Integration*, London: Pinter.

—— (1987) 'European arms co-operation: competition for resources' in Royal United Service Institute and Brassey's, *Defence Yearbook 1987*, London: Brassey's.

—— (1990) 'Defence industries in international relations', *Review of International Studies*, 16, 1, January.

—— (1991) 'Procurement in European Defence', *Utilities Policy*, 1, 2: 144–49.

US Arms Control and Disarmament Agency (1985) *World Military Expenditures and Arms Transfers*, Washington DC: USGPO.

Vredeling Report see Independent Study Team Report (December 1986) *Towards a Stronger Europe*, 2, Enclosure 7, Annex A, Brussels: the Independent European Programme Group.

Webb, S. (July 1989) *NATO and 1992: Defense Acquisition and Free Markets* Santa Monica, CA: Rand.

8 Nuclear issues

Stuart Croft

INTRODUCTION

The end of the Cold War led West Europeans to focus on political and economic integration, including foreign and defence policy. Many concrete steps have been taken, such as the formation of the common foreign and security policy and of the Eurocorps. However, one area which has not been drawn fully into this europeanisation of Western European security has been nuclear deterrence. Rather like the debates over the future of a common currency, nuclear forces have seemed to be at the heart of the debate over sovereignty. Yet, unlike debates over currencies, there have been no concrete proposals for the creation of a common nuclear deterrent.[1]

The first part of this chapter highlights the (mainly French) debate that has occurred over the europeanisation of nuclear deterrence and examines the various pressures that have led Paris to speak in these terms. The second examines four parameters limiting the development of a European nuclear identity: the relationship between the debate over a European nuclear identity and Atlantic security structures; issues related to national sovereignty; institutional impediments which exist at the European level; and, finally, problems concerning the deployment of European nuclear forces.

These parameters help to explain why the debate over the development of a European nuclear identity has been so limited. However, it would be a mistake to present a static picture of this debate and to argue that these parameters cannot change. The second half of the chapter will examine the flexibility of these parameters. It is not the case, for example, that in the nuclear field there has been no integration. West Europeans – including many of the non-nuclear states – have had a wide experience of nuclear collaboration in the NATO context. Even France, which has not been in the NATO integrated military command since the late 1960s, has experienced nuclear co-operation. Moreover, since the early 1990s there has been a programme of Franco–British nuclear co-operation. Thus, there is a habit of nuclear collaboration within Western Europe, and a practical basis for nuclear co-operation between Western Europe's two nuclear powers. The chapter will suggest that, given broad political will, there are solutions to many of the problems identified in the first section and, given the incentives for nuclear co-operation, there may be scope for further developments.

THE DEBATE OVER, AND PRESSURE FOR, EUROPEANISATION

There has been, in recent years, some debate over the Europeanisation of nuclear deterrence. Discussions were prompted by Jacques Delors, President of the European Commission, in January 1992. He argued that the EC should develop its own defence policy and that French nuclear forces should provide the nuclear deterrent capability. Some days later, President Mitterrand proposed the development of a common European nuclear doctrine. In October 1992, the French Prime Minister, Pierre Bérégovoy, argued that Britain and France should co-ordinate their nuclear policies as a step towards creating a European deterrent (*The Independent* 2 October 1992). In January 1995, Alain Juppé proposed a concerted deterrent for France and its allies, an idea endorsed by Jacques Chirac on 16 March. Chirac declared in September 1995: 'As a part of the construction of its defence, the European Union might want the French deterrent to play a role in its security. . . .'[2] Most explicitly, Juppé argued that

> Admittedly France has its own responsibilities. . . . But its action is consistent with a vaster prospect. . . . [D]oes or doesn't Europe want to exist as such? If it does, it must acquire a defence capability of its own. . . . [T]he future European defence will not be built without, in some way or other, the French – and British – deterrent playing a role in it.
>
> (Juppé 1995: 186)

Why should there be so much interest, in France at least, in the idea of Europeanising nuclear forces? There are three pressures for such developments. First, the costs of nuclear forces are such that there are inevitably savings to be made in collaborative ventures. However, with the announcement that the British would use the *Trident* system in a sub-strategic role, concrete collaboration has been put off for decades. Second, it may be that national nuclear forces are losing legitimacy, and that a Europeanised nuclear force would receive wider support. Certainly this could be seen as a British interpretation of French ideas about concerted deterrence. Ian Black of *The Guardian* reported that 'officials in London believe the French idea is mainly intended to deflect international condemnation of the Mururoa nuclear tests' (Black 1995). However, for countries such as Sweden and Finland the problem is not national nuclear forces, but nuclear weapons themselves. As the Swedish Foreign Minister, Lena Hjelm-Wallen, noted, nuclear europeanisation is 'an awful idea. . . . We've been seeking a nuclear-free Europe for thirty-five to forty years'.

The third pressure is that of the construction of Europe. Can the European Union develop its common foreign and security policy, and ultimately a common defence, without a common nuclear deterrent? For many in France, the answer is clearly no. The issue is not one that can be postponed to the longer term. As the European Union widens, so more states are eligible to join the Western European Union as full members and, as a consequence, these states receive a full security guarantee from other WEU members. But how credible is such a guarantee without a nuclear deterrent – unless the expansion of the EU is to be fully dependent upon the enlargement of NATO?

THE DEVELOPMENT OF A EUROPEAN NUCLEAR IDENTITY: CONSTRAINTS

The prevalence of Atlanticism

Perhaps above all else, the prevalence of the Atlanticist security concept limits the development of the European nuclear identity. During the Cold War, it was, above all, the American nuclear guarantee of the security of Western Europe that was at the heart of NATO and concepts of Western European security. Beyond the Cold War, there is less dependence upon the American nuclear guarantee. However, many are loath to give it up and fear that the creation of European alternatives would hasten that strategic decoupling. In the view of Atlanticist governments, such as the British, and in the view of Atlanticists in governments in Germany, the Netherlands, Italy and elsewhere, nothing should be done to damage the American guarantee, given that the West Europeans would not be able to replace that guarantee with anything comparable.

In addition to this, Atlanticists would argue that for the West Europeans to enter into a new nuclear debate would be to raise the political prominence of nuclear weapons. This would occur at a time when NATO policy has been to de-emphasise the utility of such weapons, partly in order to carry through disarmament measures in the former Soviet states, and partly to isolate rogue nuclear states such as North Korea. Even within the EU, such a debate might enhance national rivalry, rather than integrationist pressures, perhaps particularly between France and Germany. Possession of nuclear weapons has been an area of French superiority over Germany and at times a source of Franco–German tension (Schmidt 1993). It is not clear that there can be a new nuclear debate in Western Europe which does not suffer from this legacy. Finally, initiating such a debate in Western Europe might worsen the EU's relations with its neighbours to the East – Russia and Ukraine – as well as to the South in North Africa and the Middle East. After all, at whom would political leaders in those countries believe that a European deterrent would be aimed?

For the Atlanticists, then, conservatism in defence matters in general, and in nuclear matters in particular, must be the order of the day. As long as the Atlanticist approach to security remains strong, therefore, there will be a sharp brake on the development of a common European nuclear policy. Whereas there may be scope for the development of common European policies in relation to conventional forces outside the NATO context, in order to allow Europeans independent options and theoretically to reinforce NATO itself, such opportunities do not exist in the nuclear domain, for the American nuclear guarantee is at the heart of the NATO Alliance.

Challenges of sovereignty and status

One of the impediments to the creation of a common European nuclear policy most often mentioned is the threat to the status, and the challenge to the sovereignty, of the British and French. For political leaders of the only EU member states in possession of indigenous nuclear forces, state autonomy in the nuclear field has been paramount. Indeed, this view has been closely associated with the two loudest pro-nuclear leaders of those countries: Margaret Thatcher and Charles de Gaulle. Both Britain and France sought to develop independent nuclear forces in order to be able to guarantee, ultimately, their own security.

The development and maintenance of these forces was costly in both political and economic terms. Politically, the British Conservative government spent much of the early 1980s fighting an at times desperate political battle against anti-nuclear groups in Britain (Croft 1994: 228–42); while Franco–German relations were notably weakened during the 1980s by German concern over the possible deployment of the *Hades* missile – a system which, if deployed, was capable only of landing on German soil (Schlor 1993: 25–7). Both states have invested heavily in their nuclear arsenals, both financially and politically. In financial terms in 1990, Britain spent 7 per cent of its defence budget on strategic nuclear forces, while France spent 23 per cent of its defence budget on its strategic and pre-strategic forces (Boyer 1992: 117).

Despite such costs to governments in Britain and France, however, their independent deterrents have seemed to offer great advantages in both security and psychological terms. They ensured that Britain, if it ever had to stand alone again as in 1940, would have a weapon of enormous power. The French bomb spawned the belief that it could prevent a recurrence of the collapse and national humiliation of 1940. For Prime Minister Macmillan, the British bomb made the United Kingdom a great power; for Prime Minister Douglas-Home, it gave Britain a ticket of admission to the top table (Pierre 1972: 178). For de Gaulle France, as a great power, had to possess nuclear weapons in order to command its own destiny (Freedman 1989: 313). The West European nuclear arsenals were so important that London and Paris sought to ensure that their forces were excluded from Soviet–American, and then Russian–American, arms control and disarmament negotiations and agreements during the 1970s, 1980s and 1990s.

To place their national deterrents in a common European framework would, therefore, be to reverse fifty years of Franco–British history. Further, would it not strengthen arguments for the abolition of the British and French permanent seats on the United Nations Security Council in favour of an EU seat? Moreover, the creation of a common European nuclear policy would, arguably more than in any other area of European integration, asymmetrically affect the roles of the members of the EU and/or WEU. For in effect, two states would be pooling their sovereignty in this area, whereas the others would have nothing to contribute. At least with monetary union each state has to give up its own currency.

Institutional limitations

The development of a common European nuclear policy also poses institutional problems. What body would control such a nuclear force? Which institution would define nuclear strategy and doctrine? Who, centrally, would have the responsibility for launching European nuclear weapons? Unless or until the broader institutional pattern of the union of Europe becomes clearer, integrated nuclear forces seem to have no supra-national home.

In the post-Maastricht period, there is still no coherent decision-making structure within the European Union – or, indeed, the WEU – for the management of any nuclear deterrent strategy. Who would be the ultimate political authority, with the power, credibility and legitimacy to make nuclear threats, even if retaliatory ones? Following on from this, there is no structure that could define the common European Union strategy, including doctrine. There may even be difficulty with much less grandiose developments, such as a European Union system for politico–military consultation on decisions concerning the use of French and British nuclear systems, as called for by, amongst others, Roberto Zadra, and François Fillon, who suggested the formation of a European nuclear consultation group (Zadra 1992: 48). Although such a development may not face any conceptual difficulties, it may not be popular in Britain and France. In the United Kingdom, any such development will attract the opposition of the so-called 'Eurosceptics'. In France, despite a good deal of pressure from Germany, no French government has yet been able explicitly to accept that its core defence area should be extended beyond the homeland.

These problems are exacerbated by the reliance of the EU on the WEU as, in response to Article J.4 of the Maastricht Treaty, the member states of the WEU declared that 'the Union requests the Western European Union (WEU), which is an integral part of the development of the Union, to elaborate and implement decisions and actions of the Union which have defence implications.'[3] However, there is a problem with the WEU taking the lead in the nuclear field. Not all the members of the European Union are members of the WEU. This applies currently to Denmark, Ireland, Austria, Finland and Sweden.[4] Thus, one-third of the members of the European Union would not be covered by the WEU's nuclear deterrence policy. In addition, the WEU has an associate member status, conferring full rights, which would mean that non-European Union members such as Turkey, Iceland and Norway would be covered by the West European Union's nuclear deterrence policy.

Thus, the construction of Europe has not reached a point where either a legitimate authority to control nuclear launch or the detailed military planning required for a nuclear deterrent policy has been developed.

Deployment of a European deterrent force

The problems related to structure overlap into problems of deployment. For the EU to develop a common nuclear policy which, ultimately, would include doctrine and strategy, there would have to be a discussion about the necessity of deploying EU nuclear forces throughout the EU. Several problems emerge. First, in terms of membership, if the common nuclear policy is based on the WEU, the policy would be flawed by membership problems. Second, for states such as Germany and the Netherlands, where arguments over nuclear weapons were deep and bitter in the early and mid-1980s, any debate now over nuclear weapons being deployed on their territories would surely reopen old political wounds (Schmidt 1993: 48–9). Third, an EU nuclear policy that would replicate and replace that of NATO would also lead to a debate on the development of a range of new nuclear forces to allow for greater flexibility. Would that be desirable or affordable? And yet without greater flexibility, would the EU deterrent be credible in, say, Greece?

Overall, then, it can be seen that these four categories of problems set very clear parameters upon the debate over the creation of a common nuclear policy in Europe, as suggested by Mitterrand, Juppé and Chirac. However, the following section will suggest that in this area, as in so many other areas of European security since 1989, these constraints may not be as fixed as they might at first appear.

THE DEVELOPMENT OF A EUROPEAN NUCLEAR IDENTITY: POSSIBILITIES

All observers of European security have been surprised by the speed at which the previously rigid parameters of the European security debate altered: the collapse of the Warsaw Pact, Soviet Union and Yugoslavia; the unification of Germany; and the movement towards a common European defence policy as demonstrated by Maastricht and, more significantly, by the January 1994 NATO summit at Brussels were all indicative of the profound transformation underway. The four parameters identified may, therefore, be subject to movement over the years ahead.

Certainly this is true with the first: the strength of Atlanticism. The commitment to Atlanticism emphasises the essence of the transatlantic commitment – the American nuclear guarantee. Any move from Atlanticism in Europe must, at the core, question this guarantee and reinforce those in the United States Congress who are not supportive of the Atlanticist ideal. However, it may be argued that this is to put the issue the wrong way around. Many French observers suggest that the creation of a common European nuclear policy would not drive the Americans out of Europe, in the sense that the United States is already withdrawing (Boyer 1992: 117). Shifting American positions on Bosnia and on the expansion of NATO illustrate, first, that Europe is not at the heart of US foreign policy in the way that it once was and, second, that the key to US foreign policy is not fidelity to its old West European cousins but support of its new Russian friends. As the new direction of US policy becomes clearer, and as the United States and the European Union grow further apart on trade and other economic issues, West Europeans may face the natural termination of Atlanticism. In such circumstances, the development of a common nuclear policy becomes, itself, a natural development.

These comments must, of course, be kept in perspective. The end of NATO has been predicted many times before. In the early 1950s, as the NATO members failed to reach the Lisbon force goals and as West Europeans balked at the idea of West German rearmament, the Americans threatened the 'agonizing reappraisal' of the US role in Europe. In the 1960s, French dissatisfaction with the role of the US and with NATO strategy led to France's withdrawal from the integrated military structure. In the 1970s, arguments over the US use of bases in Europe during the 1973 Middle East war, and President Carter's unwillingness – from a European point of view – to lead the Alliance over the neutron bomb issue suggested that there were serious problems for the transatlantic alliance. And these problems seemed to return in the 1980s, with President Reagan's swing from confrontation to condominium with the Soviet Union – from the Strategic Defence Initiative to the INF Treaty – without consultation with the Europeans. At each of these points, observers argued that Atlanticism was in decline.

The new element in the transatlantic relationship of the 1990s and beyond is, of course, the absence of a common threat to bind the two sides of the Atlantic together. It is not suggested here that the US commitment to Western Europe will collapse; only that the limitation that Atlanticism places on the development of the common nuclear policy might not be as rigid as first appears.

If one may question the strength of Atlanticism as a long-term block on the development of a common nuclear policy, surely the same cannot be said for the second parameter – British and French concern with the status that comes with nuclear possession, and the loss of sovereignty implied in the pooling of such weapons at a European level? To many, this may seem strange. After all, nuclear weapons threaten to overwhelm far more than sovereignty if ever used. However, the power of nuclear symbolism means that this constraint seems to be a great deal more rigid than the Atlanticist one. In both states, possession of independent nuclear forces offers a good deal more than simply security. The British and French nuclear forces are part of the political psyche. How could this be surrendered? Indeed, in discussions in France about the development of a common nuclear policy, it is interesting to note that one common assumption is that ultimate decisions – when to use the weapons, and against whom – would remain in Paris.

Yet perhaps this French assumption points out one of the problems in the debate over European versus national decision making in the nuclear field. Most non-French analysts might assume that a common nuclear policy would imply common decisions taken at an EU–Brussels level. But perhaps there is a hybrid position, in which doctrine, deployment and development become European issues, but actual decisions over actual use are left in London and Paris. Would such a compromise be acceptable to anyone? This would depend, probably, on the strength of the American commitment. Thus, if the first parameter weakens so, too, might the second.

The third limitation focuses on institutional developments, and follows on from the compromise set out above. A fully integrated common nuclear policy would be defined from Brussels; yet, there are no adequate European defence institutions which could deal with the problems defining doctrine, training forces, developing concepts, or possessing the legitimacy for entering the nuclear arena. As already seen, the WEU suffers from a confused membership and a lack of experience in the nuclear field. Yet again, this limitation might not be as serious as would first appear, particularly if some compromise – the hybrid solution – is deemed to be acceptable. The latter places the emphasis on collaboration rather than immediate integration. And it could be based on the habits of co-operation developed within NATO, for only one European NATO member (Denmark) would be excluded from the full and associate member status within the WEU.

The fourth and final constraint concerned the problems of deployment associated with any European nuclear deterrent force.[5] Whereas many NATO members were prepared to accept the deployment of American nuclear forces during the Cold War, would many EU members be prepared to allow British and French forces to be deployed on their territory after the collapse of the Soviet Union? Yet, perhaps, this also is setting the standard of a common European nuclear policy too high. Are such deployments necessary? Can the common nuclear policy not be based on an existentialist notion of nuclear deterrence?

Under such a concept, possession of nuclear weapons by two members of the European Union would create a psychology of deterrence in the minds of potential adversaries who would believe that, for example, a nuclear attack on Germany would be interpreted as a nuclear attack on Britain and France. Jean-Pierre Chevènement has already suggested that 'it is not necessary for the radius of action of France's deterrence to be declaratively extended to the territory of the FRG to apply there *de facto*, according to the concept of "vital interests".'[6] Any putative rival would realise that the fate of any of the members of the Union would be deeply intertwined with the future of the nuclear powers, to the extent that there would always be enough doubt in the mind of any aggressor that the British and/or French would respond in kind. Could any putative extremist leadership in Algeria really believe it could threaten Rome with nuclear weapons without fearing a British and/or French response?

Of course, there would be problems with such an approach. The financial costs would fall disproportionately on the British and French, although it is apparent that both states would, in any case, continue to invest to maintain their nuclear arsenals. The common nuclear policy would not be fully integrated, which would represent one of the major disadvantages for those who wish to construct 'Europe'. It might place limits on future expansion of the European Union (or encourage the development of a multi-speed Europe). While Germany, Italy, and the Netherlands, for example, might be deeply intertwined with France and Britain economically and politically and, thereby, be clearly within the area of extended existentialism, would the same be true of new members?

Thus, it would seem that the limitations placed on the development of a common European nuclear policy are not necessarily fixed. Much depends on what is actually meant by a common European nuclear policy. In circumstances in which the American nuclear guarantee was widely questioned, and in which Atlanticism had lost credibility, it is possible that such a common policy might develop. Were that policy to stress commonality in terms of jointly defined strategy and doctrine, based on final decisions being taken in London and Paris, and in which existentialism was the order of the day, it is difficult to see the other parameters impeding the development of a common policy.

All of this, however, would be premised upon a willingness amongst the Europeans (and particularly amongst the British and French) to co-operate. In the nuclear field which, in the case of Western Europe, has been dominated for fifty years by the United States, this might not seem likely. Yet through the NATO nuclear planning group, habits of nuclear co-operation have developed amongst the West Europeans, many of whom have also had nuclear forces deployed on their territory. Even though the French have been outside NATO's integrated military command since the middle of the 1960s – and therefore outside the nuclear planning group – they have collaborated with the United States at a variety of levels on nuclear matters (Ullman 1989: 3–33). Equally if not more significantly, the nature of Franco–British nuclear co-operation over the past five years has provided a basis for future, and deeper, collaboration.

These contacts were initiated in early 1987 with contacts between the two ministries of defence, and led to a meeting in April 1990 between the British defence secretary, Tom King, and the French Defence Minister, Jean-Pierre Chevènement, to discuss general collaboration, including in the nuclear field (Browning 1990). In May, Prime Minister Thatcher and President Mitterrand announced that they would examine collaboration over nuclear issues. The immediate issue concerned Britain's decision over the purchase of an air-launched nuclear missile. There were American and French alternatives and a decision had been promised at the end of 1990. The French, through the president, Defence Secretary Chevènement and Prime Minister Rocard, made several direct appeals to London (Bellamy 1990; Webster 1990; Witcher 1990). It was clearly deeply symbolic: would the United Kingdom, in the post-Cold War environment, choose an American system again or turn to the French? In the event, although the British made a decision to deploy a stand-off missile system at the end of 1990, they did not make a choice between the American and French systems, a decision influenced in part by the downfall of Margaret Thatcher and her replacement as Prime Minister by John Major in November 1990, as well as the proximity of a general election.

Yet this deferral did not halt progress towards a greater degree of contact in Franco–British relations. In October 1992, Prime Minister Pierre Bérégovoy argued that Britain and France should co-ordinate their nuclear policies, and Franco–British co-operation was given explicit approval by American Defence Secretary Cheney at the NATO meeting at Gleneagles in October 1992 (*Atlantic News* 23 October 1992). Further, a joint nuclear weapons commission was established between the two countries. In July 1993, at the first Franco–British summit for almost two years which was attended by Prime Minister John Major, President Mitterrand and Prime Minister Edouard Balladur, it was announced that the Joint Commission on Nuclear Policy and Doctrine, set up the previous autumn, would be made permanent (Ridding, Stephens 1993).

The Commission's work has clearly been valued by both nations. When the British decided in the autumn of 1993 not to proceed with a dedicated sub-strategic weapon, but rather to apply the *Trident* system to sub-strategic, as well as strategic, tasks, the French reaction was muted. François Léotard, the Defence Minister, noted that the French reaction would be polite, for 'we think it would be a pity to sacrifice what has been achieved in the nuclear dialogue between France and Britain over the past two years' (Buchan 1993). And the work of the Commission may be extensive. Defence Secretary Malcolm Rifkind, for instance, was quoted as saying that discussions over joint Franco–British nuclear submarine patrols 'could not be excluded in the weeks and months to come' (Buchan 1993). The British were absolutely committed to the work of the Commission, with Rifkind emphasising the importance of Franco–British co-operation in each major speech.[7] Further emphasis on the collaborative work between the British and French came at a summit meeting at the end of 1994 and at the Franco–British summit at the end of 1995, when Major and Chirac announced: 'We do not see situations arising in which the vital interests of either France or the United Kingdom could be threatened without the vital interests of the other also being threatened' (Brown and Clark 1995; Sheridan 1995).

Thus, there exists a practical, as well as a conceptual basis for the development of a common European nuclear policy, albeit a limited one. However, suggesting that constraints are not rigid does not amount to a prediction that such a policy will develop, nor a call for such a common policy to be developed. Rather, it suggests that the reasons why debate over a common European nuclear policy has been so limited may not necessarily keep the issue off the agenda in the medium term.

CONCLUSION

This chapter has argued that there are specific reasons why there has been so little debate about the creation of a common European nuclear policy. Those reasons set four parameters to the development of such a debate in the immediate future. However, those parameters may shift and, if there is an interest in some hybrid arrangement – that is, a common European nuclear policy that is not purely federalist and fully integrationist – then there seems to be scope for its development.

Perhaps one of the most notable features of this analysis is that there is a hierarchy amongst these parameters. The least influential is the last: that of deployments within WEU members. This is not to suggest that this is not an important issue, for it is. But it could be relatively easily resolved if a decision was taken to develop an existentialist strategy. This would, however, be a significant step in its own right. Of secondary importance in terms of parameters are the institutional factors and the question of status and sovereignty to the British and French. The lack of institutional development in the defence field within the EU, and the confusing range of memberships within the WEU make the creation of a common policy enormously difficult. And yet this, too, is capable of some resolution if the hybrid model were to be suggested. Similarly, there will be strong political forces in both Britain and France arguing against the pooling of their respective nuclear forces into a European whole. However, again it is at least conceivable that, in the context of the need to develop a common policy, based on existentialism with decisions on nuclear use still remaining in London and Paris, some movement could be made towards the hybrid model.

This leaves, at the top of the hierarchy, the dominance of Atlanticism in the security debate as the primary constraint upon the development of a common European security identity. It would seem that, as long as Atlanticism is widely persuasive, moves towards developing a common nuclear policy will not occur. When there is very little threat facing the members of the European Union, with federalism within the Union under great attack in many member states, and while the United States is still prepared to maintain its NATO guarantee, the development of a European policy seems to be unnecessary. And of course to many Atlanticists, the mere development of a debate on a common European nuclear policy might provoke the US withdrawal that they fear.

Perhaps this picture would look rather different if, instead of the hybrid model of a common nuclear policy presented here, one was to suggest the creation of a full, federalist common European policy. In such a model, it might be that the question of British and French sovereignty and status would be the most important issue. However, the shape and form of such a federalist policy is extremely difficult to ascertain and, this analysis would suggest, more difficult to envisage by several orders of magnitude.

Thus, the key to the emergence of a debate over a common nuclear policy throughout the European Union depends rather more on the future role of the United States in Western Europe than it does on British and French concerns about sovereignty. But this is a two-way process; it depends not only on Washington's willingness to maintain the commitment to Western Europe; it also depends on the Western Europeans continuing to believe that the US guarantee is credible. Should either of these change, then a debate on a common European nuclear deterrence policy would surely follow.

NOTES

1 For a variety of examinations of such possibilities, see: Clarke, M. 'British and French Nuclear Forces', in Daalder, I. H. and Terriff T. (eds), *Rethinking the*

Unthinkable, London: Frank Cass, 1993, especially pp. 138–145; Bozo, F. 'Une doctrine nucléaire européenne: pour quoi faire et comment?' *Politique étrangere* Vol. 57, Summer 1992, pp. 407–21; the conclusions in Heuser, B. 'Containing uncertainty: options for British nuclear strategy', *Review of International Studies*, Summer 1993; and Yost, D. S. 'Europe and nuclear deterrence', *Survival*, Autumn 1993, pp. 97–120.

2 See note 6. For a commentary on this speech, see 'France offers "nuclear umbrella" to neighbours', *Jane's Defence Weekly*, 9 September 1995; and 'European Security', *Atlantic News* No. 2746, 6 September 1995.

3 'Declaration of the Member States of the Western European Union Issued on the Occasion of the 46th European Council Meeting on 9 and 10 December 1991 at Maastricht', reproduced in Croft S. and Williams P. (eds), *European Security without the Soviet Union*, London, Frank Cass, 1992, pp. 154–8.

4 These states have Observer status.

5 Such deployments are called for in Zadra 1992: 30.

6 Chevènement in *Le Monde* 17 October 1989, quoted in Palmer, D. R., 'French Strategic Options in the 1990s', *Adelphi Paper 260*, London, International Institute for Strategic Studies, Summer 1991, p. 54.

7 For example in his speech at King's College, London in February 1994.

REFERENCES

Bellamy, C. (1990) 'Anglo–French deal likely for missiles', *Independent*, 27 December.

Black, I. (1995) 'Nuclear offer spurned', *Guardian*, 4 September.

Boyer, J. and Stephens, P. (1992) 'French and British nuclear forces in an era of understanding', in Garrity, P. and Maaranen, S. (eds), *Nuclear weapons in the changing world*, New York and London: Plenum Press.

Bozo, F. (1992) 'Une doctrine nucléaire européenne: pour quoi faire et comment?', *Politique étrangere* 57, Summer: 407–21.

Brown, K. and Clark, B. (1995) 'UK and France in nuclear pact', *Financial Times*, 31 October.

Browning, E. S. (1990) 'Anglo–French defense talks may trigger weapons deal', *The Wall Street Journal*, 11 April.

Buchan, D. (1993) 'Paris puts on a brave face over UK's nuclear "non" ', *Financial Times*, 26 October.

Clarke, M. (1993) 'British and French nuclear forces', in Daalder, I. H. and Terriff, T. (eds), *Rethinking the unthinkable*, London: Frank Cass.

Croft, S. (1994) 'Continuity and change in British thinking about nuclear weapons', *Political Studies* 42, 2: 228–42.

Croft, S. and Williams, P. (eds) (1992) *European security without the Soviet Union*, London: Frank Cass.

Freedman, L. (1989) 'European integration and nuclear deterrence after the Cold War', *Chaillot papers* 5, Paris: Western European Union Institute for Security Studies.

Heuser, B. (1993) 'Containing uncertainty: options for British nuclear strategy', *Review of international studies*, Summer.

Juppé, A. (1995) 'Resumption of nuclear tests', *Le Figaro*, 26 August.

Pierre, A. (1972) *Nuclear politics*, London: Oxford University Press.

Ridding, J. and Stephens, P. (1993) 'France and UK signal improved relations at summit', *Financial Times*, 27 July.

Ruiz Palmer, D. (1991) 'French strategic options in the 1990s', *Adelphi Paper 260*, London: International Institute for Strategic Studies.

Schlör, W. (1993) 'German security policy', *Adelphi Paper* 277: 25–7, London: International Institute for Strategic Studies.

Schmidt, P. (1993) 'The Special Franco–German security relationship in the 1990s', *Chaillot Papers* 8, Paris: Western European Union Institute for Security Studies.

Sheridan, M. (1995) 'Major and Chirac cuddle up for entente nucleaire', *Independent*, 31 October.

Ullman, R. (1989) 'The covert French connection', *Foreign Policy* 75: 3–33.

Webster, P. (1990) 'French want to link nuclear strike force with British missile', *Guardian*, 24 October.

Witcher, T. (1990) 'France wants Britain for nuclear plan', *Daily Telegraph*, 23 October.

Yost, D. S. (1993) 'Europe and nuclear deterrence', *Survival*, Autumn: 97–120.

Zadra, R. (1992) 'European integration and nuclear deterrence after the Cold War', *Chaillot Papers* 5, Paris: Western European Union Institute for Security Studies.

9 Conclusion

Defence, states and integration

Lawrence Freedman and Anand Menon[1]

The impact of European integration on defence policies and defence policy making in the member states has been the subject of this volume. It has sought, through detailed empirical investigation, to consider the ways, if any, in which member states have found their autonomy affected by the policies and aspirations of the European Union.

This conclusion performs three functions. First, it examines the impact of the EU on national defence policies, and contrasts this with the impact of other pressures on national autonomy, illustrating how the latter have played a far more significant role than the former. Second, building on this analysis of the pressures at work on the state, it suggests why the future defence role of the Union may well continue to be limited. Finally, a short section considers the findings of this volume relative to the others in the series.

THE EUROPEAN UNION, DEFENCE POLICY AND STATE AUTONOMY

Perhaps one of the most striking themes to emerge from the preceding chapters is the fact that all the states considered in this volume have apparently increased their enthusiasm for European defence co-operation. Whilst this will probably come as no surprise in the case of states such as France and Germany, it is striking to note how even a traditionally highly 'Atlanticist' state such as the Netherlands has increasingly come to regard a European defence capability as necessary. Declarations concerning defence policy in contemporary Europe are peppered with references to the need for enhanced European capacities. Even the British, who for so long resisted such moves, have come to speak, if only in terms far more limited than those used by their partners, of the need to increase such capacities (Schnapper 1996 esp. Ch. 6). As pointed out in the introduction, however, it would be rash to assume that an increasing enthusiasm for enhanced European capabilities either represented anything more than rhetoric, or resulted from pressure exerted on national policy by the development of defence capacities within the ambit of European integration.

Whilst the rhetoric of national defence may be becoming increasingly anachronistic in the West European context, it is noticeable that the EU itself has exercised little or no direct impact over shifts in national defence policy. Certainly, we have no evidence of anything to compare with the tremendous impact of European competition law over national industrial policy, where, as shown in the first volume of this series, national industrial strategies have on occasion been stymied by Commission competition investigations (Kassim and Menon 1996). Neither have any of the preceding chapters revealed any instances of the Union affecting patterns of defence policy making (though, for other reasons, we can see a clear increase in inter-state consultation and co-operation, as Croft shows in his discussion of Franco–British nuclear collaboration).

The major reason for this is clearly the lack of EU competence over defence matters. The ambitious rhetoric of the European Union treaty disguises (or at least disguised at the time of its signing) the absence of practical progress in the defence sphere. Moreover, to the extent that defence does come within the ambit of integration, the pillared structure created in the Maastricht Treaty ensures not only that member states take decisions by unanimity, but also that the supranational institutions (unlike in the case of competition policy) have only a very minor, consultative role to play.

The picture is different, however, when we turn to look at the *indirect* impact the European Union has had on national policies. First, EU policies in areas other than defence have impinged on national defence policies. The clearest example of this is perhaps the financial stringency that has resulted from the desire of at least certain states to meet the convergence criteria for monetary integration by 1998. Without the Cold War to hold it up, defence spending throughout the EU has been a major victim in this regard, with armaments programmes cut or put back, and armed forces reduced in size.

Another facet of this kind of indirect effect has been the creeping intrusion of industrial policies on defence policy affairs. Competition policy is a case in point. The Commission has emphasised the fact that it would not hesitate to investigate cases of state aid being granted to dual-use products (Courades-Allebeck 1993) and has gradually expanded the scope of its competition-law policing activities to include more and more defence-related issues (Hayward 1994: 351). In 1990 Leon Brittan explicitly linked defence issues to the success of the internal market programme, stating with regard to 'short-sighted national defence procurement strategies' that the 'logic of the Single Market ... is perhaps more obvious here than in any other single sphere' (Brittan 1990). For all this, however, there has been no striking change in the proportion of national defence procurement budgets of the major powers spent overseas.

Another way in which the EU may have impacted indirectly on national policies is through the increased links it has fostered between states in non-military areas. As Howorth points out in his chapter on France, as the interests of states converge in other policy areas, they may well find it easier to contemplate far-reaching defence co-operation. Hence French Foreign (and later Prime) Minister Alain Juppé asked his audience, at a speech to the planning division of the French Foreign Ministry, whether the adoption of a single currency could really 'fail to have an effect on French perceptions of its own vital interests?' (Juppé 1995: 121). National military doctrines, therefore, could be easier to adapt as states find their interests and, as importantly, their perceptions of those interests, coming to converge. Similarly, as Howorth also argues, the Union may play a role in broadening concepts of security, altering the relative weight accorded to questions of purely military security and hence perhaps facilitating military co-operation as other issues rise up the hierarchy of problems facing policy makers. Again, however, far-reaching changes in defence policy, even in France, have not been subordinated to wider European considerations. Thus, despite the rhetorical tendencies, perhaps the clearest single finding to emerge from the preceding discussion is the relative unimportance of the Union as a constraint on state autonomy as compared with other factors.

During the superpower conflict, the overriding constraint was systemic, with the need to preserve security in the face of a perceived threat from the East taking precedence over other defence policy considerations, especially in geographically exposed states such as the Federal Republic. West European states were totally reliant on protection by an outside power. Defence was unattainable without the support of the United States. Such support was institutionalised through the signing of the Washington Treaty and the gradual emergence of NATO structures. Certainly NATO (despite French claims to the contrary) never amounted to a fully integrated military system, and indeed left its member states with considerable latitude for independent decision making.[2] However, the Alliance, and in particular the effects of American hegemonic leadership of the Western camp, did exercise an effect upon West European defence policies. The most severe constraint operated on West Germany, which lacked the practical ability to conduct a national defence policy in that, in the event of war, and given the absence of a German general staff, operational control over all combat units would be transferred to NATO. Smaller West European states found themselves completely dependent on the American nuclear and security guarantee, to the extent that Italy, for instance, as Andreatta and Hill point out, largely allowed NATO 'to determine its foreign policy'.

Against this, however, should be put the fact that, as the chapters on both Italy and the Netherlands illustrate, such states still maintained the ability to pursue their own, divergent policies on occasion. Moreover, the existence of NATO and the American security guarantee represented an opportunity for some states either to free-ride on the security provided by others, or to increase external influence within an intergovernmental forum. Italy is clearly an example of the first of these strategies, avoiding, as Andreatta and Hill put it, having to sacrifice butter for guns whilst benefiting from the security provided by the transatlantic Alliance.

The magnitude of the external constraint acting on West European states during the period of superpower confrontation epitomised what Stanley Hoffmann has called the 'tyranny of the external' (Kahler 1987: 289).[3] Tyranny not simply in that the state found international constraints imposing policy choices, but also in that international pressures effectively removed other constraints on state autonomy. During the period of superpower confrontation, the clarity of the threat confronting Western Europe was such as to largely 'depoliticise' questions of defence, meaning that 'strategic policy was sterilized politically and insulated bureaucratically'. (Kahler 1987: 289). Whilst domestic squabbles did sometimes erupt over military questions – witness the peace movements in Germany and the Netherlands in the early 1980s – these were infrequent and usually had little impact on policy (INF weapons were, eventually, deployed in both states, although, in the latter case, after a delay of some two years). Only as the influence of the Cold War declined did domestic impulses start to make themselves felt. Italian governments explicitly gave up autonomy to NATO in return for a depoliticisation and legitimation of defence policy. Defence budgets thus remained relatively stable, though low, with the only real internal pressure coming from within the state – notably from the armed forces who lobbied hard for a larger slice of the pie.

With the fall of the Berlin Wall and more particularly the implosion of the Soviet Union, perhaps the major constraint affecting the defence policies of West European states was removed. This was particularly clear in the German case, where, as Bohnen points out, three of the international constraints which had operated on Germany (geographical, the bipolarity of the international system and the desire for unification) were removed. The end of the superpower confrontation also witnessed the lifting of the legal constraints on Germany, with that country regaining its full sovereignty.

The end of superpower confrontation has not, however, entailed a lifting of all constraints on the state. In fact, quite the reverse has been the case, with a set of new, or reinforced pressures on state autonomy replacing the rigid exigencies of the bipolar confrontation. In the first place, these took the form of the pressure on defence budgets imposed by shifting technologies and rising costs, as Taylor makes clear in his chapter. Scholars have estimated a rise in the cost of military equipment of between 5 and 8 per cent annually, with the price of some types of weaponry increasing by much more (Fontanel 1988: 100). Further, the impact of globalisation on firms has meant that, even more than during the Cold War, states find it difficult to ensure national control over the technologies necessary to maintain efficient fighting forces (Jones 1996).

The constraint of rising costs is reinforced by that of increasing requirements. For one thing, in the aftermath of the Cold War, state-of-the-art defence systems will no longer be automatically supplied by the United States to meet military contingencies as America is no longer necessarily going to be involved in all those conflicts that affect its allies. This was the lesson to be learnt from the initial phase of the Bosnian conflict. The implications of such circumstances were outlined in a disarmingly honest manner by the outgoing Italian Foreign Minister, Beniamino Andreatta:

> the end of the Cold War has not caused a revision of the basic choices: Italy's membership of the European Community and the Atlantic Alliance. It has, however, resulted in the end of rents [from NATO bases] and free-riding. Membership is no longer enough in the new international conditions: one has to qualify oneself through presence and hard work.
>
> (Andreatta 1993)

Second, the Gulf War clearly illustrated the importance of possessing technologically sophisticated weapons systems such as cruise missiles, anti-missile defence capabilities and a space-based intelligence capacity. In addition, in order to be able to react to regional conflicts, there is a need for the European states to develop sufficient means of military transportation to ensure adequate force projection capabilities. Significant costs are involved, therefore, if these states are to be able to carry out post-Cold War defence missions.

Other pressures, however, militate against such spending. Whilst the acquisition of the means to implement defence policies commensurate with altered international circumstances implies significant costs, governmental freedom of action in this regard is increasingly hamstrung by intense domestic constraints on defence spending. As several of the chapters in this volume make clear, the Cold War legitimised defence spending and hence, whilst defence budgets were certainly a matter for debate, governments found themselves relatively unconstrained in their attempts to finance the military. The end of the Cold War, however, created increased pressure, especially from finance ministries, for the provision of a 'peace dividend'. Consequently, defence spending amongst NATO's European members has fallen from $93 billion per annum (1985) to just over $80 billion since 1990.

Constraints on the state have also increased as a result of increased public awareness of, and willingness to criticise, defence policy options. The end of the Cold War called into question the legitimacy of defence policy as a whole, and in particular a reliance on nuclear weapons, as disquiet in France concerning nuclear testing has indicated only too clearly. However, such pressures have often worked in contradictory ways. Public interest in defence questions has been particularly intense when employment issues are involved. In the first place, this has constrained governmental attempts to close down state-owned arms production facilities, whilst placing an added constraint on attempts to foster intra-European arms manufacturing collaboration (however great the perceived need for this may be). In the second, attempts to rationalise or reduce armed forces in the light of swingeing budget cuts have also provoked public outrage. Thus, whilst budgetary pressures (especially in the light of rising hardware costs) imply the need for cuts, governments must show caution when these are made in order not to provoke public anger. Effective rationalisation, therefore, remains difficult to achieve.

Domestic pressures are particularly intense in those countries which have traditionally relied on the United States to protect European interests outside Europe. The tentative German approach to the out-of-area question bears eloquent testimony to disquiet amongst both the political class and the population at large on this score. In Italy too, the reactions of the public to troop deployments overseas is unpredictable, which places constraints on the government of that state on this issue.

Interestingly, it is in relation to these alternative pressures on policy that the EU has played its final role in impinging on state autonomy. In this case, the Union has sometimes played, or is perceived by policy makers as being capable of playing, the role of enhancing such autonomy *vis-à-vis* other pressures. Thus, as Bohnen illustrates, German policy makers used European considerations as a means of overcoming domestic opposition to policy. Similarly, French officials used the arguments that the French nuclear force could eventually serve the whole of Europe to try to legitimise their renewal of nuclear testing in the face of criticisms by other states, including European partners.

NATO AND EUROPEAN DEFENCE CO-OPERATION

It could be argued that much of what has been said so far illustrates the necessity of enhanced co-operation between European states on defence policy. The combination of a United States more reticent about military involvement abroad, the increasing costs of technology and shrinking defence budgets certainly places intense pressure on the ability of nation states to achieve the objectives of their security policies alone. It is tempting to claim, therefore, that the EU will increasingly come to play a greater role in defence policy matters and will hence start to impact more significantly on national defence policies.

Certainly, as van Staden points out, certain countries such as the Netherlands have found themselves with no alternative, because of increasing budgetary constraints, to seeking enhanced European co-operation. A variety of forms of Franco–British co-operation, including in the nuclear area, also bear eloquent testimony to the pressures to co-operate. There are, however, two good reasons to be suspicious of the argument according to which increasing pressures on autonomy will necessarily lead to enhanced co-operation within the ambit of the EU.

First, states, as Taylor makes clear in his chapter, have tended to choose co-operative projects which limit the impact of such co-operation on national autonomy: hence the extremes of the principle of *juste retour* applied in the manufacturing of the European Fighter Aircraft. Alternative modes of co-operation exist which do not threaten national decision-making competence, and which can be used as substitutes for the EU. Thus, co-operative schemes can take the form of purely bilateral initiatives, such as the Franco–German corps, or the Anglo–Dutch naval force or multilateral projects such as the Eurocorps. In defence policy, 'Europe' does not, in other words, necessarily mean the EU, and the evidence points to the fact that, wherever possible, states will opt for non-institutionalised, *ad hoc* intra-European arrangements to manage defence co-operation. Moreover, whilst there is no overriding reason to expect states to prefer bilateral to multilateral co-operative ventures, it is certainly the case that it is easier to negotiate and manage such ventures when the number of partners is limited. The more partners that are involved, the less any one of them is fully in control, with obvious consequent implications for autonomy.

Second, European Union involvement in defence affairs has been limited as a result of the existence of alternative institutional structures with a proven track record through which necessary co-operation can be carried out. We have seen how NATO was the central constraint during the Cold War. Within Europe, the multi-national character of the military has been fostered over the years by NATO. It defines the contemporary military experience for most armed forces. All the possibilities of defence integration have been explored within the Alliance over the past fifty years. This has involved all sorts of co-operation from commitments to come to each other's defence, to having one country garrison its armed forces, or even nuclear missiles, on another's soil, to accepting a command structure dominated by foreign officers, to forming joint units.

However, big decisions are still national. Despite the fact that many Western governments have effectively accepted the logic of inter-dependence in the defence sphere, this has not led to a complete pooling of sovereignty of the kind that characterises several issues that fall within the ambit of the EC. Alliances definitely involve a degree of commitment to the security of others, but in the end the most fateful decisions about war and peace seem to be so fundamental that they remain the prerogative of national governments and legislatures. When and how to go to war, against and with whom, provide the touchstones of national sovereignty.

Yet since the end of the Cold War, new forms of co-operative arrangements have been developed under the NATO framework, including the new Combined Joint Task Force, which have undermined autonomy and increased the links between states. Germany has deepened the level of integration of its territorial forces within NATO. Indeed, the very cost constraints referred to above tend to militate in favour of the continued primacy of NATO, in that the member states of the EU could not afford to equip the latter with its own autonomous defence capability.[4] Further, as Croft illustrates, continued attachment to Atlanticism has proved a powerful constraint on the development of a European nuclear deterrent force.

States in some instances, therefore, may attempt jealously to guard their autonomy, even while co-operating. Where they do foster co-operation, and in so doing seem to lessen their national freedom of manoeuvre, the EU does not seem to be the chosen framework. Given recent developments within NATO, we might therefore conclude that integration is an issue that has not only been thoroughly explored and developed along practicable lines but that this has also achieved a considerable amount. European countries do not consider self-sufficiency to be an option. They have long accepted the logic of inter-dependence rather than independence when it comes to security and this is reflected in their defence policies.

In this sense, NATO is already playing the role to which some feel the European Union should aspire. This much was hinted at by one of the leading figures in the early years of European integration:

> NATO is not a classic Alliance but rather a true military confederation – an association of states that have decided on a common defence of particular territories for which purpose they have created representative bodies, as well as various common military services and a common strategy.
>
> (Spinelli 1962: 543)

Given the role of NATO, the only reason defence integration remains any sort of issue in Europe is because of its relevance to the processes of European reconstruction. It would be incorrect to view the failure to achieve more within the EU framework as indicative of a failure to respond to increasing pressure on the state by practical steps towards enhanced institutionalised co-operation and even integration. This has taken place within NATO. For the most committed, however, the European project cannot be considered complete until defence is fully included. Moreover, while they may recognise the degree to which defence integration has already been achieved, they are left dissatisfied because this comes under the NATO aegis. Although this view is less prevalent than it once was, many still believe that any institution in which the United States and Canada are so prominent can be seen as detrimental to efforts to promote European unity.

The prospect for the future therefore is likely to be a continuation of the trend of the past half century, towards closer co-operation with, and even greater dependence upon, other countries though usually outside the formal framework of European integration. Here the question of defence integration remains largely a matter of degree: it is no longer one of principle. If there is a principle to be decided it will be whether this co-operation should be geared to broader political requirements, as a means of pulling the countries of Europe even closer together, or more narrowly functional, of ensuring that governments can obtain the maximum operational efficiency through pooling resources. Hence the contrast between, on the one hand, the ambitious rhetoric used by some states concerning the building of a political union and, on the other, the British emphasis on the importance of a 'task-based approach' to defence co-operation, implying that the 'definition of a European defence policy should start with a hard-headed assessment of what the Europeans can realistically expect to do together' as basis for defining new institutional arrangements (UK Government 1995, Para 7).

It should be noted that there was never anything purely functional about the design of force structures for NATO. These were geared to a transatlantic symbolism. The key issue here however was not the march to political unity but burden-sharing. Europeans were conscious of the need to be seen to be doing enough to persuade Congress to continue to find the funds to keep troops in Europe and the security guarantee intact. They did not wish to appear to be free-riders. At the same time they did not want to be seen to be doing too much lest Congress draw the conclusion that Europeans could manage very nicely without them.

Since the end of the Cold War it has become possible to talk of different approaches to European defence integration, on the grounds that the Warsaw Pact no longer provided an excessively exacting standard against which to assess a Western European force. However, the debate became complicated by much larger questions surrounding the institutional balance within Europe, and the new demands resulting from the need to care for and involve the countries of the old communist bloc. A further complication resulted from the fact that while the stakes, in terms of the prospect of total war, had been dramatically reduced, the incidence of actual fighting increased. The move from an effectively stalemated East–West confrontation to a more disorderly post-Cold War world provided a new twist on the old debates on the possibility of European self-sufficiency.

Although, as indicated above, the formal security debate has been dominated by discussions of institutions it has been shaped not so much by the comparative and competing merits of the institutions as by the march of events, and in particular the fragmentation of the former Soviet Union and the former Yugoslavia, to some extent by the conflict in the Gulf and to an increasing extent by turmoil in North Africa.

Out of this experience the following broad conclusions can be reached:

1 The EU can be a significant instrument of security when there are shared interests, but attempts to forge a common foreign and security policy remain frustrated by the impact of particular interests, where states feel unable to compromise, and minority views (even when held by small states).

2 NATO is the only serious military organisation around and on practical matters it has been indispensable. Its first actual war-time deployments came during the Gulf War, and its first shots in anger came in support of the UN in Bosnia. Politically it remains dependent on the US, whose interest in European security has been at times selective and spasmodic, inconsistent and poorly nuanced. On the other hand, no substantial military operation is possible without the support of the US and certainly not in the face of its opposition.

3 The WEU remains an expedient institution with varying and normally transient functions. Though NATO is the only proper alliance with a serious basis for collective defence, absent the United States and the WEU could be turned into a serious alliance. This would only happen if the US stepped away from its European commitments.

4 The Organisation for Security and Co-operation in Europe, OSCE, has no authority but may have early dispute settlement and crisis management functions.

5 The UN has authority, and is an excellent source of legitimacy, but the Security Council increasingly depends on Russian connivance. It is critical to the success of any economic measures.

The most important dynamic on the institutional side has not been the influence of international events but of related institutional developments. With regard to NATO the key developments have been the tentative return of France to the fold and the effort to reach out to the countries of Central and Eastern Europe and the former Soviet Union (CEE/FSU). This effort is now pointing towards the enlargement of NATO, to bring in countries such as Poland and the Czech Republic in the first instance and others later on.

For a number of political reasons this has been a controversial matter. Most seriously it has been opposed by Russia which sees enlargement as a means by which everybody can gang up against it. It is also controversial because those countries that might have serious reasons for wanting to be members of an anti-Russian alliance are not going to be part of the first wave of members (for example the Baltic states and Ukraine), and this might lead to different types of recrimination. Another set of problems, relevant to the broader question of defence integration, is the actual practical preparation of these countries for membership of the Alliance. These problems were only appreciated at a rather late stage in the process, but they are already raising the question of whether states which cannot afford to get their training and equipment up to NATO standards can be full members of the organisation. Note the problem is not one of the actual integration of a set of national armed forces but simply their ability to fight together if necessary.

This is the essential functional criterion adopted by NATO: what is the necessary amount of inter-operability so that different forces can work closely together, sharing ammunition and fuel and spare parts. This is not always achieved within a single country's forces and needs deliberate planning over a long period if a number of countries are to work well together. Another functional necessity is for command and control systems which can ensure that the disparate units work effectively towards a common goal.

The importance of this was underlined in Bosnia. In a critical development NATO has agreed to generalise from this experience to create Combined Joint Task Forces (CJTF), which can be based on NATO infrastructure, logistics and intelligence, while involving forces which bring together 'a coalition of the willing', that is those that choose to be involved in a particular operation. This coalition may well involve non-NATO countries. The importance of these developments is that they have made NATO's practical advantages more widely available and not always dependent upon direct American involvement. So long as the NATO consensus is not actually opposed to a particular operation, its political direction can come from without NATO.

On the European Union side the role of defence in the inter-governmental conference has been shaped and constrained by the more substantial European debates on monetary union and enlargement. Monetary union has been set up as the decisive test. If it fails to happen then the integrative process will be stalled for some time and, even if it does happen, it will leave at least some states stranded (perhaps on their own volition) outside the most critical of all moves towards true unification. This effort dominates EU agendas and administrative energy. Until it is resolved other issues are likely to be pushed aside.

This includes enlargement, which at one point appeared as the central EU task. The problems here again relate to the functional as opposed to the symbolic questions of integration, although in this case the problems are more economic than military. The immediate issue raised by the prospect of enlargement is that of the EU's decision-making processes. It appears to necessitate moves towards qualified majority voting, but the countries most likely to use military power in support of wider European objectives, and in particular Britain and France, will not wish to be put in the position where they feel that they are being told to go to war by countries that are not themselves able to accept the consequent risks – nor for that matter being told to abstain from war by countries whose own specific national interests are not so directly involved.

Some enlargement has already taken place, based here more on economic than security criteria. As a result, the overlap between NATO and the EU has declined: the 'Six' were all NATO members; the 'Twelve' included only Ireland as non-NATO; the 'Fifteen' have brought in three countries (Sweden, Austria, Finland) normally associated with the neutral and non-aligned. All future candidates (with the exception of Turkey) are not currently NATO members, although a number would like to be. Of these the Visegrad Countries (Czech Republic, Hungary, Poland, Slovakia) are closest to joining both institutions, followed by Romania, Bulgaria, Estonia, Latvia, Lithuania and, eventually, Malta and Cyprus. Norway is a member of NATO but is unlikely to consider EU membership again for some time.

The combination of enlargement and the working through of the Maastricht agenda means that the EU is the most dynamic of all these institutions, but its future does depend not only on sorting out differences of perspective over degrees of integration and the conditions for monetary union, but also basic structural problems such as the Common Agricultural Policy (CAP), which cannot survive enlargement, and the structural fund. Enlargement will also involve incorporating a series of generally poor members in areas of some instability, and therefore raises a type of security issue different from those with which Western European states have been most familiar.

The existence of a CFSP means that the EU can already be considered a 'security community' in the sense that there is a degree of mutual solidarity based on shared values and an awareness that an attack on one would directly affect all, even where there is not always the firmness of an alliance obligation to come to the aid of a partner under threat. A security community is undoubtedly a looser concept than an alliance, but it may also be more appropriate to current conditions in that it depends on the quality of integration and inter-dependence among the respective societies rather than a traditional security guarantee. The problem with the latter is that it can seem provocative (in this case to Russia) and also may commit allies to supporting countries engaged in conflicts in which they are not necessarily the most aggrieved party. The creeping enlargement of a security community, as general inter-dependence grows, may be preferable to the sharp drawing of lines by an alliance, which inevitably confines some countries to an uncomfortable non-alignment.

For the Visegrad countries this may not be an either/or situation, as NATO is now committed to enlargement and is discussing how this might best be achieved. However, these are not the countries most under threat. These largely lie within the former Soviet Union and, apart from the Baltic States, are not candidates either for the EU or NATO. Thus security guarantees to countries which do not need them may heighten the insecurity of those who do need them but cannot get them.

Any move to a common defence policy (CDP) must reflect this wider set of problems. It can be seen either as a way of turning this creeping security community, which now shares a number of common borders with Russia, into an alliance, or as a way of developing European co-operation to perform a more decisive role within NATO. The traditional argument in favour of strengthening the European contribution to NATO and rendering it more coherent has normally been based on the 'two pillars' concept. However, this meant one thing when the US pillar was strong. When it is weak it means something else altogether, for a strengthening of the European pillar can then mean an imbalance in the whole structure.

Furthermore, NATO has of late lost its clear focus and has become a secondary contractor to other institutions, particularly the UN in Bosnia, rather than a prime contractor. Its current value is threefold: it helps freeze alliance formation, always a sign of instability and possibly danger in great power politics; it provides a vehicle for the expression of American interest in and influence over European affairs; third, it has a well-developed integrated military command.

This third factor has shown its worth in recent conflicts, even when NATO itself has not been directly involved. It helps with inter-operability of equipment, standard operating procedures (such as identification of friend or foe) and good personal contacts which can ease the most impro-vised military operations. With the current reductions in forces, the joint deployments and exercises at the heart of the integrated command are under stress. This has led to concern about a possible 'renationalisation' of forces, whereby NATO operations will start to acquire the *ad hoc* and improvised characteristics of other multinational operations.

However, it may be that in practice a more likely pattern is a collection of more or less specialist groupings of nations. This can be seen in the Franco–German Eurocorps, the recent Anglo–French agreements on co-operation on air and naval groups, as well as the long-established Anglo–Dutch commando units and the more substantial rapid reaction corps, plus the new CJTFs.

All this suggests a way forward on the basis of strengthening the EU as a security community while relying on NATO as a source of multinational military capacity. This leaves a question mark against the Western Euro-pean Union. At the moment its military capacity is extremely limited and, while its central staff has been strengthened recently, there is really no comparison with NATO. Moreover, there is agreement that the WEU cannot be anything other than a sub-group of NATO, in that it cannot take on EU members who are not also members of NATO. This would seem to constrain significantly its future utility. On the other hand, there is no way that France is going to allow it to be killed off, and the British government has shown no interest in such a course.

The best way forward depends on closer bilateral and multilateral military relations within the established institutional framework. There is currently sufficient flexibility within this framework to pursue any military operation which has widespread political support. Rather than a swift move to an overt common defence policy, it makes sense to start by strengthening the security dimension of the EU, without worrying over-much if this moves into areas normally considered to be the domain of defence. This is appropriate because it allows for an active diplomacy to consider not only the use of political and economic instruments, with which the EU is already well endowed, but also military instruments.

There has long been a separate case for a greater sensitivity to the defence implications of industrial developments, particularly with regard to the recent rationalisations and joint ventures within the European defence industry, and concern about issues related to the proliferation of instruments of mass destruction, such as dual-use technologies. It would be unwise to expect a truly common policy here, because of the competitive elements, but there could be far more co-ordination and work on guidelines for the transfers of weapons and technologies. Again it would be prudent to start with such work in an advisory rather than directive role.

The basic test of any defence integration is a readiness to go to war together. This requires considerable mutual confidence and trust. There is nothing more damaging to long-term relations than the sense of having been badly let down by a supposed ally. This sort of mutual confidence comes through training together and operational experience. It has to be forged through the officer corps and not through governments. Officers will have little interest in arrangements designed to make a show of conspicuous integration with another country if they are not going to be realised in any imaginable contingency. This has dogged Franco–German co-operation, as the French have come to realise that they do not have sufficient spare capacity for largely symbolic gestures and they must design their forces with operations in mind.

Compared with the pre-NATO years, Europe has now achieved an extraordinarily high level of defence integration. Very few European states would now be able, even if they were willing, to fight by themselves. They have the habit of co-operation. They regularly train and exercise together, buy the same equipment and occasionally set up joint units and headquarters. If they fail the test of war (or of any of the variety of missions that now comes under the general heading of 'peace support') it is not going to be because they have not prepared together but because they disagree on the nature of the conflict that has stimulated action and do not have a shared stake in its resolution.

CONCLUSION

What does the preceding analysis tell us about defence in comparison to the other policy sectors examined in this series and to broader questions concerning the state and integration in Europe? One evident peculiarity of the defence sector is the distinction between decision-making authority and implementation capacity, in other words between the sovereign right of the state to make decisions concerning war and peace and the autonomy of the state to translate decisions into effective action. The volume on industrial policy pointed out that one of the crucial limits to the impact of the EU resides in its fundamental dependence on the nation states to implement decisions taken (sometimes against the will of the member states) at European level. In the defence sphere, we have seen how the West European states, even the smaller ones such as the Netherlands, have remained wedded to the notion of national control over decisions. Indeed, this is one of the reasons why they have, in recent years, expressed a clear preference for NATO as the most appropriate forum for co-operation, thereby reducing the possibility of any supranational influence over, or watering down of national vetoes concerning, defence policy. However whilst the sovereign right to make decisions remains intact, the ability of individual European states to implement these decisions with military action has been rendered almost negligible. This is certainly true in the case of the smaller states and of states like Italy which systematically neglected their armed forces during the Cold War. Yet even the larger, more militarily powerful states have also come to realise the limits of purely national military action, as Howorth makes clear in his chapter on France.

On the surface, the purely intergovernmental nature of decision making in the defence sphere, along with the highly limited direct impact of the EU on national policy, may well be seen as reinforcing the claims of those, drawing inspiration from the realist school of international relations theory, who argue that states will not sacrifice national control over 'high politics' (Hoffmann 1966). The reality of increasing dependence on others for successful military action, however, reveals this to be something of a facade. States seem to be more worried about maintaining the right to take the formal decision authorising military action than about acquiring the possibility of carrying out such actions. It is striking that, in contrast to those who have claimed that states will co-operate only in the face of a clear military threat which requires far-reaching co-operation amongst allies (Joffe 1992: 48), developments within NATO since the Cold War indicate otherwise. Indeed, the irony from the theoretical perspective resides in the fact that it is the very threat of a return to the kind of balance of power politics highlighted by realist theorists that is often explicitly used in rhetoric supporting further inter-state co-operation and even integration (Art 1996).

Yet whilst the push towards the creation of ever more multinational structures within NATO points to a weakness of traditional realist analyses of defence policy, it clearly does not vindicate the picture painted by those who have foreseen a steady increase in the role of the institutions of European integration. Admittedly, the kinds of connection between different aspects of governmental activities known to the neofunctionalists as 'functional spill-over' can be seen to apply to defence in the way that economic pressures (in some cases resulting from the constraint of the convergence criteria) seem to impel states towards greater co-operation. It may well be, therefore, that some kind of functionalist logic holds for defence questions in that particular problems in certain sectors lead to regional institutional arrangements. The problem is, however, that certain such sectors and many such problems transcend regional boundaries and thus do not lead to the kind of integration that will necessarily further the cause of *European* integration. NATO remains popular amongst European states because, even in the absence of a massive threat which required the intervention of a superpower to preserve West European security, the West European states remain wedded to the notion of maintaining US involvement in European security. In the end it has also proved to be the institution of choice of the post-communist countries of Eastern Europe.

The state, then, has not been exposed to substantial pressures from the EU as far as defence policy is concerned. To the extent that the Union does exercise and influence national policy, this is via indirect channels and in many cases has the effect of increasing the margin of manoeuvre enjoyed by national policy makers. The heaviest constraints on state autonomy in fact emanate from sources other than the EU, be they the international environment, or financial pressures, or the influence of domestic groups anxious to influence the nature of policy. Yet for all the fact that these have, in many cases, undermined the capacity of individual West European states autonomously to carry out military action, they have not led to an increase in the EU's prerogatives, nor to enhanced EU impact on national policies. The central importance of the existence of alternative fora for interstate co-operation is thus made abundantly clear. For all the decrease in national defence autonomy that we have pointed out, West European nation states can still choose the institutions within which to compensate for their relative weakness, and there is every reason to suspect that they will continue to prefer NATO over the EU in this regard, not least in order to ensure continued national control over the big decisions concerning national defence.

NOTES

1 The author would like to acknowledge the support provided by ESRC Research Grant R000221254 which has enabled him to carry out research on the pressures affecting national defence policy.
2 All the allied powers retained the sole right to decide upon the engagement of their forces, and their placing under Nato integrated command. The stipulations in the Washington Treaty regarding the obligations of signatory states towards each other in the event of external aggression are remarkable limited, especially in comparison to those contained within the Brussels treaty which created the West European Union. Moreover, neither France in Indochina and Algeria,

nor Britain in Malaya, nor Greece and Turkey in their regular and bloody skirmishes over Cyprus, had any difficulty in providing the necessary forces.
3 Whilst Davidson may well have been right in his characterisation of the scope of the external threat, his analysis raises an analytically important point. NATO never, in fact, represented the kind of ambitious integration he refers to. West European states did not feel themselves compelled to take such a drastic step. In many cases, whatever the scale of the pressures on nation states, they will fail to react with what observers take to be clearly the most appropriate policy response. States may, in other words, fail to realise the implications of the constraints on their autonomy facing them.
4 The estimated costs of achieving an autonomous European defence capacity were estimated by the Royal United Services Institute at around 1.5 per cent of GDP on top of current expenditure on defence by member states for around ten years (*The Economist* 25 February 1995).

REFERENCES

Andreatta, B. (1993) 'Una politica estera per l'Italia', *Il Mulino*, November–December.
Art, R. (1996) 'Why Western Europe Needs the United States and NATO', *Political Science Quarterly* 111, 1, 1–39.
Brittan, L. (1990) 'A European Security Community?', speech delivered to the British Atlantic Group of Young Politicians, London, 17 May.
Corrades Allebeck, A. (1993) 'The European Community: From the EC to European Union', in H. Wulf (ed), *Arms Industry Limited*, New York: Oxford University Press.
Fontanel, J. (1988) 'Defence Costs and Budgeting in France', in P. Lellouche, Y. Boyer and J. Roper (eds), *Franco–British Defence Co-operation*, London: Routledge.
Hayward, K. 'European Union Policy and the European Aerospace Industry', *Journal of European Public Policy* 1, 3: 347–65.
Hoffmann, S. (1966) 'Obstinate or obsolete? The fate of the nation-state and the case of Western Europe', *Daedalus*, 95, 3.
Joffe, J. (1992) 'Collective Security and the future of Europe: failed dreams and dead ends', *Survival*, 34/1, 36–50.
Jones, C. (1996) 'Aerospace' in Kassim, H. and Menon, A., *The European Union and National Industrial Policy*, London: Routledge.
Juppé, A. (1995) Speech on the occasion of 20th anniversary of the Centre d'Analyse et de Prévision, Paris, 30 January 1995, text provided by the French Foreign Ministry.
Kahler, M. (1987) 'The Survival of the State in European International Relations' in Maier, C., *Changing boundaries of the political: essays on the evolving balance between the state and society, public and private in Europe*, Cambridge: Cambridge University Press.
Kassim, H. and Menon, A. (1996) *The European Union and National Industrial Policy*, London: Routledge.
Schnapper, P. (1996) *Les Infortunes du Pragmatisme: La Grande-Bretagne et la Sécurité Européenne 1989–1995*, thèse présentée en vue de l'obtention du diplome de doctorat de l'Institut d'Etudes Politiques de Paris.
Spinelli (1962) 'Atlantic Pact or European Union', *Foreign Affairs* 40, 4, July.
United Kingdom Government (1995) *The United Kingdom's Approach to the Treatment of Defence Issues at the 1996 Intergovernmental Conference*, 1 March.

Index